# Understanding Thin-Client/Server Computing

Joel P. Kanter

**Microsoft** Press

# Understanding Thin-Client/Server Computing

Published by **Microsoft Press**
A Division of Microsoft Corporation
One Microsoft Way
Redmond, Washington 98052-6399

Copyright © 1998 by Citrix Systems, Inc.

All rights reserved. No part of the contents of this book may be reproduced or transmitted in any form or by any means without the written permission of the publisher.

Library of Congress Cataloging-in-Publication Data
Kanter, Joel.
　　Understanding Thin-Client/Server Computing / Joel Kanter.
　　　　p.　cm. -- (Strategic technology series)
　　Includes index.
　　ISBN 1-57231-744-2
　　1. Client/server computing.　　I. Title.　　II. Series.
QA76.9.C55K36　 1997
004'.36--dc21　　　　　　　　　　　　　　　　　　　　　　　　97-31953
　　　　　　　　　　　　　　　　　　　　　　　　　　　　　　　CIP

Printed and bound in the United States of America.

1 2 3 4 5 6 7 8 9　 WCWC　 3 2 1 0 9 8

Distributed to the book trade in Canada by Macmillan of Canada, a division of Canada Publishing Corporation.

A CIP catalogue record for this book is available from the British Library.

Microsoft Press books are available through booksellers and distributors worldwide. For further information about international editions, contact your local Microsoft Corporation office. Or contact Microsoft Press International directly at fax (425) 936-7329. Visit our Web site at mspress.microsoft.com.

Citrix, ICA, and WinFrame are registered trademarks and MultiWin is a trademark of Citrix Systems, Inc. Macintosh is a registered trademark of Apple Computer, Inc. Intel is a registered trademark of Intel Corporation. BackOffice, FoxPro, Microsoft, Microsoft Press, MS-DOS, PowerPoint, Visual Basic, Visual C++, Windows, Windows NT, and Win32 are registered trademarks and ActiveX and Visual J++ are trademarks of Microsoft Corporation. NT is a trademark of Northern Telecom Limited. Java is a trademark of Sun Microsystems, Inc. Other product and company names mentioned herein may be the trademarks of their respective owners.

Companies, names, and/or data used in screens and sample output are fictitious unless otherwise noted.

**Acquisitions Editor:** Stephen G. Guty
**Project Editor:** Sally Stickney
**Technical Editor:** James W. Johnson

*This book is for the members of the Citrix community—
the people responsible for the great WinFrame
thin-client/server software—as well as for their families.*

*Special thanks to Compaq Computer Corporation
for supporting this project with hardware and
excellent technical assistance.*

# Contents

Foreword ......... ix
Preface ......... xiii
Acknowledgments ......... xv

Chapter One
## The Thin-Client/Server Computing Model ......... 1

What Is Thin-Client/Server Computing? 3
How Does Thin-Client/Server Computing Work? 4
What Do You Need to Do, and Where Do You Need to Do It? 7
Addressing the Issues: Management and Scalability, Access, Performance, Security, and Total Cost of Ownership 14

Chapter Two
## Comparing Computer Architectures ......... 21

Network Operating Systems and Application Servers 23
Distributed Computing Architectures 30
Thin-Client Computing 41

New Technologies:
Competition or Continuum?  45

Chapter Three
# Key Components of WinFrame and Windows NT Server ................... 49

System Foundations for
a Multiuser Environment  50

The Components of
Thin-Client/Server Architecture  56

How the Components Work Together  63

Connecting an ICA Client
to a WinFrame Session  65

Running Applications Using
the Thin-Client/Server Model  68

Chapter Four
# Form Follows Function: A Computing Continuum ................. 73

Thin-Client/Server Hardware:
Form Follows Function  74

Getting the Most Out
of Yesterday's Computers  86

Other Solutions  87

Chapter Five
# Setting Up Your Thin-Client/Server Computing Environment ................... 91

Licensing Considerations  91

Configuring and
Publishing Applications  97

| | |
|---|---|
| Network Integration | 101 |
| Security | 109 |
| Accessing Thin-Client/Server Sessions | 113 |

Chapter Six
# Planning Your Thin-Client/Server Environment ... 119

| | |
|---|---|
| A Typical Planning and Deployment Scenario | 121 |
| Reallocating Budgeting Priorities | 125 |
| Hardware and Software Requirements | 130 |

Chapter Seven
# Thin-Client/Server Computing on the Web ... 143

| | |
|---|---|
| Overview of WinFrame Web Computing | 146 |
| The Server Side: WinFrame for Web Computing Support | 147 |
| The Client Side: The ICA Web Client | 155 |
| Running an Internet Browser on a Thin-Client/Server System | 158 |

Chapter Eight
# Case Studies ... 161

| | |
|---|---|
| Accounting and Financial Reporting | 162 |
| Sales Automation | 173 |
| Health Care Services | 177 |
| Thin-Client/Server on the Web | 186 |
| Human Resources Management Applications | 189 |

| | |
|---|---|
| Communications and Remote Computing | 195 |
| Legal Services | 200 |
| The Public and Nonprofit Sectors | 203 |
| Education | 212 |

Chapter Nine
# The Future of Thin-Client/Server Computing ............ 219

| | |
|---|---|
| Changes to the Thin-Client/Server Landscape | 221 |
| The Future of Thin-Client/Server Computing | 223 |
| Where Will the Technology Go from Here? | 229 |

Appendix
# The Thin-Client/Server Community ............ 231

| | |
|---|---|
| Application Providers | 232 |
| Connectivity Providers | 240 |
| Platform Providers | 242 |
| ICA Licensees | 243 |
| | |
| Index | 245 |

# Foreword

When Citrix opened for business in 1989, we envisioned a computing paradigm that would simplify the deployment of enterprise applications and enable universal information access from every conceivable desktop and device. The idea was to empower users while providing centralized application deployment and administration for IS professionals. As a result, our mission to deliver on the thin-client/server computing architecture was under way long before terms like "network computers," "intranet," and "total cost of ownership" were popularized.

Today, thousands of organizations with millions of information-hungry users around the world connect to Microsoft Windows–based business-critical applications using Citrix WinFrame thin-client/server system software. The rapid adoption of WinFrame is changing the way IS managers think about enterprise computing and application delivery because thin-client/server computing simplifies the IS application environment, reduces cost of ownership, and increases the value of corporate information. It's a simple idea that is evolutionary in nature but profound in its benefits.

Thin-client/server computing means that 100 percent of all application execution lives on the server. Users gain universal access to these applications from powerful desktop computers using thin-client software or through truly thin devices such as the Windows-based terminal. Enabling this computing architecture is the Independent Computing Architecture (ICA) protocol, which is an emerging de facto standard for thin-client/server computing. The ICA protocol provides a standard way of exchanging application presentation services between powerful servers and a limitless range of information appliances, with minimal traffic over the network. ICA-based protocol support allows any desktop PC, NetPC, Windows-based terminal, Network Computer, Personal Digital Assistant (PDA), or other information appliance to be part of the mission-critical computing infrastructure. The WinFrame thin-client/server environment, built on Microsoft's powerful Windows NT Server technology, is the solution that many thousands of IS professionals have already chosen to overcome obstacles to delivering the latest software solutions across the enterprise.

Thin-client/server computing facilitates the immediate deployment of corporate applications, information, and software updates by providing a single point of management on the server. This, in and of itself, allows IS professionals to do their jobs more efficiently and effectively. With thin-client/server computing, IS professionals no longer have to touch every desktop to deploy new applications. Users can access applications from anywhere, but the IS professional administers the server from only one location. And support professionals can use tools built right into the server to provide users with training and technical services.

In addition to simplified management, IS professionals are using the thin-client/server model to deliver applications and solutions anywhere in the enterprise network regardless of bandwidth or type of desktop hardware. As a result, homogeneous desktop hardware and unlimited network bandwidth are no longer on the critical path to deploying mission-critical applications.

As you'll see in the case studies provided in this book, application and data security is outstanding. Because application code and corporate data never leave the server, application configurations are secure, corporate information is protected, and data replication is eliminated. In fact, thin-client/server computing is the simplest, most secure way of delivering mission-critical applications . . . period.

*Understanding Thin-Client/Server Computing* is the first book that offers a detailed look at this innovative approach to delivering Windows-based applications. I first met the author, Joel Kanter, when he was the Academic Programs Manager in Microsoft's Internet Platform and Tools Division. While he had initially discovered that hardware was a barrier to using the latest software tools for supporting technical curricula, he also recognized that school and university IS managers were stretched to their limits. Actually, we thought Joel was pushing the outer limits of thin-client/server computing when he approached us about using WinFrame for making development tools such as Microsoft Visual Basic and Microsoft Visual C++ available to instructional labs. So we humored him and sent copies of WinFrame to him as well as to Professor Corey Schou at Idaho State University. We were pleasantly surprised when Dr. Schou demonstrated how well WinFrame worked for his instructional labs, making not only Visual Basic and Visual C++ but also Visual J++ available for various courses. Dr. Schou was even able to leverage some of his legacy hardware equipment. (See the case study about Idaho State University in Chapter 8.)

After Joel left Microsoft, he continued to work with Mark Templeton, our Vice President of Marketing, to look at ways for reaching all kinds of businesses, organizations, and individuals with the thin-client/server computing message. The result is this book. We greatly appreciate Joel's early vision to see the implications of thin-client/server computing, his enthusiasm, and his efforts to make this book possible.

I hope that you use *Understanding Thin-Client/Server Computing* to help you understand how the thin-client/server computing model can fit with your present computing infrastructure and how it can help you to maximize your IS personnel resources, extend your computing investments, increase network efficiency, and enhance information security. The simplicity of thin-client/server computing can help you take your computing environment and your business even further. And this book will help you begin that process.

*Edward I. Iacobucci, Chairman*
*Citrix Systems, Inc.*
*Fort Lauderdale, Florida*

# Preface

Until my immersion in the topic of thin-client/server computing, I hadn't fully understood either the impact on IS professionals or the complications involved in supporting networks with a mix of devices that included PCs with rapidly changing hardware and software technology. The more familiar I've become with this topic—by writing this book and by providing support to my clients—the stronger my convictions have become about an increasing role for the thin-client/server computing model within the information infrastructure of large corporations, small businesses, government institutions, health care organizations, educational institutions, and other organizations. The prognosis for thin-client/server technology to rapidly deliver computing solutions to further the business goals of any organization is extremely positive.

> Thin-client/server computing helps IS departments to cost-effectively manage and rapidly deploy applications across an enterprise.

This book introduces the topic of thin-client/server computing. Simply put, the thin-client/server computing model is a multiuser server-based computing model in which 100 percent of the application executes on a server. Mouse and keyboard input are sent from the client device, with the server returning only the display. The implementation by Citrix Systems allows applications to be efficiently delivered to any hardware platform, regardless of network bandwidth. Using this technology, familiar applications using the Microsoft Windows graphical user interface can be rapidly deployed faster and further. *Understanding Thin-Client/Server Computing* is not intended as an exhaustive volume; rather, it explains how this computing model works, its potential for rapid application deployment, and the way that it helps computing infrastructures evolve efficiently and cost-effectively.

> This book provides an introduction to thin-client/server computing.

> The book is intended for anyone who is required to make a network technology decision.

IS professionals, administrators, and technology planners will find the information in this book invaluable. If you are responsible for furthering the goals of your organization but have been stymied by the human resources needs and equipment costs of computing infrastructures, you should also read this book. Whether you read the entire book straight through or just skip around the chapters, you'll gather a lot of vital information.

> The book was written in cooperation with Citrix Systems.

This book is the result of extensive cooperation with Citrix Systems, Inc., the leader in thin-client/server computing. The company opened its archives and provided the conceptual and technical source materials that went into building this first book devoted to the topic of thin-client/server computing. Citrix Systems opened its doors in 1989 when it began development of a multiuser version of OS/2. WinFrame, the company's first multiuser-based product for Windows NT, shipped in 1995.

Citrix Systems became a public company in 1995. Citrix technology added a great deal of value to the Windows NT platform and caught Microsoft's attention. Microsoft certainly validated thin-client/server computing when it licensed the Citrix multiuser technology for its multiuser version of Windows NT, code-named Hydra.

> Thin-client/server technology provides a foundation for businesses to live long and prosper.

The emerging thin-client/server technology discussed in this book will continue to evolve for years to come, improving access to the latest computing technologies. At the same time, it will present the opportunity for new markets to benefit from computing solutions. This book will jump-start your thinking in terms of how formerly unattainable computing solutions for meeting your organization's goals are now within reach. It should also provide hope in terms of your being able to easily and continually take advantage of new computing solutions that will allow your organization to prosper and to grow.

*Joel P. Kanter, Ph.D.*
*Kanter Computing, Inc.*

# Acknowledgments

In this era of projects with ever-increasing scope and compressed schedules, acknowledging the contributions of everyone involved along the way is more and more important. All too often, we move on to new projects without remembering to thank the people who have helped us on the current one. A contribution that might on the surface seem small can in fact make or break a project or present a fresh way of solving a problem. It's important not only to thank people personally but also to find every opportunity to recognize their contributions publicly.

My investigation of thin-client/server computing began while I held the position of academic programs manager in the Internet Platform and Tools Division at Microsoft (a group that has probably changed names at least two or three times since I left the company). George Norris, who at the time worked in a Microsoft group doing strategic planning for education using the Microsoft Windows 95 platform, steered me toward Citrix Systems and the company's technology as a potentially great solution for educational institutions. Although George was unable to pursue this technology, we both felt that its use in education would not only benefit schools but would serve as a pilot to help Microsoft understand how thin-client/server computing could positively impact Microsoft's business. I have a deep respect for George, his vision, and his desire to create a real win-win-win situation for education customers, Microsoft, and Citrix Systems.

George steered me to Mark Templeton, vice president of marketing at Citrix. Mark exudes an infectious enthusiasm and passion for evangelizing Citrix's thin-client/server products. He was very willing to work with me while I was at Microsoft in trying to set up pilot projects that removed both the IS management and hardware barriers preventing use of the latest versions of development tools in higher education. After I left Microsoft, Mark and I continued to talk. Our talks inspired me to write this book. I value Mark's time, attention, and input as well as his insight and vision.

Daniel Heimlich, a Citrix product manager, served as my main contact and Citrix project lead for this book. Daniel's enthusiasm, passion, attention to detail, and devotion to thin-client/server computing paid off quite well as the final version of this book went to press. At this point in my career, I've decided to put my energy into worthwhile projects that provide an opportunity to work with great people. I would work with Daniel again in a heartbeat.

The information provided in this book was assembled from the archives at Citrix. I especially want to thank the company as a whole for allowing these materials to be used for this book.

I would also like to thank consultants Ursula Habermacher and David Carroll for their writing assistance with the more technical chapters in this book. Both Ursula and David, former Citrix employees, have extensive experience with WinFrame and now provide thin-client/server consulting and training services. It was their assistance and willingness to form a team around this book that got it through some of those critical early stages. I look forward to teaming up with Ursula and David again.

During my Microsoft career, which spanned almost eight years, the people at Microsoft Press always stood out as real stars. Jim Brown, Microsoft Press Publisher, who is not only a colleague but also a personal friend for whom I have high regard, was willing to take a look at this project. He noted its strategic value and along with Acquisitions Director Steve Guty gave enthusiastic consent. The project rapidly picked up pace when Sally Stickney became the project editor. Working with Sally provided a real shot in the arm. Her insights, ability to work as a team member, flexibility, and obvious experience in the publishing industry—and daily phone calls—really brought this project to fruition. I would also like to thank Jim Johnson and Lisa Theobald for their astute editorial comments and Travis Beaven for the graphics. Travis's particular talents with Adobe Photoshop greatly enhanced my picture in the back of the book; he removed my beard (although I had just shaved) and the dark circles under my eyes. Thanks also to Cheryl Penner, principal proofreader/copy editor, for polishing the final drafts of the galleys and pages, and to Peggy Herman, principal desktop publisher, for laying out the pages so competently.

Compaq Computer Corporation was especially generous. The company not only furnished a server, allowing me to test software, but it was also very gracious about providing product support. William Casperson, a Compaq systems engineer stationed at a local "Redmond, Washington," software company made sure that the server ran like a top. He would stop by the Kanter Computing headquarters (my house) when needed. I would also like to thank F. G. Seeburger and Dave Mauldin for their assistance in assuring that the equipment required to complete this project was available.

Getting reviewers to look at your materials can be a real challenge, even when you're employed by the same company at the same location. The level of cooperation that I received from the members of the Citrix community would have been incredible if I were an on-site employee. It was even more incredible considering that we worked at opposite ends of the country—with them in Fort Lauderdale, Florida, and me in Redmond, Washington. The quality of their reviews was outstanding as well. I would like to thank not only Daniel Heimlich, but also Kurt Moody, Ed Janaczek, Russ Naples, and Seng Sun, who were always available to provide technical assistance and were real cheerleaders for this project. I also deeply appreciate the time spent by Bill Madden, Bob Williams, Tammy Olivia, Dave Manks, David Weiss, James Marsala, Bill Brown, Linda Cohen, Jane Regan, and Bob Faerman. The Citrix reviewers were subject to regular calls from me as I tried to verify technical details and track down information. Everyone was quite generous with time and very willing to answer questions. If someone didn't know an answer, he or she helped me find a source. I also appreciate the support and assistance for the different aspects of this project provided by Deepa Swamy, Fay Wilmot, Craig Bernstein, Eric Thav, Erich Steller, Jeff Krantz, Josh Drachman, Vicky Harris, Ken Downs, Marc Andre Boisseau, Janet Hansen, and Peter Savino. I'm also grateful to Liz Bullington at Sicola Martin for her assistance in obtaining art source files. I hope that I haven't left anyone out, but if so, please accept my apologies and also my appreciation for your help.

In addition to the technical help from Citrix, Solveig Whittle, product manager in the Microsoft Windows NT group, also reviewed materials and answered questions. I appreciate Solveig's support and look forward to working more closely with her as Microsoft's Hydra project reaches maturity.

I would very much like to thank Ed Iacobucci, chairman of Citrix Systems, for providing the Foreword to this book. I would also like to thank Roger Roberts, CEO of Citrix Systems, for fostering a corporate culture that encourages people to go above and beyond mere duty in assisting with a project of this type.

I'm very grateful for all of the help provided by MooseLogic, Inc., one of Citrix's resellers. Scott Gorcester and all of the professionals at MooseLogic might be best described as "technical support saints." They understand the use of WinFrame inside and out and have been most generous with their assistance.

In Chapter 8, you'll find a case study from Idaho State University. This case study shows how you can make programming tools available on a WinFrame server. ISU Professor Corey Schou is responsible for making this happen. Corey's an incredible person and a great teacher. He knows how to create an educational experience for his students that not only imparts the requisite theoretical concepts but also provides students with practical skills for the real world. When you ask Corey for help, he'll tell you that his students can do miracles, but the impossible might take a few days. I value my association with Corey very much.

During the course of this project, Kevin Fisher of Contour Data, a FoxPro developer and a colleague of mine, turned from skeptic to believer with regard to thin-client/server computing. I want to thank Kevin for all his input. I also want to thank members of the Lake Washington schools—Dan Phelan, Hugh Mobley, George Ainsworth, Jeff Bowers, Cheryl Chikalla, and Dean Irvine—for envisioning ways in which thin-client/server computing can revolutionize the use of information in schools and for their patience while I focused on this project.

I'm most appreciative of the support provided by Mark Templeton's and Daniel Heimlich's families. Last year, I proposed the first incarnation of this project in a meeting at Mark's house, with a second meeting on his boat (yes, life can be rough sometimes). I want to thank Mark's wife, Yvonne, for her hospitality when we met. I very much enjoyed our exchange of stories about software industry survival. Mark's kids, Warren, Pinckney, and Pierce, really added a nice perspective and dimension to those meetings. I also want to thank Cheryl Heimlich, Daniel's wife, who has also been gracious as Daniel received my frantic calls on evenings and weekends, and I'd like to wish them both the best of luck with their new baby, Julia Angel Heimlich.

With regard to my own family, my mother, Nettie Kanter, along with my aunt, Enid Weinberg, kept the Boca Raton, Florida, offices of Kanter Computing open for the duration of this project. You can't imagine how much I appreciated their help.

Most of all, I want to thank my wife, Minna, and my boys, Sam and Matt. Sam and Matt are a real source of inspiration; they're very sharp and insightful considering their ages of 8 and 5, respectively. They've made working at home a very worthwhile experience. Minna has endured my doctoral dissertation and eight years of Microsoft life. She's not only my wife and a wonderful, devoted full-time mother but also the legal counsel, administrator, and business manager for Kanter Computing. Minna is an extremely bright and caring individual who is concerned with her family and with the community at large. Without her love, support, and all the work she does on a daily basis to keep this family moving, I would not have been able to complete this project.

*Joel P. Kanter, October 1997*

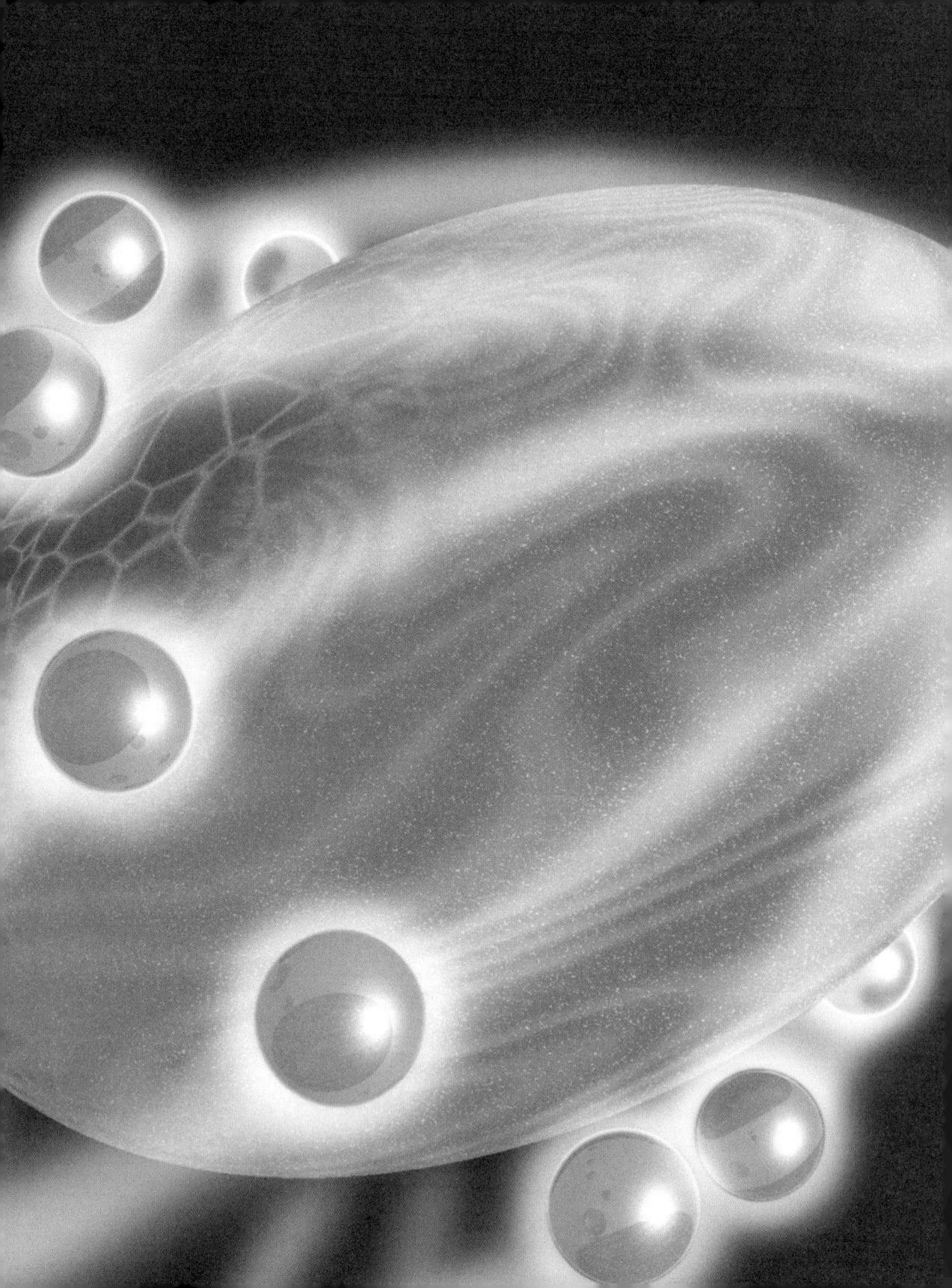

Chapter One

# The Thin-Client/Server Computing Model

During my tenure as a Microsoft product manager, members of the Windows Strategy group introduced me to Citrix Systems' thin-client/server computing model, which consists of the WinFrame server and Independent Computing Architecture (ICA) client software. To me, the greatest appeal of this model was the removal of hardware barriers to the introduction of the most current 32-bit software, which included both development and productivity tools. I immediately realized the impact this computing model would have on total cost of ownership, including application access from any hardware platform, bandwidth-independent performance, and additional levels of data security. I could envision the model having important benefits for small and large corporations, organizations, schools, system administrators, and even the user relationship to an Internet Service Provider (ISP). Although WinFrame was already an authorized extension to Microsoft Windows NT Server, Microsoft further validated the thin-client/server model by licensing Citrix's MultiWin technology for future versions of Windows NT Server, a project referred to by Microsoft as "Hydra."

*Thin-client/server computing enables single-point application management, universal application access, bandwidth-independent performance, and additional levels of data security.*

The phrase that everyone is working with these days is "total cost of ownership" (TCO), which really boils down to getting the most out of your technology investment with the least amount of unnecessary effort. To that end, a thin-client/server solution might well be the best thing that ever happened to your IS department. With thin-client/server computing, your IS people can deploy applications instantly, without ever needing to "touch" every desktop. No, you're not dreaming: mission-critical applications can be deployed and updated on one central server. This TCO benefit saves IS organizations literally months in rollout time. Such rapid application deployment is just one of the many management benefits that can revolutionize your IS department and your way of doing business. I'll cover the management issues that pertain to the thin-client/server model in more detail in the "Addressing the Issues: Management and Scalability, Access, Performance, Security, and Total Cost of Ownership" section later in this chapter.

*Applications can be deployed.*

Another boon to your company as a result of adopting the thin-client/server model will be your ability to give your employees access to the most current software applications without breaking your budget. Currently, corporations that supply their employees with personal computers must upgrade or purchase new hardware before testing and rolling out new, more robust 32-bit software applications. If the Information Systems (IS) department wants to deploy custom internal applications, it needs to create and test client software for each operating system and version thereof that the company uses. The thin-client/server model, using technologies from Citrix Systems built on Microsoft Windows NT Server, allows rapid application deployment regardless of platform. The application executes completely on the server—only mouse clicks and keystrokes are sent to the server for processing, and video display is returned to the client device via an efficient networking protocol and thin-client software on the local device. As I've become more familiar with the technology and seen it implemented across a variety of business situations, I've seen how quickly IS departments become better able to serve their users: the deployment of applications becomes easier to manage; users have greater access to applications and data, which increases their performance; and security is enhanced because all data is maintained on the network.

In this chapter, you'll be introduced to the basics of thin-client/server computing. Chapter 2 gets into the relationship of the thin-client/server model to two- and three-tier client/server computing and the download-and-run model used for Java computing. But for now, let's start with an overview of thin-client/server computing—a model of computing that's sure to catch on because it allows IS professionals and organizations to maximize their resources and save time while providing quality services to their users.

## What Is Thin-Client/Server Computing?

The thin-client/server computing model involves connecting thin-client software or a thin-client hardware device with the server side using a highly efficient network protocol such as Citrix's ICA. The thin-client/server architecture enables 100 percent server-based processing, management, deployment, and support for mission-critical, productivity, Web-based, or other custom applications across any type of connection to any type of client hardware, regardless of platform. The client hardware can include Windows-based terminals, PCs, NetPCs, network computers, Apple Macintosh computers, or UNIX devices.

Applications execute 100 percent on the server.

Using the thin-client/server computing model, you won't need to purchase or upgrade hardware just to run the latest software—instead, you'll be able to let it comfortably evolve, leveraging your existing hardware, operating systems, software, networks, and standards. Thin-client/server computing extends the life of your computing infrastructure considerably.

Update your computing infrastructure as applications become available.

## How Does Thin-Client/Server Computing Work?

To see how thin-client/server computing really works, you need to start with the server part of the model. To put it simply, in thin-client/server computing, all your applications and data are deployed, managed, and supported at the server. In addition, 100 percent of the application executes at the server. The application logic is separated from the user interface at the server and transported to the client. (See Figure 1-1.) This separation means that only screen updates, mouse clicks, and keystrokes travel the network to the server.

**FIGURE 1-1** *The application executes on the server, and screen updates are sent to the client device.*

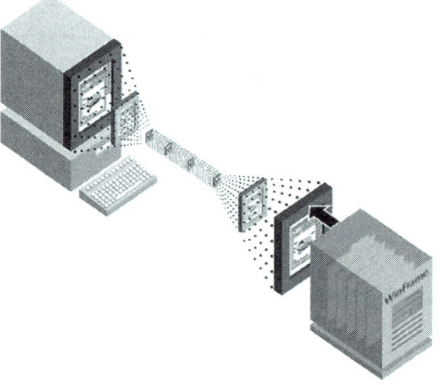

*Citrix MultiWin allows multiple concurrent users to log on to a Windows NT Server.*

The thin-client software accesses and takes advantage of the server system software. MultiWin, the extension to Windows NT Server, allows multiple concurrent thin-client users to log on and run applications in separate, protected Windows sessions on the server.

*ICA allows client devices to run applications without special emulation software.*

The ICA thin-client software that works with MultiWin enables a wide variety of client devices to access the same applications—without special emulation software, changes in system configuration, or application rewrites. Figure 1-2 depicts a server running with four different computing devices that use thin-client/server software.

FIGURE 1-2   *The Citrix WinFrame product line with the Citrix MultiWin technology enables a wide variety of devices to access your applications.*

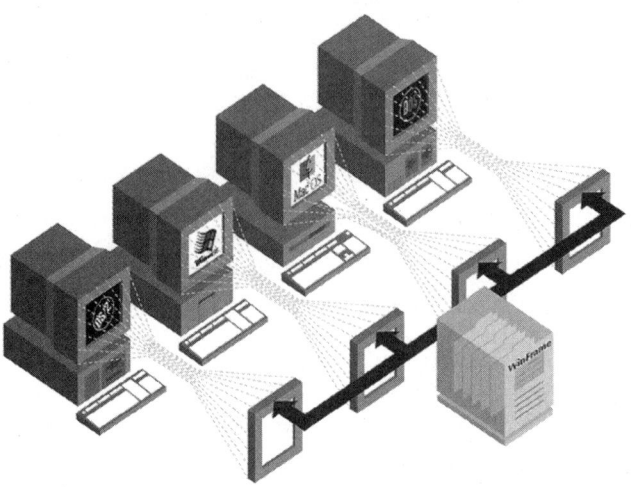

With the server splitting the execution and display logic, only keystrokes, mouse clicks, and screen updates travel the network. Thus, applications consume just a fraction of the normal network bandwidth usually required. Because applications require fewer resources, they can be extended from one location across any type of connection to any type of client with exceptional performance.

*The server splits execution from display logic.*

### About Citrix MultiWin

Citrix created MultiWin as an authorized multiuser extension to Microsoft Windows NT Server for its WinFrame server. The MultiWin technology is currently available from Citrix Systems in WinFrame Enterprise version 1.7, built on the Windows NT Server 3.51 platform. In mid-1997, Citrix licensed the MultiWin technology to Microsoft as part of a cooperative development agreement for creating native multiuser capabilities in Windows NT Server version 4 and future versions.

*METAFRAME*

If you compare bandwidth requirements across shared Ethernet, wireless Ethernet, ISDN (Integrated Services Digital Network), and modem speeds, you'll find a thin-client/server protocol such as Citrix ICA extremely efficient. (See Figure 1-3.)

**FIGURE 1-3** *Using just a fraction of network bandwidth, ICA enables robust 32-bit applications to generate consistent performance through any connection.*

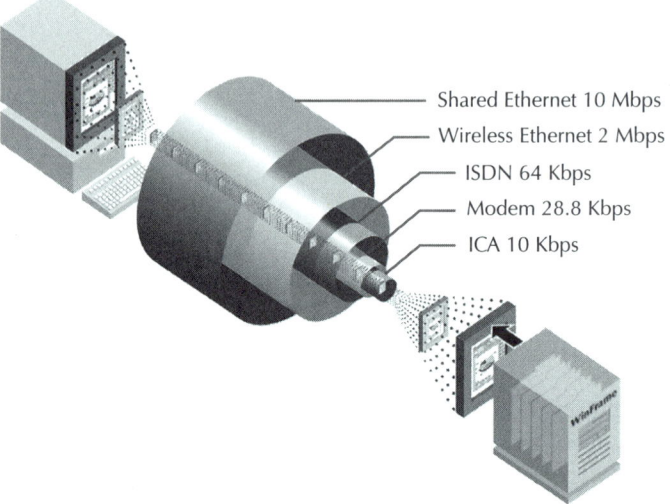

*You can cut and paste between thin-client and local sessions.*

Using a protocol such as ICA with a local area network (LAN) or a wide area network (WAN) connection, the user experience with many software applications is the same for applications running on a WinFrame server as it is for applications running on a local computer with a full complement of application and operating system software. In a thin-client/server session, users can cut and paste between sessions, save to local storage devices, and print to local or network printers.

In summary, the thin-client/server architecture includes three components sitting on top of the Microsoft Windows NT Server:

- MultiWin, a multiuser layer on the server that simulates local application processing

- ICA display services on the multiuser layer that divide the application execution from the display logic
- Thin-client software, such as the ICA client, on the client device that sends mouse movements and keystrokes to the server while accepting display images

Separation of the application execution from the display logic reduces the amount of data that needs to be communicated across the network, allowing efficient use of available bandwidth—and in the case of ICA, very efficient use of low-bandwidth situations.

## What Do You Need to Do, and Where Do You Need to Do It?

Thin-client/server computing is not necessarily for everyone, everywhere, all the time. It should not be perceived as a religious technology war to see which company survives the next great era in the information age. Less of that type of noise would help customers make better decisions about what they need to accomplish. Ideally, to figure out what form of technology is best suited to a particular business situation, an IS department should conduct a functional assessment of the company's installed base and projected needs. To that end, the thin-client/server computing model allows the use of most recent versions of line-of-business, mission-critical, or information applications on different devices along with existing native applications. IS departments will be able to deploy and integrate these applications on existing systems where needed.

*With technology, form should follow function.*

The thin-client software, especially the Citrix ICA client, can reside on any device: a handheld computer, a network computer, JavaStation, NetPC, a Windows terminal, a PC running any Microsoft Windows operating system (Windows 3.*x*, Windows 95, or Windows NT), a Macintosh, or a UNIX workstation. You can also choose to run Windows applications either locally or from a server.

*You can run thin-client sessions on any device, anytime, anywhere.*

## A Personal Experience

In my previous positions as product manager, instructional designer, and technical writer at Microsoft, I always outgrew the capacity of the equipment issued to do my work. Arriving at Microsoft in December 1988, I was given a Compaq 386/20E with a 120-MB hard drive and a Mac II with 5 MB of RAM and an 80-MB hard drive for my technical writing. By the time I left Microsoft in October 1996, I was using a Toshiba notebook with a P75 processor, 24 MB of RAM, and an 850-MB hard drive. Between testing different Microsoft products in alpha and beta stages and dealing with huge e-mail files and an ever-increasing number of internal custom information and requisition types of applications, my machines were forever at maximum capacity. My e-mail files often reached the 100-MB limit.

Microsoft internal information and eform applications were written at different times with different tools by various groups within the company and often increased the size of my system directory. Occasionally, the applications conflicted because of different DLL versions and didn't work well together. At the same time, I regularly used Microsoft Office applications such as Microsoft Excel, Word, PowerPoint, Access, and Internet Explorer and development tools such as Microsoft Visual Basic. As a knowledge worker with creative application needs, I was always working with macros or using Office applications in some exotic manner for which they weren't intended. While I couldn't imagine giving up local control of my applications, I would have been far better off not only keeping my e-mail files on a server but also executing the mail client there as well and viewing my mail through a thin client. I could also have better accessed a number of the many Microsoft internal applications (for example, benefits, Help desk, product information) using a thin client residing on my desktop. And rather than running Internet Explorer locally, I would have made better use of my hard drive space and system resources if I had run Internet Explorer on a server and accessed it with thin-client software on my desktop.

At Microsoft, thousands of users worldwide are serviced by ITG, Microsoft's IS group. ITG is responsible for deploying and maintaining corporate applications. The thin-client/server model would facilitate the rollout of the myriad applications used by Microsoft employees. At the same time, this model would help maximize the use of each employee's computing resources.

The following table lists various user scenarios for thin-client/server computing. In the next four sections, you'll see how each type of user mentioned in this table might actually work within a company or organization.

## User Scenarios

| User | Devices | Tasks, Settings, or Job Titles | Application Type | Thin-Client/Server vs. Local Apps. (%) |
|---|---|---|---|---|
| Mobile task-based user | Handheld or mobile thin-client device | Writing traffic tickets, monitoring car rental returns, taking restaurant orders, reading gas/water meters, tracking deliveries | Line-of-business applications | 0% local/ 100% thin-client |
| Office task-based user | Windows terminal, NetPC, or network computer | Traditional office environments, with workers ranging from temporary to administrative; bank tellers, telemarketers, insurance claim adjustors; fast food service; automobile service departments; information kiosks | Word processing, line-of-business applications, information applications | 0% local/ 100% thin-client |
| Knowledge workers | Notebook PC and/or desktop PC, handheld devices | Project management, financial reporting, proposal writing, sales, presentations, e-mail, scheduling, contact management | Productivity applications; groupware and communications; Internet, intranet, and extranet information; documents and applications | 50% local/ 50% thin-client |
| Power users with creative, analytic, or engineering task needs | Notebook PC and/or desktop PC, and/or high-end workstation; handheld devices | Knowledge worker tasks, with the addition of statistical or scientific analysis and research; periodical or book publishing; graphics; multimedia and Web authoring; software application development | All of the software used by the knowledge worker with the addition of desktop publishing applications, graphics software, and software development tools | 70% local/ 30% thin-client |

### Mobile Task-Based User

An example of a mobile task-based user is a police officer with a thin-client mobile device in her car. As the officer requires information, she can access any of the applications on the server through her terminal via wireless communications. For example, she might be giving a traffic ticket and need to check with the registry of motor vehicles. Other officers might use maps or other information that is updated daily. The server that the police officers are logged on to can be powerful and robust and connected directly to national databases through high-speed lines. The device in the police car doesn't carry any confidential information; all transactions are executed on the server and displayed on the mobile device.

An express delivery carrier is another excellent example of a person who uses a mobile client device with thin-client software. As this person picks up and delivers packages, he enters the latest tracking and status data into his handheld device. The thin client in the handheld device encrypts and transmits the information back to the driver's base of operations, where all data is consolidated for quick processing and where the carrier has access to the most up-to-date data. Again, no confidential information exists on the local device because 100 percent of the application executes on the server.

### Office Task-Based User

*Use dedicated thin-client devices for task-based users.*

Imagine that you're the head of IS at a large insurance company. You need to provide the claims department access to customized forms and tables, and you need to allow the company access to a centralized database that contains current data. Although the claims workers and other company personnel might need to use e-mail or scheduling software, they would be unnecessarily distracted by any other software. These users don't need to spend any time with the intricacies of an operating system. In settings such as this, employees could be using a Windows-based terminal, NetPC, or network computer with the applications completely developed, deployed, and maintained by an internal IS department. Your company could even use Citrix ICA thin-client/server software with some older PCs and effectively turn them into Windows terminals with just a network card and a VGA video card and monitor. The insurance industry is certainly not the only type of industry that can greatly benefit from using thin-client/server–based applications. IS professionals who plan, deploy, and support systems for all types of customer service professionals can increase their productivity and streamline their computing infrastructure with this new technology. Whether providing information, taking orders, troubleshooting, tracking customer information, or using group scheduling and communications, customer service professionals are a segment of task-based workers whose computing needs can be most efficiently met with thin-client/server technology.

### Knowledge Workers

Are you responsible for providing IS services to knowledge workers? Knowledge workers might include writers, editors, planners, managers, lawyers, doctors, clergy, and faculty teaching at any level of education. Knowledge work is work that is based on researching, extending, applying, and distributing information in one form or another. This type of worker might prefer to use a desktop or notebook PC with a full complement of productivity software. Even though the work of knowledge workers doesn't tax the limits of the operating system or of locally run software, these workers might prefer storing documents locally and having the choice of using this software with or without a network. They could be using their notebook computers not only at work but also while on the road or at home. On the other hand, many of these professionals might be equally well served by a thin-client/server device and software solutions. It's a matter of how you, the IS professional, balance the needs and work habits of your user base with IS resources.

*Use a combination of thin-client and local solutions for knowledge workers.*

As the table on page 9 indicates, knowledge workers might prefer to have about half their tasks executed locally and half through a thin-client/server solution. I would say that tasks might logically be divided along these lines: frequently used productivity tools are used locally, and infrequently used productivity tools are run on the server. This split assumes that other kinds of tasks—such as e-mail, information management, scheduling, and any applications specific to the company—can save local resources by being run in a thin-client/server scenario. Desktop icons for e-mail and other thin-client/server applications would look identical to the icons for starting local applications. The only difference would be in the execution: whether the application executed locally or on the server. Again, deciding how and when to use thin-client/server technology is a matter of optimizing the professional's time and computing resources, and of making sure that mission-critical applications are always available, regardless of the proverbial rain, snow, sleet, or hail.

### Power Users with Creative and Analytic Task Needs

Power users share certain characteristics: they are often professionally interested in technology; they push the limits of the software they regularly use; and they sometimes need high-end tools that require robust, high-powered hardware that can handle intensive local application processing. Because of their interest or their job requirements, some knowledge workers also reach the limits of their computing capacity and become a population of power users demanding not only performance but also storage capacity. These users might require creative, analytic, or engineering applications. They often push productivity tools beyond the limit that an IS group is prepared to support. Power users can include artists requiring high-end graphics applications; researchers and engineers running modeling, simulation, or intensive number-crunching applications; and software engineers using development tools to create software for distribution to a small group or a wide audience.

> Preserve cycles and storage space for CPU-intensive applications by running other applications, such as e-mail, scheduling, and information, from a server.

Hardware used by the power user can include high-end PCs, high-end notebook computers, and dedicated workstations. Power users might even use a combination of devices along with a handheld PC. Although power users would prefer to have a complement of tools on their local devices, they might be best served if applications such as e-mail, scheduling, an Internet browser, internal information, and form applications are run from a server in a thin-client/server scenario. These applications need not take up either system resources or space on the local computer. Power users would also benefit from having a backup set of tools on a server that they could access through thin-client software. All tools executed on the server are the ones that would be most easily supported by an IS department. Rather than having to go to user sites, the support staff would be able to deploy, maintain, and troubleshoot these applications from the server. In the table on page 9, the speculation that power users might run up to 30 percent of their applications through a thin-client/server scenario is a guess that these users spend most of their time with a core set of tools that are best run locally. It also suggests that they would be best served if the other applications, such as e-mail, scheduling, and information applications, didn't detract from either CPU usage or storage; and software that didn't need to be on the local computer would not conflict with applications that were required to be there.

*Power users often use multiple devices.*

Figure 1-4 illustrates how thin-client/server computing holds a place within the computing environment of almost any user

**FIGURE 1-4**  *This figure compares different user types, showing an estimate of the proportion of time spent with locally run applications vs. thin-client/server solutions.*

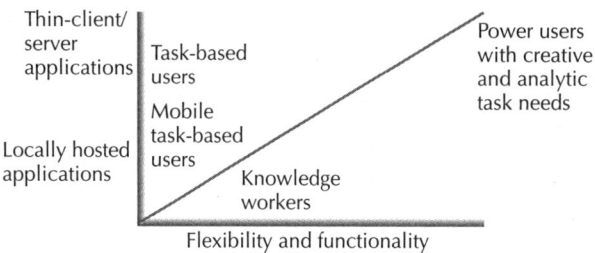

within an organization. From 100 percent of the applications for task-specific functions to approximately 30 percent for the most intense power user, this computing model can help you make the most of your available computing resources.

## Addressing the Issues: Management and Scalability, Access, Performance, Security, and Total Cost of Ownership

So now you know the basics of how the thin-client/server model works, where it might be used, and who might use it. You've also seen how this model will allow you to use your computing equipment efficiently and your IS support and maintenance resources wisely. In this section, I'll present the issues involved in using the thin-client/server model from the IS perspective. Certainly, TCO is important to IS professionals. But just as key to them is what the thin-client/server solution can offer to the company in terms of management and scalability, access, performance, and security.

### Management and Scalability

*Deploy fully configured workstations where necessary.*

IS professionals clearly prefer single-point control. They don't want to travel around a company providing support for each desktop computer that has an operating system. The thin-client/server architecture allows IS departments to consolidate databases, file servers, and application servers in the same location in which they manage user access. This consolidation means that users worldwide can access the same centralized information and that companies can avoid the security, cost, reliability, and management issues involved in having widely dispersed databases. At the same time, workstations with a full complement of software, including a desktop operating system and locally run applications, can be deployed as required for a particular job. Figure 1-5 illustrates the way in which the server is connected to file, application, and database servers.

**FIGURE 1-5** *Using the thin-client/server model, you can consolidate databases, file servers, and application servers at one location while managing user access.*

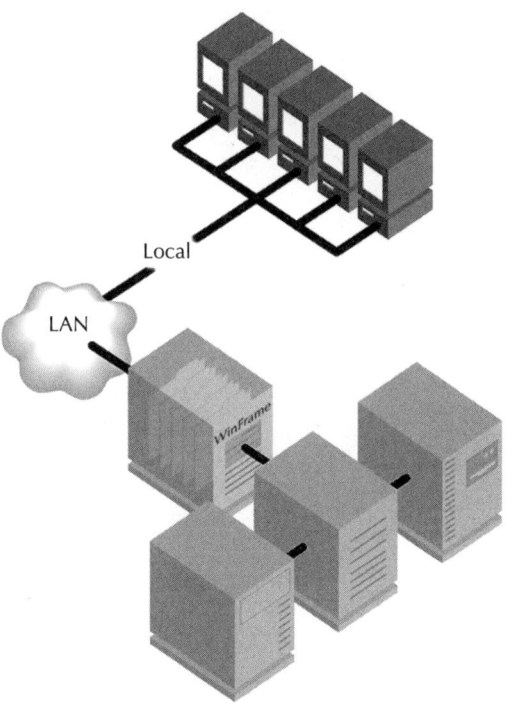

Scalability presents another challenge to IS professionals, who might need to scale a growing enterprise from dozens to thousands of users. You'll find that Citrix's WinFrame load-balancing option allows for extremely reliable deployment of thin-client application solutions from a server "farm." With the WinFrame load-balancing scenario, users are dynamically routed to the WinFrame server that offers the best application performance. System administrators will still see and manage a single system image for the entire network. Figure 1-6 shows a cluster of clients attached to a server farm using WinFrame load balancing.

**FIGURE 1-6** *The Citrix load-balancing feature enables multiple WinFrame Servers with the Citrix add-on to be grouped together to meet the needs of thousands of users.*

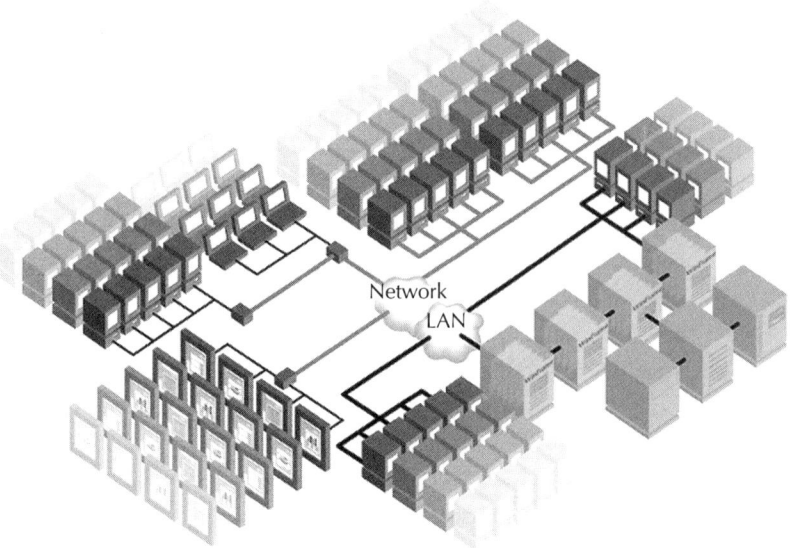

### Access

From that single location that houses all of your application servers, file servers, and databases, you can manage not only the users on your LAN but also the users in branch offices, telecommuters, and mobile professionals. Because of the efficiency of not only processing on the server but also of using network bandwidth, applications run extremely well over existing remote-node servers and branch-office routers. Figure 1-7 shows a WinFrame server farm.

### Performance

In developing WinFrame and the ICA client, Citrix has optimized network performance for connections as low as 9600 baud for use over a cellular modem. Because ICA clients are sending only mouse clicks and keystrokes to the server and receiving only screen updates, ICA clients maximize the use of your bandwidth whether you're on a LAN or using an analog or ISDN modem.

**FIGURE 1-7** *The thin-client/server computing model gives you the power of single-point control to extend applications over any connection to any client with increased performance and security.*

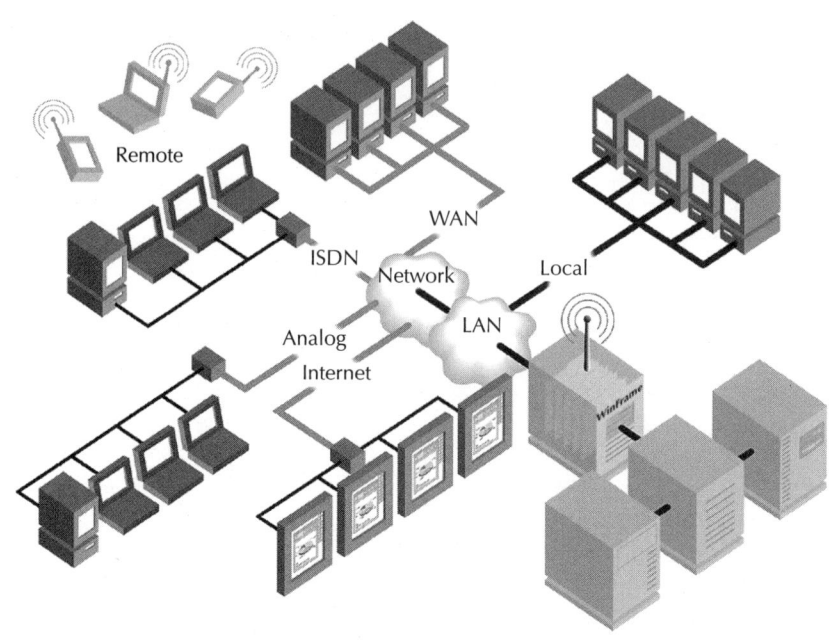

Ironically, it takes a while for users to understand how this system software works because application performance is something they take for granted. However, when you add the ICA client to an old 386 with 2 MB of RAM and demonstrate the use of the latest 32-bit version of your software, eyes light up.

## Security

Security for thin-client/server computing comes from WinFrame's base of services provided by Microsoft Windows NT Server. Windows NT Server provides security through individual and group accounts, user profiles, and the differing levels of security required for the U.S. Department of Defense's C2 security specification. In addition, regardless of whether the user has the latest PC or a Windows-based terminal, sensitive data can be maintained in a single secure place on the server.

## Performance Research

Citrix commissioned the Tolly Group to evaluate the performance and scalability of the Citrix WinFrame Enterprise (version 1.6) application server when supporting clients running 32-bit Windows applications. Among the tests, the Tolly Group measured the time required for a Windows 95 client using a 28.8 modem connection to complete some common Microsoft Excel tasks when an increasing number of LAN clients were running on the WinFrame server.

The results showed that up to 30 clients—29 LAN clients and 1 WAN client—could run Excel from a dual-processor Pentium 90 WinFrame server without significant degradation. The WAN client took about 30 seconds to perform a group of common Excel tasks with no other clients accessing the WinFrame server. With 19 LAN clients simultaneously accessing the WinFrame server, the WAN client's response times in Excel were degraded by less than 10 percent. With 29 LAN clients simultaneously accessing the server, response time on the dial-up client was degraded by less than 35 percent.

The Tolly Group found that the WinFrame server provides a scalable solution that is capable of supporting up to 30 clients on a dual-processor Pentium server, without significant degradation in response times for any one client. The Tolly Group also found that the WinFrame architecture makes efficient use of bandwidth, indicating that it is a good solution for bandwidth-constrained environments such as dial-up analog modem connections.

### Total Cost of Ownership

Zona Research, quoted on both the Boundless and NCD Web sites, calculates a 54–57 percent savings by using the thin-client/server model over a comparable number of networked PCs. The savings were projected over a five-year period by comparing the costs of setting up and maintaining 15 PCs and 15 Windows terminal solutions using ICA clients and a WinFrame server.

Leading research firms are seeing the impact that thin-client/server computing can make in extended enterprises. Gartner

Group, Intelliquest, IDC, and Zona Research are all conducting comprehensive studies on the market potential and user and enterprise benefits of the thin-client/server computing solution.

In summary, the thin-client/server architecture provides IS departments and professionals with an excellent solution for managing databases, file servers, and application servers in one location while providing a central point for user configurations and security. It provides access to different types of users, including local users, remote users, and telecommuters. In addition, IS professionals will be able to scale services from a small number of users on a LAN to thousands of users worldwide. Corporations currently deploying applications using Citrix's WinFrame include AT&T Wireless, Chevron, GE Capital Services, and Sears. In the case studies in Chapter 8, you'll find even more companies that are taking advantage of thin-client/server computing using Citrix technology, including LaSalle Partners, Omnes, Honeywell Europe S.A., Pyramid Breweries, Standard Forms, Anne E. Biedel & Associates, Clarion Health, Mecon, Claimsnet.com, Pro Staff, Relo-Action, Bell Mobility, and Vodac. Organizations as varied as the Orange County Public Defender's Office, Florida Water Services, Goodwill Industries of Southern Arizona, the Tulsa City-County Library, and Idaho State University are also benefiting from this technology.

## In Conclusion

The thin-client/server architecture can bring the best of different computing models and architectures together. You can instantly provide access to virtually any business-critical application, including 16-bit and 32-bit Windows applications, across any type of network connection to any type of client. You get the power of single-point control for deploying, managing, and supporting applications, including enterprise-wide rollouts, updates, and additions. Users get the universal access to the applications they need, the exceptional performance they require, and the familiarity and ease of use they're accustomed to. Plus, this technology is cost-effective and secure. IS administrators can optimize resources by providing thin-client/server solutions to task-based users via thin-client devices, or thin-client/server software solutions to knowledge workers and power users.

Chapter Two

# Comparing Computer Architectures

On one hand, the design and implementation of personal computers offer users a great degree of freedom and flexibility. On the other hand, the PC's proliferation throughout organizations has resulted in premature gray hair for many IS professionals at those organizations. As with many products, the usage envisioned by the creator of any piece of hardware or software can be quite different from how the customer actually uses the product. For example, other than holding sheets of paper together, what can you do with a paper clip? I've used paper clips to unlock a bathroom door when one of my kids tried to hide, to remove a 3.5-inch disk from a Macintosh computer, as a fishhook for a kids' carnival game, and as a tie to hold together parts of my lawnmower's handle. As the old saying goes, "Necessity is the mother of invention."

Necessity, along with curiosity, creativity, a wide range of choices, and a little bit of knowledge, has pushed the limits of the personal computer and created an ever-expanding and almost uncontrollable job for the IS professional. In the "old days," an IS professional would connect a terminal to a minicomputer or mainframe and then not touch the terminal for years. Applications and user

> The freedom offered by PCs, along with users' curiosity, creativity, and choice, has made life difficult for IS professionals.

accounts would be deployed and maintained centrally on the server. But even in those good old days, IS professionals needed to know what they were doing, since most of the available applications were not particularly intuitive and required a fair amount of support until users became proficient.

*Users just want to get the job done; they don't care how the computer works.*

In today's computing environment, a combination of new and old computing models that leverage user-interface advances and bring back the old model of mainframe computing can help IS professionals do their jobs. The "Using Terminals at Citrix" sidebar looks at one aspect of application deployment and product evolution that occurred within Citrix Systems.

Most computing environments are mixed. The thin-client/server model combines ease of use for users and single-point management for network administrators.

## Using Terminals at Citrix

As recently as 1993, Citrix's entire product support database was stored on a computer with a 486 processor that ran a multiuser version of OS/2 connected to several IBM Model 3151 terminals. At the time, the biggest problem in the system was finding an asynchronous cable for connection to a terminal. The network software consisted of Microsoft LAN Manager and Novell NetWare 3.11. As times changed at Citrix, the company's users—along with the rest of the industry—started demanding Microsoft Windows–based applications, which meant a move away from using terminals.

Citrix users were mainly concerned about the work they could accomplish with their applications. Ursula Habermacher, a thin-client/server consultant, attributes the following quote to one of her friends: "Don't tell me how a combustion engine works; just show me how to drive the car." Citrix users wanted the same thing with regard to their applications. At work, they wanted access to the same applications they used on their home PCs, but the dumb terminals could not run these new personal productivity applications. In response to the changing times and needs, Citrix released WinView, the successor to its multiuser OS/2 system, with the addition of support for Microsoft Windows.

What applications exist in your computing environment today? There's a good chance that you use a combination of applications, which might include MS-DOS–based applications, 16-bit and 32-bit Windows-based applications, and legacy mainframe and UNIX applications. I would further guess that your preference is to learn and use applications that provide a graphical user interface (GUI). While it might be easier for your organization to provide application training to users because of consistencies across GUI applications, GUI-based applications can take up a lot of network and communication bandwidth, depending on your system's architecture and configuration.

In an effort to understand the evolution, origins, and coexistence of the thin-client/server model with other architectures and technologies, in this chapter we'll look at network operating systems and application servers. We'll also examine models of distributed computing that are attempting to evolve toward a thinner client. Then we'll consider two different thin-client models and various technologies provided by different vendors. We'll conclude by looking at how you can combine the thin-client/server model with models of distributed computing and new technology to meet the needs of your organization.

## Network Operating Systems and Application Servers

Throughout the years, network operating systems and the deployment of applications have evolved. In some cases, the application model evolved to take advantage of the network operating system; in other cases, the operating system adapted in response to application requirements. The UNIX system seems to be designed with the application in mind—for example, UNIX is an excellent platform for engineers who require lots of horsepower to run their applications. UNIX taught us the value of file and data sharing across a network. But with the 1980s came the PC revolution, the advent of personal productivity applications, and the GUI. At that time, Novell designed its network operating system with file-and-print-sharing capabilities. Microsoft Windows NT combined the best of UNIX and Novell's NetWare product to target the evolving enterprise.

*Application servers have evolved from network operating systems.*

Now that we've discussed the evolution of network operating systems, let's talk about their relationship to an application server. The definition of an application server differs from vendor to vendor and from paradigm to paradigm. UNIX, now considered the original application server, used to be thought of as a time-sharing system. Novell's UnixWare was touted as a "powerful UNIX operating system for deploying line-of-business applications on departmental and enterprise server systems…designed to support the server end of client/server applications, to run line-of-business applications in NetWare environments, or to run multiuser applications that have traditionally run on proprietary mainframe or mid-range systems."

Since the introduction of UnixWare, companies such as Citrix Systems and Microsoft have again redefined the application server. For example, the Citrix WinFrame server operates as an application server in a way similar to how a UNIX server operates. Applications execute on the server, with display sent to the user's workstation. Microsoft has envisioned more of a distributed model for an application. In the Microsoft scenario, processing is distributed between the client application that executes on a local machine and a back-end Windows NT server that processes database information and possibly business rules.

In the following sections, we'll take a closer look at some of these systems.

### UNIX

*UNIX has powerful multiuser capabilities.*

UNIX is an interactive time-sharing operating system that was invented in 1969. It was originally created to allow engineers to play games on their scavenged DEC minicomputers, according to the On-Line Computing Dictionary at:

> http://wagner.Princeton.edu/foldoc

A powerful system, UNIX has long satisfied the requirements of demanding applications and engineers because of its architecture and features. Among the many features of UNIX are 32-bit and 64-bit architectures, preemptive multitasking, robustness, and networking capability.

Where UNIX and Windows NT part ways is with the diversity of UNIX vendors. With the Microsoft–Citrix announcement of May 12, 1997, Microsoft will remain the only Windows NT vendor. Conversely, there are hundreds of UNIX vendors with no "standard" flavor of UNIX among the different brands, which has hurt its market acceptance. In comparison to supported operating systems such as MS-DOS, Windows, or Windows NT, you'll find that UNIX is quite expensive, with the exception of Linux. But despite the number of vendors and the cost, by 1991 UNIX had become the most widely used multiuser general-purpose operating system in the world.

### Novell NetWare

For a number of years, NetWare was synonymous with networking. However, Windows NT is giving NetWare some stiff competition. NetWare, an exceptionally fast file-and-print server, allows desktop clients to share files, data, and printers. A typical distributed processing environment is shown in Figure 2-1 on the following page.

*NetWare's strength is in its file-and-print services.*

From its inception, Novell's redirector implementation strategy reflected the need for speed. The NetWare redirector was designed to intercept and redirect system calls for disk access; as an afterthought, Novell decided that client/server computing was also important. However, Novell's client/server implementation was problematic. The implementation was based on a 16-bit MS-DOS operating system that did not run in a protected mode. If one user session locked up, the server needed to be rebooted. Windows NT and OS/2 ran each user's session in protected mode; if one user's session locked up, the server didn't need to be rebooted.

**FIGURE 2-1** *A typical distributed processing environment with centralized data storage, as used in Novell's NetWare*

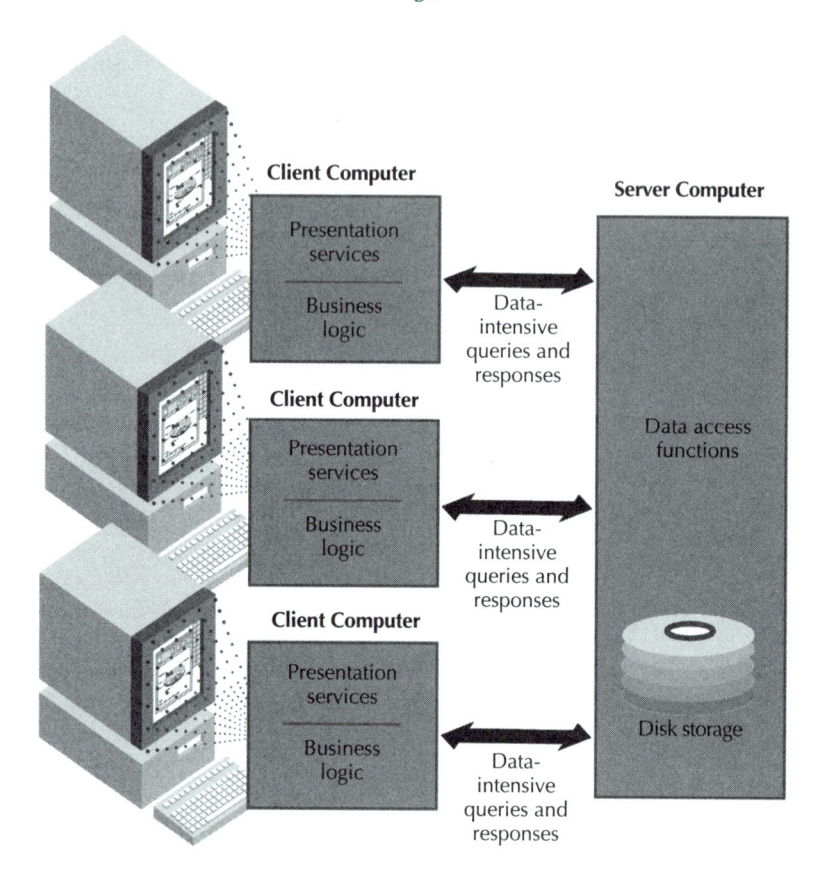

## Microsoft Windows NT Server

*Windows NT Server leverages the Windows GUI into the world of networking.*

Microsoft Windows NT Server, a 32-bit operating system, has evolved from code originally intended to be used for OS/2 version 3.0. OS/2 was jointly developed by Microsoft and IBM before the companies' development agreement ended.

After one of the longest beta tests anyone could remember (according to the Usenet groups), Microsoft Windows NT version 3.1 was released in September 1993. Unlike Microsoft Windows 3.1, a graphical environment that runs on top of MS-DOS, Windows NT is a complete operating system. To the user, the interface for

Windows NT versions 3.1 and 3.5x make the products look just like Windows 3.1; the Windows 95 GUI is used for Windows NT version 4.0. But while Windows NT uses the same interfaces as Windows 3.x and Windows 95, it surpasses these systems with true multithreading and built-in networking, security, and memory protection. While users get the desktop GUI they are accustomed to for personal productivity applications, they also get the power of a UNIX-type operating system.

When Microsoft conceived of Windows NT, the company had several market requirements in mind:

- Portability
- Multiprocessing and scalability
- Distributed computing
- POSIX compliance
- C2 security

The underlying capabilities of Windows NT echo those of OS/2 and UNIX. Windows NT was offhandedly described as "OS/2 and Windows combined, but on steroids." This obviously was not a coincidence, since many of the engineers who had worked on Windows NT had also worked on OS/2, and many of the technical capabilities of UNIX were explicitly included. What Microsoft left out of its Windows NT product was also intentional: it disregarded the diversity that existed among UNIX vendors. Windows NT has consistent GUI, application features, and API (Win32), regardless of the hardware it's used on.

## Citrix WinFrame

As we briefly discuss the different network operating systems and application servers, we come to Citrix WinFrame, which supports thin-client/server computing. Citrix WinFrame offers yet another type of application server specifically designed for use in a thin-client/server architecture.

WinFrame builds on Windows NT and adds multiuser capabilities.

WinFrame is a multiuser Windows-based application server that's built on Windows NT Server version 3.51. As I mentioned in Chapter 1, applications execute on the server and are accessed using universal, thin-client Independent Computing Architecture (ICA) software that works in conjunction with the WinFrame multiuser application server software for display on dedicated thin-client devices or over local area network (LAN), wide area network (WAN), Internet, or dial-up connections. The local device sends mouse clicks and keystrokes to the server, with display transmitted from the server to the local device. The thin-client architecture provides users with consistent, high-performance, and universal access to any type of application, including MS-DOS–based applications, Windows 16-bit and 32-bit applications, and client/server applications, regardless of available bandwidth or client hardware. The multiuser application server design provides IS managers with an economical and manageable way to deliver applications across an extended corporate network or public Internet. The WinFrame application server configuration is shown in Figure 2-2.

**FIGURE 2-2**  *The WinFrame application server configuration*

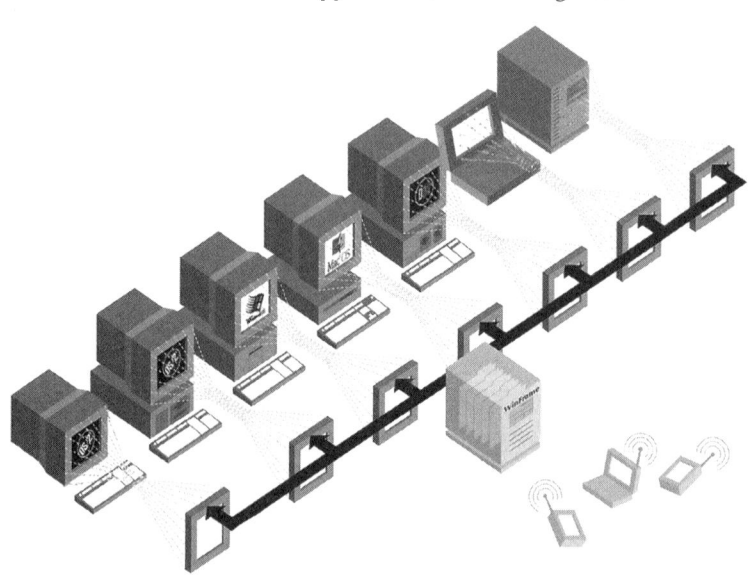

The thin-client/server model functions similarly to an *n*-tier client/server application that has been partitioned such that all business logic executes on intermediate application servers, leaving client workstations to display the user interface, with databases residing on file servers. With the thin-client/server architecture, however, the actual execution of display services also occurs on the server. IS managers who are familiar with UNIX will recognize this approach's similarity to the X Window System, which centralizes business logic and data access for UNIX applications. In contrast to the X Window System, the thin-client/server architecture that uses WinFrame application servers can run 16-bit and 32-bit Windows-based applications with a GUI that's familiar to users.

The thin-client/server model lets the IS department deploy a single copy of the mission-critical application at a central site in the enterprise network. Local and remote clients, in turn, connect to the central application via LAN, WAN, or dial-up connections. In the thin-client/server model that uses WinFrame, since all application execution takes place on the server, you can use almost any device as the client machine, including a very low-end PC.

### Using an IBM AT at a Trade Show

In 1995, Citrix introduced WinFrame at several major trade shows. Citrix representatives set up an old IBM AT with 2 MB of RAM to illustrate this capability. The machine had been dragged out of storage—cobweb-covered motherboard, dead CMOS battery, and all. It even required use of those old 5.25-inch setup disks. Once these problems were corrected and the machine was set up, they were ready for a demo. Floor traffic came to a stop next to the AT running what appeared to be Windows 3.1. The demo effectively illustrated how a thin client could work.

Now you can stop using old computers as doorstops.

# Distributed Computing Architectures

*The thin-client/server model builds on distributed computing models.*

Distributing the processing functions among different computers has been an evolving idea. Once you realize how the basics of thin-client/server computing work from the operating-system level, you can extend the thin-client/server model by accessing client/server systems with parts distributed among different servers. Let's look at the different client/server paradigms.

## Client/Server Paradigms

In an age of information overload, client/server computing emerged as the method of choice for culling the ever-growing mountain of data. Relational database engines such as Microsoft SQL Server and Oracle continued to give more and more control over how we viewed and manipulated this data. However, as this newfound power to manipulate data from a PC increased, so did the power necessary to drive these engines.

The client/server architecture seemed to provide the answer. Building on the concepts of modular programming, in which the fundamental assumption is the separation of a large piece of software into its constituent parts ("modules"), engineers developing client/server applications recognized that these modules need not all be executed within the same memory space or even on the same device. In a client/server application, the client module requests a service and the server module provides it.

*Client devices still require powerful computers.*

**Two-tier client/server** The predominant architecture today, two-tier client/server (shown in Figure 2-3) divides applications into two parts. The presentation services and the business logic functions execute at the client PC, while data access functions are handled by a database server on the network. Because two-tier client/server applications are not optimized for dial-up or WAN connections, response times are often unacceptable for remote users. Application upgrades require software and often hardware upgrades to all client PCs, resulting in potential version control problems.

FIGURE 2-3   *The traditional two-tier client/server environment*

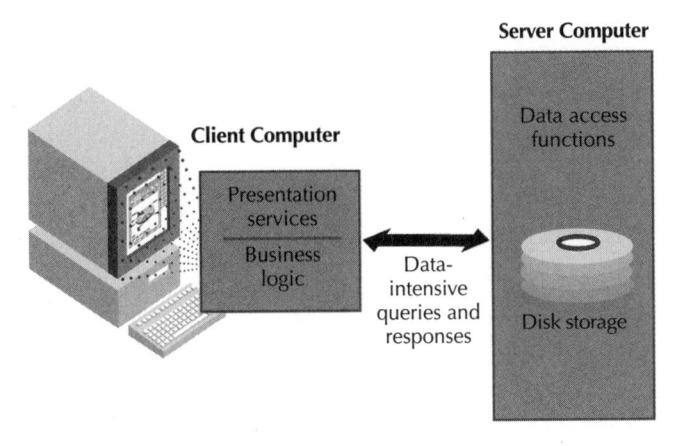

## A Client/Server Problem

Ursula Habermacher's consulting experience at a manufacturing company in New England illustrates the limitations of the traditional two-tier client/server model. In the early stages of the worldwide rollout of an integrated supply-chain management package, the company found that performance over the WAN was unacceptable. Windows NT 4.0 Workstation running on a Pentium or Pentium Pro with 32 MB of RAM was required to run the client locally. The client workstation was required to do some serious number crunching.

The problem arose as the client needed to pull all of that number-crunching data down to the local machine. While the application ran beautifully on the local LAN, European-based employees were required to run this application across the WAN, which meant pulling down all the data across a 56-KB line. This was further exacerbated by the reality that most United States–based companies, including this one, upgraded hardware at the foreign offices after home office upgrades occurred. Most of the desktop machines in the European office were well below the recommended specification necessary to run the client. Even if the WAN had not been a problem, the hardware available at the European offices was an issue. (In the sidebar titled "The Thin-Client/Server Solution" on page 44, you'll see how thin-client/server architecture, using Citrix WinFrame, resolved this company's WAN issues.)

In today's widely distributed enterprises, two-tier architecture breaks down as the client moves farther away from the server and as the local machine's computing requirements increase. These problems are inherent to the traditional client/server architecture, which emphasizes client-side computational power.

To address some of the limitations of the two-tier architecture, three-tier (sometimes called *n*-tier or multitier) client/server architecture was born. Figure 2-4 shows an example of three-tier architecture. Three-tier or multitier client/server architecture requires the restructuring of an application into three or more parts. The presentation service application executes on the client PC, which may also perform a portion of the business logic functions. Application servers or intermediate servers are inserted into the infrastructure, executing the rest of the business logic. The data access is handled by one or more back-end database servers.

If your company requires a multitier client/server architecture, you'll find the thin-client/server model an extremely helpful method for delivering these applications. You can distribute the

**FIGURE 2-4** *A three-tier (multitier) client/server environment*

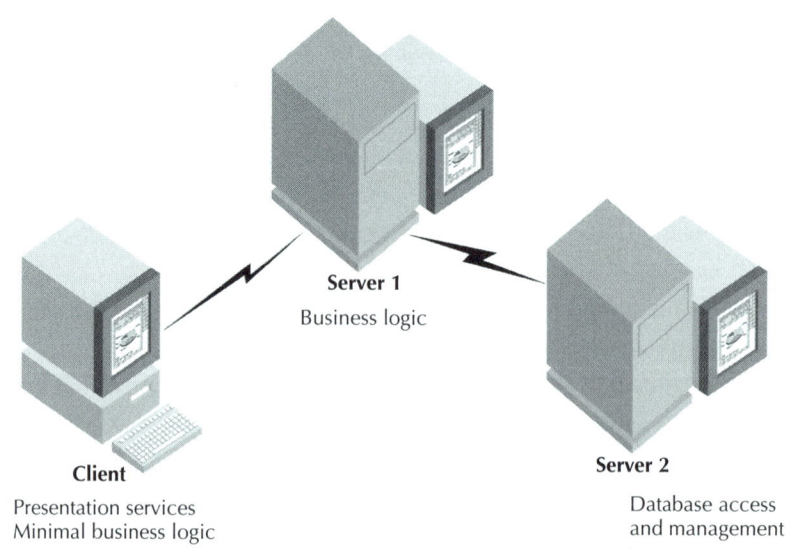

processing in any manner you deem necessary to get the optimal performance. You then use the thin-client/server architecture to deliver the presentation services. Rather than the presentation services application residing on and executing on the user's local machine, you can use either a thin-client display protocol such as ICA or a dedicated hardware device such as a Windows-based terminal, a NetPC, or a network computer that runs ICA for viewing the display generated by the thin-client/server (such as WinFrame). Using the thin-client/server model to complement a multitier client/server architecture allows for rapid deployment of these applications on any device and through any type of network. I'll tell you more about ICA later in this chapter.

*Three-tier client/ server architecture separates the presentation services, business logic, and data on different devices.*

## Web-Based Paradigms

According to the META Group, a major focus of application delivery for the next two years will be to support specific extended enterprise requirements. These extended enterprise requirements include intranets and extranets, which are built on standards set for the World Wide Web. The META Group predicts that intranet applications will predominantly utilize the three-tier model, while extranet applications will require models with four or more tiers. The implication is that big business is taking the Internet seriously.

*Web models are becoming a popular way to distribute applications.*

The World Wide Web is technically an Internet client/server hypertext-distributed information system. You might view it as a very large multimedia client/server network. The browser (the client) downloads remote text and graphics files from a server to the local computer and then displays them on the local computer's screen. The text file is written using Hypertext Markup Language (HTML), which the local computer translates for display along with graphics files and any scripts that have been downloaded. The speed of this process depends on a number of factors:

*HTML pages are downloaded from networked servers and translated by the browser.*

- Speed of the modem in the local PC
- Speed of the Internet Service Provider's (ISP's) modem to which you are connected
- Size of files for downloading

- Activity on the server providing the files
- Amount of traffic on the Internet

The speed with which a system displays the graphics also depends in part on the power of the workstation. Much like the two-tier and three-tier client/server models, some of the computing burden still resides on the client. Quite frankly, Internet browsers utilize quite a bit of a system's resources.

IS professionals can provide information and applications using the Web paradigm—with the browser client accessing data from a server with HTML pages via the Internet, the intranet, or the extranet. You might ask, "What's the difference between these three? Aren't these just buzzwords made up by marketing professionals to ensure that they make their review objectives and get their bonuses and yearly portion of stock options?" Well, that's not quite the answer. While all three require use of an Internet browser to access data distributed by Web-based servers, the intended audience and security differs in each case, as the following table shows.

### What's What on the "Nets"

|  | Internet | Intranet | Extranet |
| --- | --- | --- | --- |
| **Access** | Public | Private | Semiprivate |
| **Who are the users?** | Anyone | Limited to members of a single organization or company | Group of companies joined together in an alliance |
| **What type of information?** | All types of data | Proprietary and/or confidential data specific to the company | Proprietary and/or confidential data for only those in a specific relationship |
| **Examples of use** | Getting stock quotes, headline news, or distributing general information | Getting internal job openings at the company, a technical white paper for support, status information, or group or departmental information | Supply-chain management |

**The Internet** These days, the terms "Internet" and "World Wide Web" refer to the same entity. CERN, the European Particle Physics Laboratory, proposed the World Wide Web (WWW) project in 1989 and developed the first prototype in 1990. Its purpose was to share papers and data with physicists all over the world. The WWW project was intended to share information across computer networks as simply as possible. Before the WWW and the use of HTML with a browser, users would access information with text-based tools.

Since 1990, Web servers have evolved from their original purpose of sharing scholarly research to disseminating all kinds of information—from marketing brochures to interactive applications. For many companies, these applications are becoming mission-critical components for conducting business. The Web allows companies to take advantage of this low-cost, low-maintenance means of deploying applications across low-bandwidth and high-bandwidth connections. In addition, organizations' IS departments use the Internet to provide mobile users and those working from their homes with access to e-mail, support material and information, and even corporate data. Some of these users even access their particular company's production network via an ISP, although this presents an additional layer of complexity due to the necessary security.

Big business is not the only entity benefiting from this low-cost means of deploying applications across the country and around the world. For example, in southwest Texas, several small regional libraries have banded together through the Internet to provide people in small towns with online access to all the resources available at major metropolitan libraries.

*Web models aren't just for business.*

All of this is possible because of HTML—the standard, platform-independent language used to lay out and format Web pages. The Web server transmits these HTML files on demand over the Internet to a client machine running a Web browser (such as Microsoft Internet Explorer or Netscape Navigator), which displays the data or text according to the formatting commands.

**Let's keep a consistent standard.**

Because HTML is a standard language, pages written in HTML theoretically can be viewed by any browser, making the Web the perfect cross-platform vehicle for disseminating information and applications. (See Figure 2-5.)

In support of Web-based computing and HTML, Sun Microsystems created the Java language to work with Internet browsers and utilize the download-and-run method of application deployment from Web pages. I'll discuss this in detail later.

**FIGURE 2-5** *The Internet is used on all types of computer systems and configurations.*

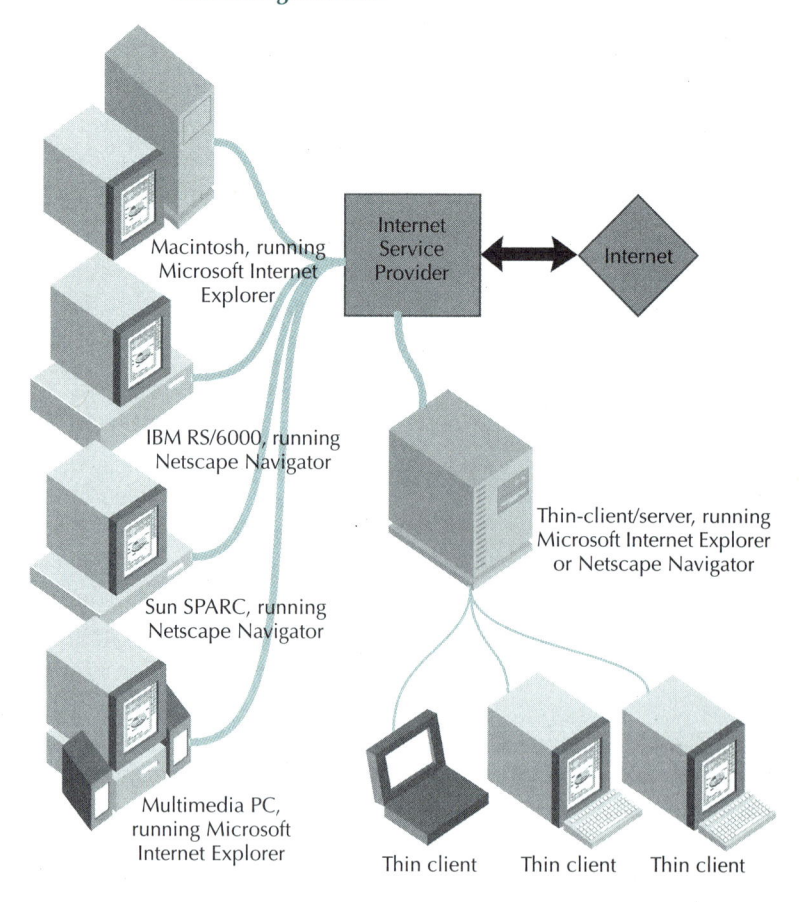

## The Difficulty with Standards

Remember back in your college marketing class, when you learned about commodities and differentiation? I am reminded of this when I think of browsers—or, more precisely, when I try to decide which one to load on my system or on my clients' systems. Both Microsoft Internet Explorer and Netscape Navigator have virtually the same functionality. Each product's extensions (and proposed extensions) differentiate it from the other by giving the programmer additional capabilities with HTML, but only if the page is viewed with that product's browser.

In response to this attempt to divide the Internet into distinct camps—or to force you to make a choice—users, fueled by Jesse Berst of Ziff-Davis, "revolted." Berst circulated a petition protesting the differing proprietary Web standards that threatened to divide the Internet and force consumers to choose sides. It asked Microsoft and Netscape to stop developing proprietary extensions and adhere to open Internet standards. "Define revolt," you say? Berst received more than 10,000 signatures within the first 12 hours of his campaign, and within three weeks more than 35,000 people had signed the petition. The result was the Web Interoperability Pledge and WIP logo program signed by Web developers, including Microsoft and Netscape.

How does this all relate to the thin-client/server model? While it seems that a browser is a simple piece of software, it requires quite a bit of the system's resources to run. If you want to run the latest browsers and take advantage of the latest innovations on the Internet, you still need to use a relatively powerful computer, even if it's a network computer. However, you can run a computer browser on a server and use thin-client software such as ICA to view the browser. This way, you don't tie up local system resources. On the other hand, you might choose to run one company's browser on your local computer and control another browser running on a server through a thin client.

> You can run a browser on a server and connect with a thin-client device.

**Intranets** You can think of an intranet as a private, small-scale internet that isn't accessible to anyone outside your company. Most companies use intranets to make important corporate information available to employees. A typical intranet will display

> Intranets are a great way to distribute information within an organization.

internal phone lists, job notices, a marketing events calendar, human resources forms, and other information typically found on bulletin boards in break rooms at offices around the world. Figure 2-6 shows a typical intranet configuration.

**FIGURE 2-6**  *An intranet distributes information within an organization.*

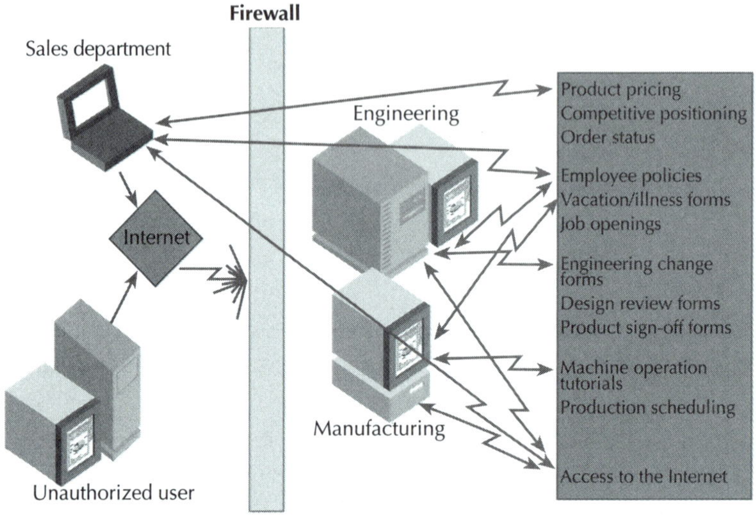

[Figure 2-6: Diagram showing an intranet configuration with a Firewall separating the Internet (with Unauthorized user) from internal departments (Sales department, Engineering, Manufacturing). Services listed include: Product pricing, Competitive positioning, Order status, Employee policies, Vacation/illness forms, Job openings, Engineering change forms, Design review forms, Product sign-off forms, Machine operation tutorials, Production scheduling, Access to the Internet.]

However, a truly useful intranet—one that's worth the development time and money spent on it (which, according to research from the META Group, would be significant)—would potentially tie database information into Web pages and add full-text document search capabilities. An example of a useful intranet would be one that uses a Web browser as a query front-end for a Microsoft SQL Server database. In a real-world situation, a medical diagnostics company in south Florida uses its intranet to give users access to its SQL database, via their browsers, to run queries against the database. The application front-end is a Microsoft Visual Basic application, but by deploying the application to users via a Web page, rather than deploying the Visual Basic application itself, the client piece is small and easy to use. In cases like this, the Web paradigm eliminates the need for custom client-based programs or at least reduces the amount of maintenance and programming required to keep an intranet running.

Other intranet advantages include the simplicity of browsers and their cost effectiveness. Most users are comfortable with Internet browsers such as Internet Explorer or Netscape Navigator, and Internet browsers are distributed at little or no cost.

Viewing HTML Web pages through a browser gives users a consistent implementation and delivery of corporate information. Because the "clients" viewing your data work for and with you, you control the type of browser and the operating system used to view the information. However, Web pages must be written in HTML with applications written in Java or one of the available Web scripting tools in order to be accessed from a standard Web server. Provided Microsoft, Netscape, Sun Microsystems, and others stick to their promise of an open Internet standard, as mentioned in the previous "The Difficulty with Standards" sidebar, the conversion to an intranet offers a viable alternative for some IS implementations.

As the Web paradigm is used for corporate intranets, applications are getting more sophisticated. However, you can use either thin-client/server software or hardware clients for viewing these applications, with execution on the server, in the same way that you can access applications on the Internet.

**Extranets** An extranet extends an organization's intranet out onto the Internet, for example, to allow customers, suppliers, and mobile workers to access data and information about the organization via the World Wide Web. In the past, developers and companies created systems to be used exclusively within the company. When people outside the organization needed access to the same data or functions, developers built other applications for outside use. Again, according to the META Group, during the next two years, electronic commerce over the Internet will grow as developers come up with more sophisticated enterprise application packages. In short, extranets are in. Figure 2-7 on the following page shows a typical extranet configuration.

*Extranets deliver information and applications to geographically disparate organizations.*

**FIGURE 2-7** *An extranet delivers information and applications to geographically disparate organizations.*

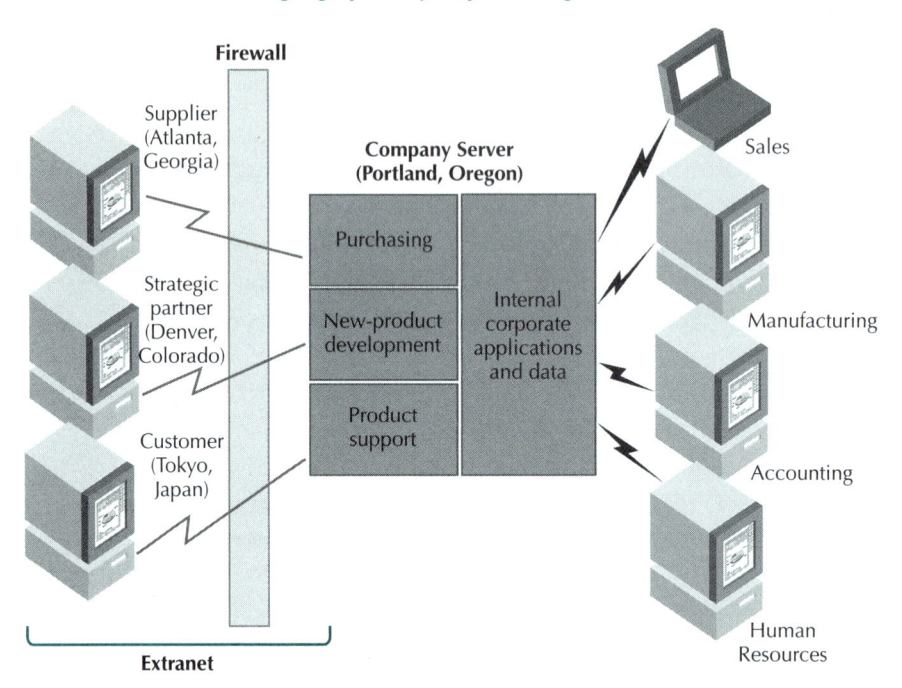

According to Netscape, the extranet, fueled by open Internet software, changes our whole communications paradigm. These new extended enterprise networks take an organization's existing intranet and extend it beyond the enterprise, enabling outside organizations to collaboratively engage in business applications. These organizations hope to deliver applications that can be used across multiple communications platforms, namely the Internet, as well as internally. By extending applications across the "firewall," companies are building applications just once and allowing their business to grow. The obvious issue and challenge with this type of implementation is security, a topic we'll examine in detail in Chapter 5.

# Thin-Client Computing

One solution to the enterprise-wide application deployment challenge lies beyond, but still supports, the traditional client/server model. Thin-client/server technologies are creating a new, network-centric computing paradigm. The thin-client technology is experiencing explosive growth and attention, as each camp attempts to absolutely define thin-client computing. On one side is a group led by Netscape, Oracle, and Sun Microsystems that advocates Java-based thin clients downloading and running on network computers. The other side, championed by Microsoft and Intel, leverages traditional desktop applications originally intended to run on stand-alone desktop computers. The thin-client/server architecture brings together the technology of these two camps.

*The thin-client model brings together disparate computing visions.*

### Java: Download-and-Run on Any Device

Java has been described as a "revolution" in business computing. This high-level programming language was developed by Sun Microsystems and was designed for handheld devices and set-top boxes. Java was originally called Oak. Because the Oak product never made it to market, in 1995 Sun changed course and went after the Internet, changing the product name to Java.

*Java is a download-and-run model for the Internet.*

Java is an object-oriented language similar to C++ but much simpler to work with. It was designed with the network environment in mind. According to Kim Polese, former Java product manager, Java's unique network features include:

- Platform independence
- Dynamic code downloading
- Multithreading for multimedia performance
- Compact code designed to move quickly across the Internet

Java works differently than desktop software applications that are currently available. Java applications, or "applets," are not

> You can run any application from a server to any computer with a Java Virtual Machine.

necessarily stored on your PC. Instead, these small programs are usually stored on a central network server. Figure 2-8 shows how the Java applet works. When your browser encounters a Web page in which a Java applet is stored, the applet is downloaded (as requested by your browser). Since these applets are designed to be relatively small programs, they should load more quickly than larger applications do. Version control is made easier with the central storage model of Java applets.

According to Java evangelists, one of the big perks for the IS professional is Java's ability to both vastly simplify application creation and deployment while maintaining existing legacy computers and software. Once written, Java programs can run without modification on most computers with an Internet browser or on a Java Virtual Machine. The underlying operating system makes no difference to Java.

**FIGURE 2-8**  *Java applets execute on devices that have Java Virtual Machines.*

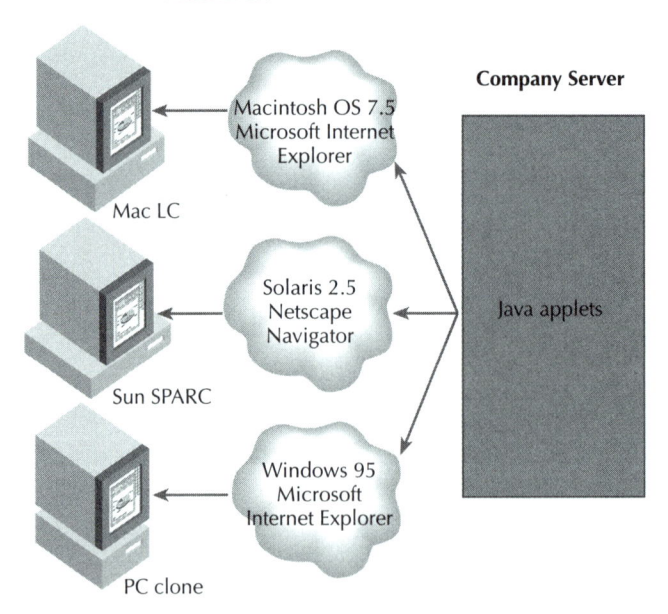

## Citrix Independent Computing Architecture Client

In Chapter 1, I mentioned ICA as the technology from Citrix Systems that enables use of the WinFrame multiuser operating system. In this section, I also want to mention ICA client software while reviewing other available technologies. In the next chapter, I'll talk about ICA in more depth.

The ICA client serves as a general-purpose presentation services protocol for Microsoft Windows. Basically, any device having an ICA client embedded or installed on it can run applications written for the following platforms:

*ICA client software runs on any computer.*

- Windows NT (32 bit)
- Windows 95 (32 bit)
- Windows 3.*x* (16 bit)
- MS-DOS text
- OS/2 text
- POSIX text
- X Window System applications (used with emulator software)

The ICA protocol presents only the user interface on the client machine, while keeping all application execution on the server. This provides a thin-client software solution since no application execution is performed on the client. ICA also delivers true location independence by running the Windows operating system and the application program at one location (at the server) and displaying the program's user interface somewhere else (at the client).

Conceptually, ICA is similar to the X Window System protocol. ICA allows an application's logic to execute on a WinFrame application server, while only the user interface—keystrokes and mouse movements—are transferred between the server and the client device across any network or communications protocol, resulting in minimal client resource consumption. (See Figure 2-9 on page 45.)

## The Thin-Client/Server Solution

Earlier in this chapter, I described a New England–based manufacturing company with a two-tier client/server application that performed very poorly across a WAN. The employees based in Europe were reporting load times of several minutes. The application vendor called in Ursula Habermacher to install a WinFrame server, even though the application vendor's team lead was not convinced that this would help. The goal was for users in Europe to launch an ICA client session for running the application instead of executing the client software directly on their workstations. The icon properties on the users' desktops were changed to launch the Citrix ICA thin client, which was then connected across the WAN to the WinFrame server. Once logged on to the WinFrame session, the client portion of the application would execute on the server. It seemed like the answer to the company's performance and hardware issues.

The users on both ends were skeptical of this solution, which seemed impossible. Before Ursula could even begin the integration, she had to upload the client software to the German users, set up a meeting with the U.S. project team, and then make a conference call to the employees in Germany. She was told, "Don't even think of leaving without having the director see the performance for himself." Ursula gathered the United States–based employees around a large monitor and connected to the WinFrame server. Once the conference call was initiated and the remote user logged on to WinFrame, Ursula began shadowing the remote user; the entire United States–based team was seeing what the remote user was seeing. As the German user launched the application, there were gasps—even from the application vendor. They could not believe this application could perform at near local speeds across a WAN.

You have to love the thin client. No change to the application was required. The application, which was virtually unusable in a WAN, is now being sold as a remote solution as well.

**FIGURE 2-9** *The Citrix ICA protocol separates application logic from the user interface.*

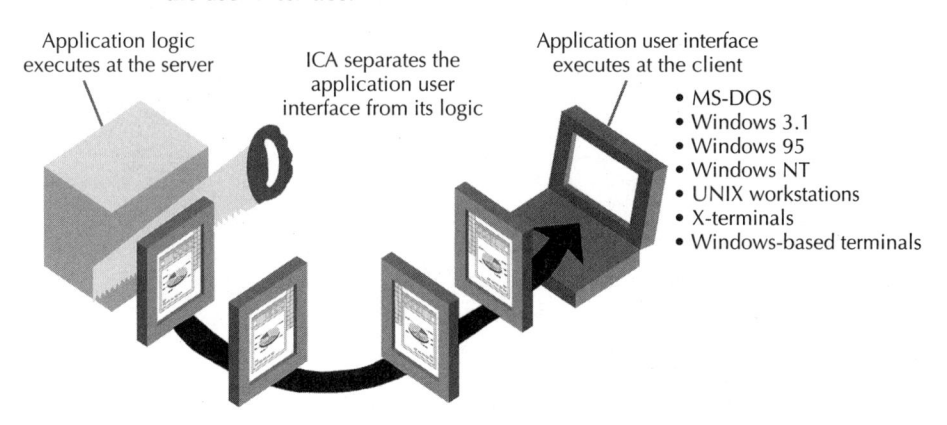

Application logic executes at the server

ICA separates the application user interface from its logic

Application user interface executes at the client
- MS-DOS
- Windows 3.1
- Windows 95
- Windows NT
- UNIX workstations
- X-terminals
- Windows-based terminals

## New Technologies: Competition or Continuum?

Each of the operating systems and architectures discussed in this chapter has its place, and each has been used successfully. However, the IS professional's main concern is to find solutions that optimize the organization's computing resources. Ultimately, you'll find uses in your computing environment for many of the various technologies. The next sections briefly examine some of these operating systems and architectures.

New technologies will work together under the thin-client/server model.

### Visions of Network Computing by Sun, Netscape, and Oracle

Sun, Netscape, and Oracle view the Java technology as the next logical step in the evolution of enterprise computing. The basic premise of using Java for enterprise computing is that the "fat-client" desktop (the PC) is replaced by a thin-client hardware device, the network computer (shown in Figure 2-10 on the following page), which could be a Sun JavaStation or an Oracle version of a network computer. For example, press releases by Sun and Netscape describe the JavaStation (the Java terminal) as having a much simpler hardware design than fat clients, and,

Network computers will download Java applets.

**FIGURE 2-10** *Network computing allows Java applets to download from a central server and run on a Network Computer (NC).*

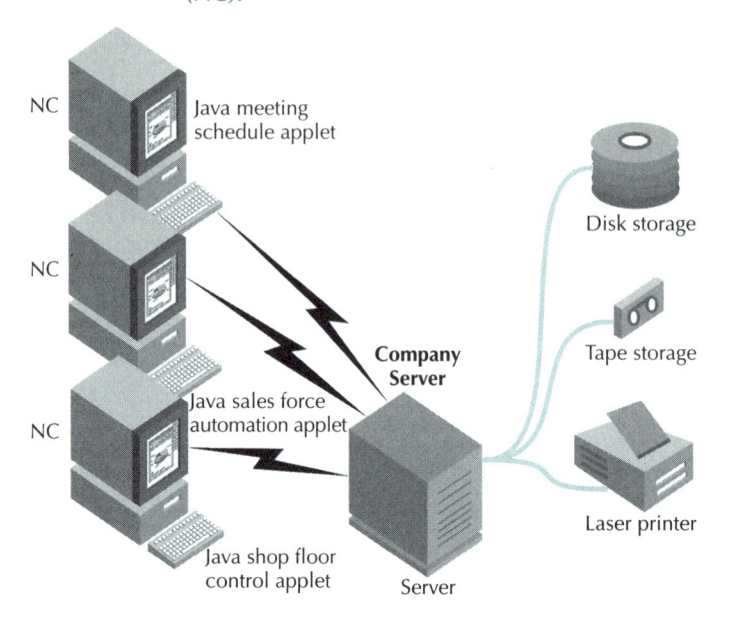

more importantly, the JavaStation is a stateless device. This further extends the concept of storing Java applets on a central server to a model in which all data, applications, and configuration information are stored on a central server.

## Multiuser Versions of Windows NT, ActiveX, and Windows on the Internet

*With Citrix WinFrame, the Windows NT platform is evolving toward a multiuser system.*

Citrix has successfully developed and marketed WinFrame as a thin-client/server adaptation of Microsoft Windows NT. Microsoft further validated the Citrix concept of thin-client/server computing when it licensed the MultiWin technology as the multiuser technology to be used for the Hydra server. For Microsoft, this multiuser technology supplements the existing family of Windows operating systems, and it allows Microsoft to use Windows to compete with network computers.

Microsoft also embraced the Internet and Web technologies by introducing ActiveX, a technology that can be used either with or instead of Java. ActiveX was developed by Microsoft for sharing information and components among different applications. (See Figure 2-11.) It is an outgrowth of two other Microsoft technologies: OLE (Object Linking and Embedding) and COM (Component Object Model). ActiveX supports new features that enable it to take advantage of the Internet. For example, an ActiveX control, much like a Java applet, can be automatically downloaded and executed by a Web browser. A fundamental difference between ActiveX and Java, however, is that ActiveX is not a programming language. ActiveX defines how applications can share information and can be used with several different programming languages, including C, C++, Visual Basic, and Java.

*ActiveX is a technology that facilitates sharing data.*

**FIGURE 2-11** *ActiveX controls can be used in Web pages.*

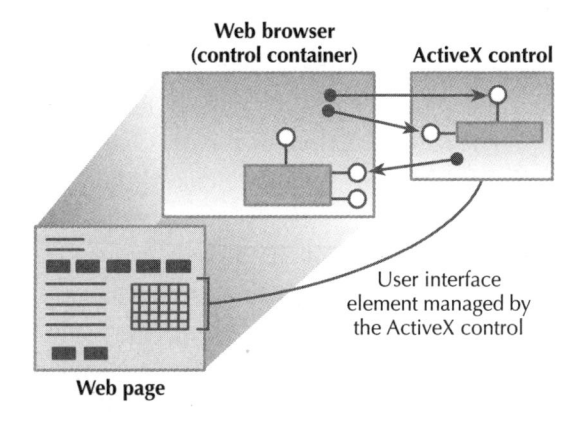

Let's tie ActiveX and multiuser technologies together. As developers create ActiveX controls or components that talk to each other and work together, they can be deployed through an Internet browser that's running in a thin-client scenario on a server. In this case, if a control must be downloaded, it's downloaded once and then made available to all users accessing that browser. The bottom line is that regardless of the technology, the architecture can be optimized and delivered over a thin-client scenario to a wider audience with various hardware devices.

## In Conclusion

With today's emphasis on the Internet, intranets, extranets, and Web-related tools, the bulk of the workload falls on the server. Java and ActiveX technologies that are downloaded to local devices and run via a browser can help balance client/server processing loads either on the Internet or in an intranet. However, a significant amount of data still needs to be transmitted to the client machine—which makes bandwidth an issue—and some of the computing power must come from the browser. Browsers are slow, and so is the connection (via networks or modems) that many users have to their data. On the other hand, you can further leverage your investments in servers and networking infrastructure with the thin-client/server architectures built on multiuser technologies.

Regardless of vendor technology visions, you need to design your computing infrastructure based on the work your users need to conduct, rather than on some religious computing issue. Chapter 1 provided an overview of the thin-client/server computing model and its relationship to different types of users. This chapter discussed the relationship of the thin-client/server architecture to network operating systems, distributed computing architectures, and Web-based computing. It also discussed the applications and architectures that are being positioned as competing technologies. Ultimately, based on the planned growth of your company, the user requirements to sustain that growth, and the available resources, you'll build a computing infrastructure that leverages existing resources, takes advantage of technologies that converge with your needs, and extends your infrastructure so that you can respond rapidly to any change.

Chapter Three

# Key Components of WinFrame and Windows NT Server

In November 1992, Citrix Systems licensed Microsoft Windows NT Server source code from Microsoft to build WinFrame. By adding multiuser capabilities to Windows NT, Citrix added the last piece needed for Windows to compete with UNIX. On May 12, 1997, Citrix and Microsoft announced a licensing agreement that enables Citrix MultiWin to be incorporated into upcoming releases of Windows NT 4.*x*. Microsoft has code-named this new multiuser operating system Hydra. On this same day, Citrix also announced the upcoming release of its thin-client/server enabling product, code-named pICAsso. The pICAsso system software will provide significant management, performance, and security enhancements to Hydra as well as universal client access. The combination of pICAsso and Hydra will provide the same thin-client/server functionality seen in today's WinFrame, but with the Windows NT 4.0 user interface.

In Chapter 2, we saw how WinFrame evolved in terms of developments in network operating systems. We also looked at the value added by this thin-client/server solution for different methods of deploying client/server, Web-based, and productivity applications. In this chapter, we'll examine the strong foundation provided by Windows NT and the key components of the Citrix thin-client/server solution.

## System Foundations for a Multiuser Environment

*Windows NT provides a strong foundation for the development of a multiuser system.*

Windows NT provides a strong foundation for a multiuser system largely because the network operating system is integrated with the native operating system. With WinFrame, Citrix Systems took advantage of this foundation and created a system of multiuser primitives (low-level APIs), extending and exploiting these foundations. Citrix further enabled these foundations by adding the Independent Computing Architecture (ICA) system services, protocol, and client to the mix. Bob Williams, Director of ICA Architecture at Citrix Systems and Chairman of the Open ICA Forum, lists these features intrinsic to Windows NT that enabled Citrix to build concurrent multiuser access:

- *User profiles* A collection of configuration data that applies only to a specific user. Each time the user logs on, the system retrieves this information and configures the environment to that user's settings.
- *Embedded logon* Users must log on to access a Windows NT–based computer. The logon generates an access token containing the user's security and group identifiers. Every action that takes place on Windows NT has an attached access token to create barriers between different users' contexts.
- *Symmetric multiprocessing support (SMP)* SMP is a feature of Windows NT that lends itself to the power required for multiuser access. SMP allows multiple processors on one machine to work together for increased system performance. Each processor has full access to hardware, bus, and memory actions.

### Configuring and Managing User and Group Accounts

*Centralization of user accounts is key to a thin-client/server multiuser system.*

Both Windows NT and WinFrame utilize the domain organization for managing users and accounts. The domain organization creates a pool of resources that are available to a defined group of users across workstations, servers, and network devices. Users can reach all the domain's resources with a single username and password. User administration is centralized on one machine—the domain controller. Centralization of user accounts is ideal for a thin-client/server multiuser system such as WinFrame. Because Citrix took advantage of the features already built into Windows NT Server, system administrators will find it easier to leverage their knowledge to get a thin-client/server multiuser system up and running.

The User Configuration Manager configures and manages users on Windows NT Server and on WinFrame. Because the WinFrame server can join an existing Windows NT domain, the administrator doesn't need to add usernames to the user database on the WinFrame server. Likewise, the Migration Tool for NetWare allows the administrator to transfer user and group accounts from a NetWare server to WinFrame. The Migration Tool automatically transfers the accounts to the server's domain controller. At the end of the transfer process, accounts are replicated automatically to the backup domain controllers.

*WinFrame takes advantage of the Windows NT domain structure.*

Citrix integrated its user management tools into the User Manager for Domains. Leveraging this centralized use of profiles was key to lowering the cost of ownership when deploying information services and applications across the enterprise. Citrix added the Config button at the bottom of the User Properties dialog box in the User Manager for Domains utility (shown in Figure 3-1 on page 52) to access the WinFrame User Configuration dialog box (shown in Figure 3-2, also on page 52).

*The User Configuration Manager adds specific WinFrame functionality to your system.*

Citrix added the User Configuration dialog box to manage the characteristics unique to deploying a mission-critical application in a thin-client/server multiuser environment. These characteristic features address security when the user logs on to an application, fault tolerance through system recovery, and ease of use and customization when accessing an application by bypassing the Windows Program Manager. The user configuration enhancements Citrix made are listed on pages 53–54.

FIGURE 3-1  *The Config button in the User Manager for Domains, which accesses the WinFrame User Configuration dialog box*

Config button

FIGURE 3-2  *The WinFrame User Configuration dialog box*

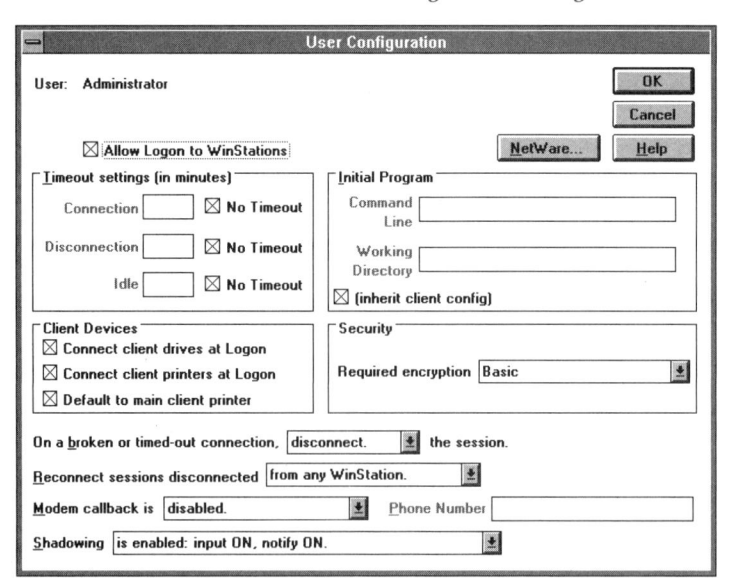

- *Restrict user logon to WinFrame WinStations* Remote control of ICA clients' WinStations allows a remote system administrator to provide access to users across a multiuser system. An individual user can be configured for a network logon to use the Windows NT services for disk and printer access that ship with the WinFrame Enterprise. Limiting access via Windows-based terminals provides an added level of security to the applications on the server.
- *Recover a session* WinFrame, by default, preserves a user's session if the physical connection between the client and the server is broken. This feature is especially useful during client-site power outages or when a remote connection is severed due to a disconnection or other interruption of carrier services. The feature can be disabled or limited to a specific duration (in which case, a session will be available for a specified number of minutes and then discontinued).
- *Bypass Program Manager and automatically launch a program* By default, all users launch the familiar Windows NT Program Manager after successfully logging on to WinFrame or Windows NT. WinFrame allows you to launch a different program for specific users, such as Microsoft Word, Microsoft Excel, or a custom application. When the user exits this "initial program," he or she is logged off the system. This customization feature is particularly useful for limiting a user's access to a line-of-business application.
- *Access client workstation printers and disk drives* This feature leverages the user's comfort with his or her own computing device, making the integration between local printers and drives and the printers and drives on the thin-client/server hardware seamless. The ICA client allows users to access their local printers (those attached to the remote workstation) or local drives (the CD-ROM, disk, and diskette drives on the client PC or notebook computer). This feature can be disabled through the User Configuration Manager utility.

- *Monitor a user session with "shadowing"* Shadowing allows one user to view the video, keystrokes, and mouse movements of another user's session. System administrators, support professionals, and trainers find this feature extremely valuable. Specifically, ICA clients that are attached to a WinFrame server and that have administrator rights or specifically assigned rights can view a user's video and keyboard on the WinFrame server. When setting up the configuration, administrators can specify whether individual user sessions can be shadowed and whether the shadowed user is to be notified when being shadowed.

- *Synchronize NetWare password with the Windows NT logon domain* This feature provides seamless integration with NetWare logon. The system administrator can configure a user so that his or her password is verified against the specified NetWare server before it is checked on the logon domain. If the password on the logon domain is different from the user's NetWare password, the user's logon domain password is updated to match the NetWare password.

### Creating Profiles

*User profiles can specify machine settings.*

Each application for MS-DOS and Windows needs its own configuration file; however, Windows NT centralizes program initialization variables and settings parameters in the Registry (a special-purpose operating system database). Again, even Windows NT 4.0 and 3.*x* have multiuser capabilities, since part of the Registry is user-specific and is referred to as a "user profile."

By using user profiles, an administrator can control each user's desktop, environment, and access permissions whenever a user logs on to the domain from any workstation, whether virtual or real. To create a profile for a particular user, the system administrator must log on as the user or create a "default" user account. For example, if I want to change the wallpaper to circles for some but not all of my users, I create an account named "default" and log on as *default*. Then I change my wallpaper to circles and save the current environment as a profile named "circles.usr" or "circles.man." After logging off, I log back on as the administrator and assign the appropriate users the profile "circles.man" or I copy "circles.usr" to a profile named "*username*.usr" (since a personal profile should be unique to each user).

The ability to create profiles is a huge improvement over the Windows 3.*x* and Windows for Workgroups days, but it has a major drawback: the profiles don't allow the administrator to capture environment settings without being logged on to the

---

### Using Profiles Effectively

One of Ursula Habermacher's recent consulting assignments was to assist an insurance company in using WinFrame 1.6, built on Windows NT 3.51, to deploy a custom insurance policy tracking application across a WAN. The company's IS group didn't want the users to run any application on the WinFrame server except the custom application. However, members of the IS group needed to be able to run all the system utilities and productivity applications on WinFrame while dialing in from home.

The easiest way to achieve this capability on WinFrame 1.6 was through the use of profiles. The administrator created a profile for the users—granting them access to the custom application only—and then assigned users to this profile. As each user logged on to the system, the system verified that the user was able to log on, retrieved the user's profile, and then restricted the user's ability for executing programs to the custom application. Meanwhile, the IS group created its own profile, which granted group access to execute all applications installed on the system for users—without making all group members administrators.

environment. For example, if I want to change user *Jane*'s environment so that she has no wallpaper, there is no "switch" in the User Profile Editor to allow this. Likewise, I can't remove icons from her desktop without either logging on as Jane or logging on as my default profile and changing my desktop (deleting the icons and so on) and then *resaving* the profile and assigning or copying it to *Jane*'s profile. The process is rather cumbersome.

## The Components of Thin-Client/Server Architecture

As you saw in the first two chapters, WinFrame supports enterprise application deployment using a thin-client/server architecture. The key pieces of the WinFrame system, as it exists today, include the ICA protocol, the universal thin client, and the WinFrame MultiWin multiuser application server technology. This WinFrame architecture is illustrated in Figure 3-3.

### The Operating System and MultiWin

*MultiWin works with the Windows NT kernel to support multiuser sessions.*

Windows NT provides the basic operating system components; adding Citrix MultiWin allows multiple concurrent users to access the WinFrame system. Essentially, users remotely control the WinFrame server—in effect, they virtually "sit" at the console of the WinFrame server and share all systems resources with other concurrent users, making further use of the preemptive multitasking features of Windows NT.

As illustrated in Figure 3-4 on page 58, preemptive multitasking means that the kernel (in this case, the Windows NT kernel plus MultiWin) acts as the gatekeeper and determines which thread gets processor time and when. Preemptive multitasking ensures that each thread gets its turn and that no particular thread or process can dominate system resources at the expense of other processes or threads, as opposed to a model that yields the processor to the application until execution has completed. In the latter scenario, an application that "hangs" can bring down the entire system.

**FIGURE 3-3** *Current WinFrame architecture*

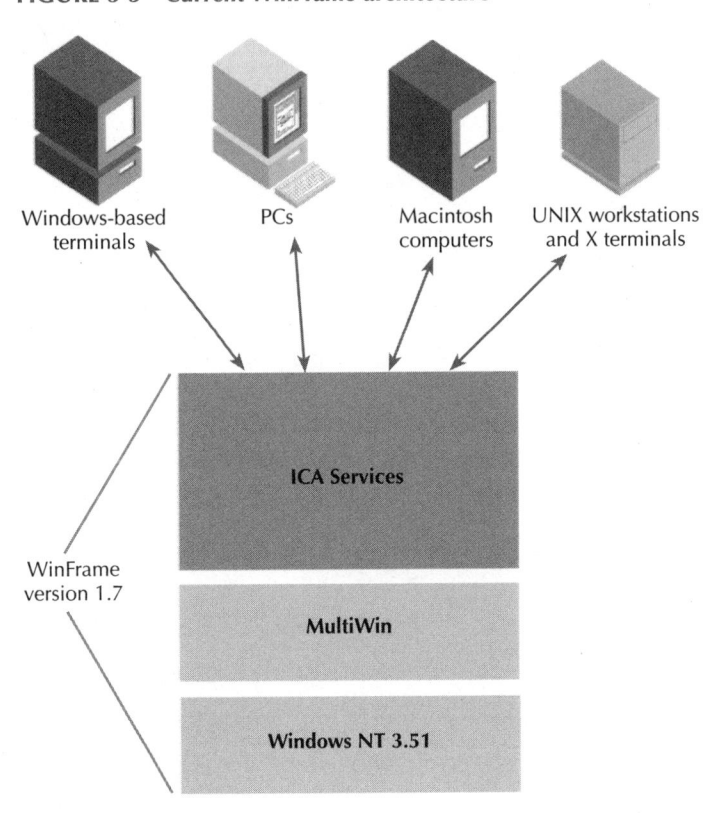

Windows-based terminals | PCs | Macintosh computers | UNIX workstations and X terminals

WinFrame version 1.7:
- ICA Services
- MultiWin
- Windows NT 3.51

Preemptive multitasking is critical for a multiuser environment in which you want the system to perform like a single user system. It makes it seem to each user that he or she is the only person using the system.

## The ICA Thin Client and ICA Services

The other pieces of the picture are the universal ICA thin client, the ICA protocol, the ICA Platform, and ICA Services. Citrix developed the ICA universal thin-client model and protocol—a general-purpose Windows-based protocol. The ICA protocol provides true location independence for Windows-based applications. It also allows Windows-based applications to run at one location and display the program's user interface somewhere else.

ICA comprises a universal thin client, a protocol, a platform, and system services.

**FIGURE 3-4** *Preemptive multitasking in a multiuser system*

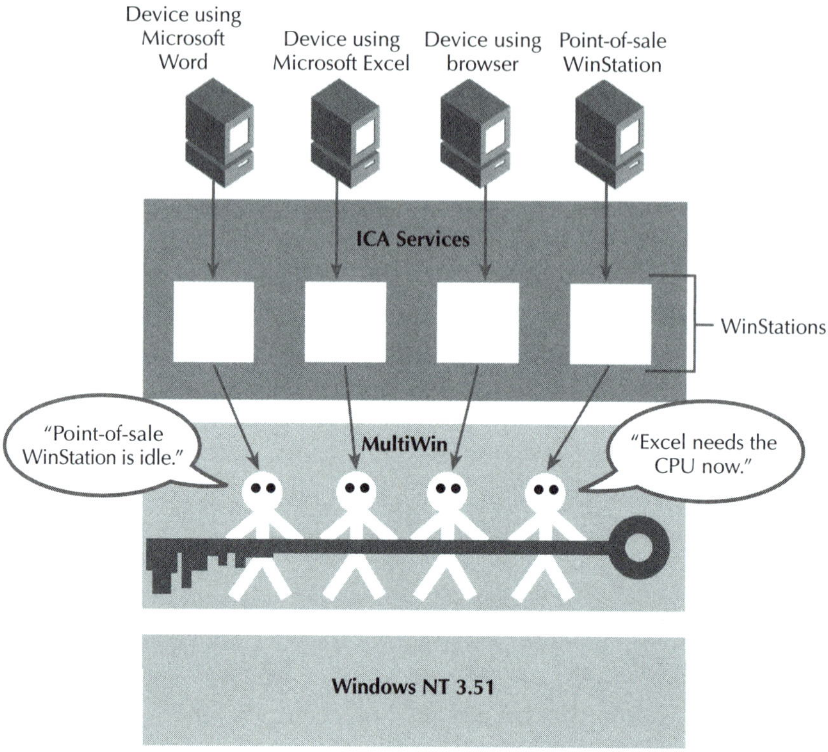

![Figure 3-4 diagram showing devices using Microsoft Word, Microsoft Excel, browser, and Point-of-sale WinStation connecting through ICA Services and WinStations to MultiWin layer with figures holding a key, running on Windows NT 3.51. Speech bubbles read "Point-of-sale WinStation is idle." and "Excel needs the CPU now."]

Designed to provide high-performance display of Windows-based applications over local area networks (LANs), wide area networks (WANs), or dial-up devices while minimizing network traffic, the ICA protocol—in conjunction with ICA services—and the ICA client can deliver complete Windows-based applications even over low-bandwidth connections. A robust and extensible protocol, ICA includes definitions for the following capabilities:

- Full-screen text presentation
- Graphical screen presentation of Windows-based applications
- Keyboard and mouse input
- Session control

- Framing for asynchronous connections
- Error detection and recovery
- Encryption
- Compression hooks
- File system redirection
- Print redirection
- Multiple generic virtual channels
- Cut and paste across servers
- COM port redirection
- General purpose WinFrame server browsing
- Virtual channels for custom extensions

Through its customers, ICA licensees, and organizations such as the Open ICA Forum, Citrix keeps gathering feedback and ideas for ICA development.

## A Recap of the ICA

As you'll recall from Chapter 1, Citrix Systems' Independent Computing Architecture (ICA) is a general-purpose presentation services protocol that is optimized to run applications based on Microsoft Windows. Conceptually, ICA is similar to the X Window System protocol used in UNIX systems. ICA allows an application's logic to execute on an application server. Only the user interface, keystrokes, and mouse movements are transferred between the server and the client device over any network or communications protocol, which results in minimal client resource consumption. ICA is designed to run over industry-standard network protocols, such as TCP/IP, NetBEUI, IPX/SPX, and PPP (Point-to-Point Protocol), using industry-standard transport protocols, such as asynchronous connections, ISDN, frame relay, and ATM (Asynchronous Transfer Mode).

**ICA packet overview** An ICA packet consists of a required 1-byte command followed by optional data. This packet can be prefixed by optional preambles that are negotiated at connection time to manage the transmission of the packet. The nature of the transmission medium (LAN vs. asynchronous) and user-defined options (such as compression) influence the total packet definition.

All ICA commands have the following format:

- *Frame head* Optional framing protocol header; a preamble for framing stream-oriented transport data.
- *Reliable* Optional reliable transmission protocol header; a preamble for error detection and recovery.
- *Encrypt* Optional encryption protocol header; a preamble for managing encrypted data.
- *Compress* Optional compression protocol header; a preamble for managing compressed data.
- *Command* ICA command byte; beginning of base ICA protocol packet.
- *Command data* Optional data bytes associated with the specified command. The length of the data is dependent on the command and can be 0. Command data can also contain Virtual Channel protocol packets.
- *Frame trail* Optional framing protocol trailer; a postamble for framing asynchronous transport data.

Figure 3-5 illustrates the format of an ICA command packet.

**FIGURE 3-5** *The format of an ICA command packet*

| Frame head | Reliable | Library | Encrypt | Compress | Command | Command data | Frame trail |
|---|---|---|---|---|---|---|---|

The command is always present in the packet and is the only required field. The preambles and postambles depend on the transport and negotiation that take place during initialization. The presence of command data depends on the command itself.

**ICA commands** There are several different categories of ICA command packets. These categories—control commands, full-screen text commands, keyboard commands, and mouse commands—are discussed in the following paragraphs.

*Control commands* are a category of ICA command packets that manage the connection to the application server and the relationship to the local client user interface. This category includes:

- Server browsing
- Connection initialization and negotiation
- Screen control between the application server and the local client user interface
- Keyboard and mouse input to the application server
- Control of the local keyboard LEDs

The *full-screen text* category of ICA command packets allows the application server to control the local client display in full-screen text mode. These commands are rarely used for Windows-based applications. However, they are important for the support of low-end devices, such as a point-of-sale device like a cash register. These commands involve less data transfer and, thus, improved display performance. Packets are sent from the server to perform the following functions:

- Set the text modes
- Write characters
- Adjust character attributes
- Scroll the window
- Control the cursor

With *keyboard commands*, PC scan codes are transmitted from the client to the server application. An ICA command packet can contain multiple scan codes.

The ICA command set includes *mouse commands* to input the position of the mouse using normalized coordinates. These commands can also track the mouse button status.

**Virtual Channel commands** The ICA protocol provides multiplexed management of multiple virtual channels. A virtual channel is a session-oriented transmission connection that can be used by application-layer code. Virtual channels are used to add functional enhancements to the client, independently of the ICA protocol itself. There is a set of ICA Virtual Channel commands that are used to send and receive this ICA protocol–independent data. These commands enhance the users' experience by integrating closely with functions on the local device, such as printers, serial and parallel ports, drives, and the clipboard. Each type of virtual channel—ThinWire, Printer Spooling, Drive Mapping, Parallel Port, Serial Port, and Clipboard—is described in this section.

The *ThinWire* protocol is an ICA Virtual Channel protocol used to transmit presentation commands from Windows-based applications running on the application server to the client. The application appears to the user as though it's running on the local device. The ThinWire protocol is highly tuned to transmit the display of Windows objects over low-bandwidth connections. The ThinWire protocol transmits the display using the following methods:

- Command-specific and object-specific intelligent compression with state persistence, such as run-length encoding for bitmaps
- Outboard complex clipping and complex curve drawing
- Intelligent caching of Windows objects, such as bitmaps, brushes, glyphs, and pointers
- Remote SaveScreenBitmaps
- Cross-session persistent caching

ICA also includes a *Printer Spooling* Virtual Channel protocol, which transmits printer data to a client, and a *Drive Mapping* Virtual Channel protocol, which transmits file system functions between the WinFrame server and the client. The *Parallel Port Mapping* Virtual Channel protocol provides outbound access to the client's parallel ports from server applications and the spooler. The *Serial Port Mapping* Virtual Channel protocol provides full duplex access to the client's serial ports from server applications and the spooler. And, finally, the *Clipboard* Virtual Channel protocol provides support for the Windows clipboard, allowing users to cut and paste between server and client applications.

## How the Components Work Together

Communication between the client PC (or any other ICA-enabled client device) and the WinFrame server takes place via ICA—the physical line protocol. The application's graphical screen image is exported as a logical datastream that is encapsulated in ICA by ThinWire, the data protocol. (ThinWire is not a physical protocol.) The physical protocol—ICA—must guarantee the delivery of the ThinWire datastream with no errors and no missing or out-of-sequence data.

From the perspective of the WinFrame application server, the major portion of the ThinWire component is part of the graphical device interface (GDI) and video driver subsystem. This ThinWire component, in conjunction with key elements in the WinFrame Win32 subsystem, generates highly optimized drawing primitives called the "ThinWire protocol." The output of the ThinWire protocol driver is a logical datastream that is sent back up a virtual channel API, which takes the datastream and encapsulates it into an ICA packet. Once the ICA packet is formed, it optionally passes through a series of protocol drivers to add functionality such as encryption, compression, and framing. It is then placed on the transport layer and sent to the client. Once at the ICA client, the data packet passes through the same layers in the opposite order, resulting in the graphical display of the remote application user interface on the client. This flow of information is shown in Figure 3-6 on the following page.

FIGURE 3-6  *Flow of information between the WinFrame application server and the ICA client*

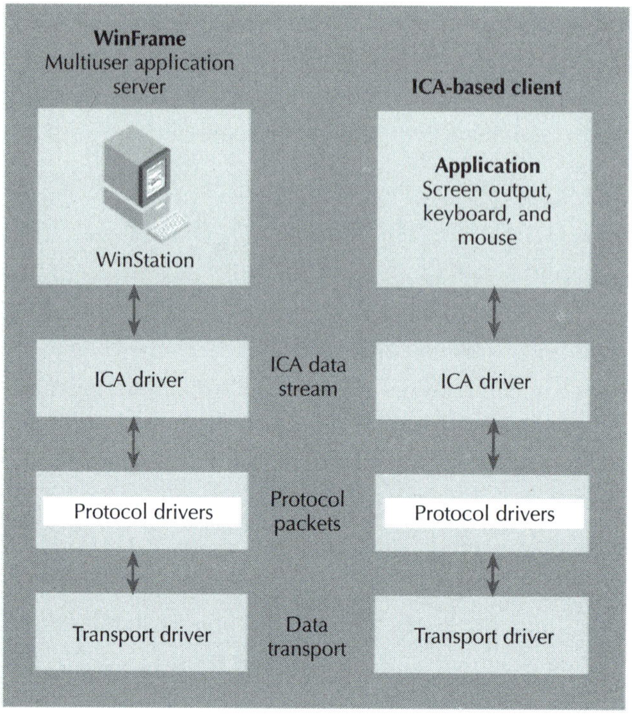

[Figure 3-6: Diagram showing WinFrame Multiuser application server (WinStation → ICA driver → Protocol drivers → Transport driver) communicating with ICA-based client (Application: Screen output, keyboard, and mouse → ICA driver → Protocol drivers → Transport driver) via ICA data stream, Protocol packets, and Data transport.]

## ICA Protocol and Transport Driver Layers

Beneath the ICA data packets are several optional protocol driver layers. ICA does not depend on these layers; their existence and use is negotiated during the ICA handshaking period that occurs at the start of a session. Because these layers sit below ICA, they can be removed or replaced, and additional protocol drivers can also be added. A wide range of supplied protocol modules allow ICA to work with all of the most prevalent transport technologies, such as TCP/IP, NetBIOS, IPX/SPX, and PPP/SLIP (Serial Line Interface Protocol), supplying true protocol independence to ICA.

## ICA Extensibility

ICA is a flexible and extensible protocol. The protocol is designed to accommodate varying degrees of client capability. During handshaking, the ICA client communicates information including screen resolution, color depth, and cache size. The ICA server receives these parameters from the client and adjusts to this information by providing the appropriate drivers and other settings to make the application perform as though it's running on a local workstation. This communication allows for a wide variety of ICA clients, ranging from fixed-function monochrome terminals to high-end workstations.

Through its virtual-channel architecture, ICA can be extended to include new data types, such as sound and video. Virtual channels can also be used to support auxiliary client devices such as badge readers, wands, and scanners.

The modular design of the ICA protocol allows the supporting layers below it to be expanded. For example, the existing encryption layer can be augmented with RSA (Rivest-Shamir-Adleman) encryption or DES (Data Encryption Standard) encryption. Converters, such as those converting an ICA protocol to X.11, can be added in, and new transport protocols, such as ATM, can easily be supported.

*You can augment ICA with encryption, new transports, and new protocol extensions from third parties.*

## Connecting an ICA Client to a WinFrame Session

To take advantage of the ICA protocol features, ICA clients must connect to a WinStation, a user session on the WinFrame server. The configuration of the WinStation defines the attributes of a remote-control session that runs on the WinFrame server. A WinStation is primarily associated with a network connection, but it can also be associated with a serial COM port to provide direct ICA dial-up access to the WinFrame server.

### Accessing a WinFrame Server Through LANs and WANs

To attach to a WinFrame server across a LAN or a WAN, WinFrame requires that a network transport (such as IPX/SPX, TCP/IP, or NetBEUI) exist between the ICA client and the WinFrame server.

Once this transport is in place, the ICA protocol builds a list of available WinFrame servers. The ICA client then connects to the server via the transport specified in the ICA client configuration.

The ICA protocol stack is dynamically configured to meet the needs of each transport protocol. For example, the IPX protocol by itself does not guarantee packet delivery, so WinFrame adds a protocol driver to ensure that the data is reliably transmitted between the ICA connection and the host and that it is received by the client. However, because IPX is a frame-based protocol, a frame driver is not included in this particular ICA protocol stack. The Transmission Control Protocol (TCP), however, is a stream protocol; in this case, a frame driver is included. TCP is reliable; therefore, the Reliable protocol driver is not added to the stack. Figure 3-7 illustrates the ICA protocol stack and drivers.

**FIGURE 3-7** *The ICA protocol stack and drivers*

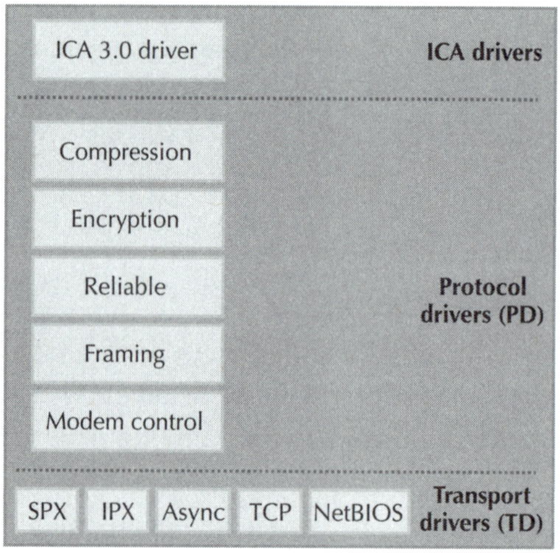

```
ICA 3.0 driver                          ICA drivers

Compression
Encryption
Reliable                                Protocol
                                        drivers (PD)
Framing
Modem control

SPX  IPX  Async  TCP  NetBIOS    Transport
                                 drivers (TD)
```

The ICA protocol stack includes the following protocols:

- *Compression*  The Compression protocol can encapsulate an encrypted ICA packet. This protocol is system replaceable and is not strictly defined in the ICA protocol definition.

- *Encryption* The Encryption protocol can encapsulate an encrypted ICA packet. This protocol is system replaceable and is not strictly defined in the ICA protocol definition.
- *Reliable* The Reliable protocol is a transmission packaging protocol used to detect transmission errors and to request resends of data. This protocol is used in conjunction with any transport mechanism that does not provide guaranteed delivery. Two such mechanisms are Novell's IPX protocol and standard asynchronous connections.
- *Framing* The Framing protocol is a transmission packaging protocol used to manage stream-oriented communications, such as asynchronous communications and TCP. It is used in conjunction with the Reliable protocol to provide error-free data transmission.
- *Modem Control* The Modem Control protocol allows for modem detection and initialization prior to connection.

## Accessing WinFrame Remotely

WinFrame can be accessed remotely via either a traditional remote node (a network emulation that causes the remote connection to emulate a LAN connection) or a direct dial-in (in which the user's modem dials directly to a modem attached to the WinFrame server). WinFrame supports Remote Access Service (RAS), but RAS is not required for a user to dial into a WinFrame server. To take advantage of the features of ICA, the user must be attached to a WinStation on the WinFrame server. Once the initial connection is made via remote node such as RAS, the user must initiate a remote control or an ICA session with the Remote Application Manager on the client hardware device.

**Remote Access Services** RAS, Microsoft's remote-node server product (included with Windows NT), runs a network transport stack via telephone lines, converting your serial port and modems into a network "extension cord." RAS can use IPX/SPX, TCP/IP, or NetBEUI to give users access to servers running these protocols. RAS supports SLIP and PPP. The remote-node client software

> You can use RAS to access the WinFrame server.

establishes a remote-node connection to a WinFrame server by making a PPP connection to RAS. The system administrator is able to configure the client and RAS to use the transport protocol that is needed. Once the remote network connection has been established, the administrator can access the WinFrame client to start a network remote-control session. The default WinFrame server installation allows you to install Microsoft RAS, or you can install it after you install WinFrame.

Citrix has extended the RAS client support beyond that currently provided with Windows NT 3.51 to include extended compatibility with non–Microsoft network environments as well as older clients running 16-bit MS-DOS and Windows.

To minimize both the number of steps a user must take to connect to an ICA session and the layers involved, WinFrame supports direct asynchronous dial-up. An asynchronous WinStation can be created with the WinStation Configuration utility to inform the ICA server that a modem is attached to a serial device and that a WinStation should be enabled. Users connecting to this WinStation use the ICA client to dial directly to the modem attached to the server and are presented with a logon prompt. Once a user is authenticated, either a Windows NT desktop on the WinFrame server or the first window of the published application appears.

## Running Applications Using the Thin-Client/Server Model

Any application can run under the thin-client/server model using WinFrame with no rewriting of code. This section looks at how you can set up applications to run using this computing model.

### Client/Server Applications

Client/server applications have become increasingly popular. The bandwidth requirements for these applications have continued to change, however. As more and more IS departments deploy client/server applications across low-bandwidth connections, an increasing number of these IS teams use the thin-client/server model to improve system performance. Because users are already familiar with their applications, the IS department's objective should be to configure the universal thin client to be as transparent as possible.

Using the ICA thin client, an IS professional can completely hide the WinFrame server and technology from the user. This is commonly accomplished through the auto-logon and application-launching features of WinFrame and the ICA client. For example, let's assume that a group of users with laptop computers running Microsoft Windows 95 regularly access a client/server application named "test.exe." Currently, the users dial up the server using RAS accounts and log on to the network. Then they launch test.exe from an icon on their laptops, which accesses an Oracle database on an HP5000. Over RAS, the performance is slow. In this situation, you can introduce a thin-client/server solution with WinFrame to speed things up. Once WinFrame is in use, the users do exactly the same things they did over RAS, but instead of the application executing on their laptops, it executes on the WinFrame server.

> A user can execute a thin-client session from an icon on the desktop.

To set up an application (for example, test.exe) under WinFrame, follow these general steps:

1. Install the application (test.exe) on the WinFrame server.
2. Install the ICA client on the user's laptop.
3. Create an entry in the ICA client on the user's laptop; include username and password (unless the application doesn't have its own security, in which case, you would probably leave the password area blank). Figure 3-8 on page 70 shows the Properties dialog box for the client as it would appear on either the Windows 95 or the Windows NT 4.0 platform.
4. Specify *test.exe* as the application to launch when the user logs on to WinFrame, as shown in Figure 3-9 on page 70. When the user logs on to WinFrame, the test.exe

**FIGURE 3-8** *ICA client entry with description of entry, network protocol, server address, and optional username, password, and domain*

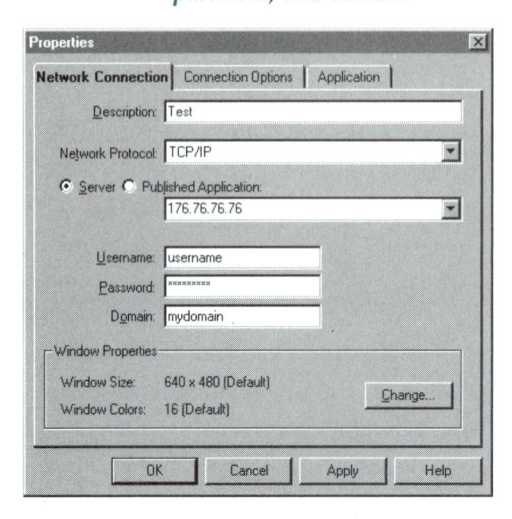

**FIGURE 3-9** *Specifying the executable file that will run when the client logs on to WinFrame*

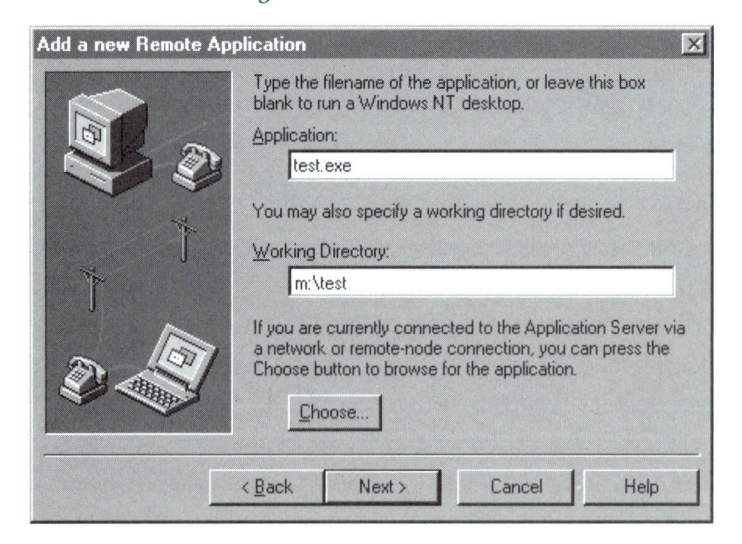

application will launch directly, without launching the Windows desktop. When the user exits the test.exe application, the user logs off the system.

5. Select the icon for the test.exe application that users are accustomed to seeing.

These simple steps make the addition of WinFrame into a client/server environment virtually seamless. When users want to run the test.exe application, they follow the same steps that they used when logging on before the thin-client configuration options were set: they simply dial into RAS, log on to the network, and double-click on the application icon. The test.exe application is launched, and it appears as it would if it were running on the user's desktop.

In this new scenario, however, the user actually launches an ICA client, which accesses the WinFrame server, logs the user on, and runs the test.exe application. The ICA client session establishes a three-tier environment, executing the client's application on the WinFrame server, with business rules, and any supporting database elsewhere.

## Remote Applications and Productivity Applications

From the client/server example beginning on page 68, you can see how easily a thin-client/server solution using WinFrame can fit into your existing environment with little or no change in how users access the applications. These same features can be applied to applications accessed on the LAN as well as remotely, regardless of whether the application is a client/server application or a productivity application.

*You can launch any type of application from a WinFrame server.*

The same steps used for the test.exe example could have easily been used to run Microsoft Excel, Microsoft Word, Microsoft Internet Explorer, Netscape Navigator, or the Lotus SmartSuite applications under the same scenario. If transport exists between the user's workstation and the WinFrame server, you can create an icon on the user's desktop to take the actions listed at the top of the following page.

- Automatically launch the ICA client
- Connect to the specific WinFrame server (or group of servers if using load balancing)
- Automatically log on the user
- Automatically launch the program

## In Conclusion

One of the main benefits for IS administrators or decision makers that was described in this chapter is the great extent to which your department can leverage its knowledge of Windows NT. As you begin to deploy a thin-client/server solution, especially using the WinFrame server, you'll want to make sure that the other members of your IS department receive training on Windows NT Server before they receive WinFrame training.

In addition, the ICA client software, ICA protocol, and ICA system services are available today. Citrix Systems and others will continue to develop and extend their functionality.

And finally, when you begin deploying a thin-client/server solution using WinFrame, you'll gain a tremendous amount of control over how you deploy applications to your users.

Chapter Four

# Form Follows Function: A Computing Continuum

So far in this book, you've learned about what thin-client/server computing is, about what it takes to deploy client/server and Web-based applications using a thin-client/server model, and about how Microsoft Windows NT Server provided a great foundation on which Citrix Systems built WinFrame. You've also seen how well the Independent Computing Architecture (ICA) works on any client platform—whether MS-DOS, Microsoft Windows 3.*x*, Microsoft Windows 95, Microsoft Windows NT, Apple Macintosh, or UNIX—regardless of available bandwidth.

*ICA works on any client platform regardless of available bandwidth.*

In this chapter, I'll describe the range of computing platforms and hardware devices that are enabled by the Citrix ICA client. As you can see in Figure 4-1 on page 74, you have a lot to choose from. The purpose of this book is to provide information that will help you decide where and when to add thin-client/server computing to your IS infrastructure. The thin-client/server model allows you to deploy applications rapidly regardless of available hardware and provides you with the flexibility to choose the hardware

*With thin-client/server solutions, you can choose a hardware device in the form required for a job function.*

**FIGURE 4-1** *Using the ICA thin-client/server software allows access from almost any type of device.*

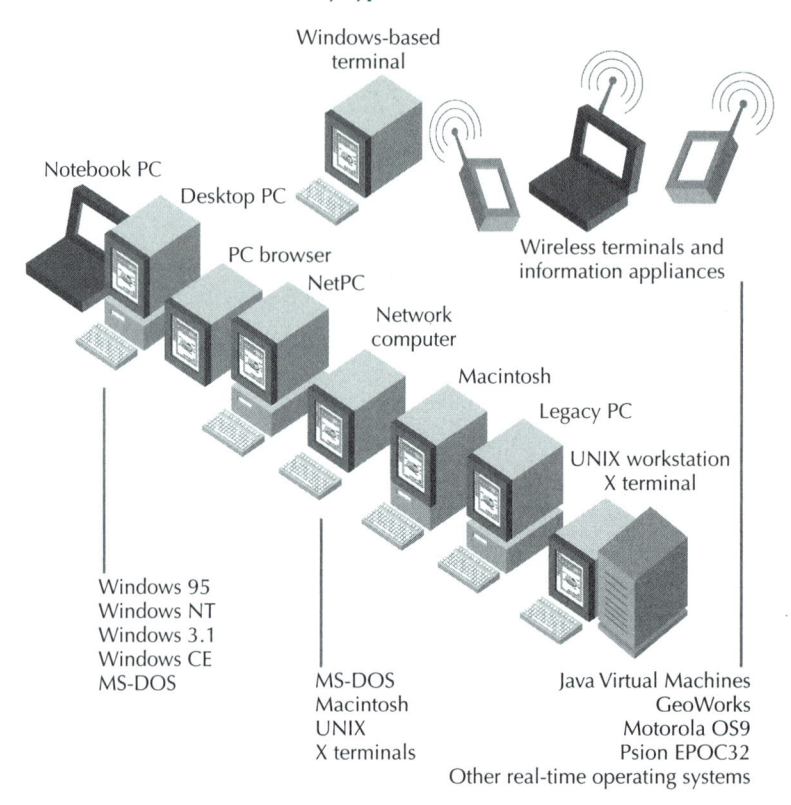

device, thick or thin, that's best suited to your users' job requirements. Because of this freedom to choose among a range of devices, you can allow the form of the device you select to follow the function required for the job—a choice far preferable to shoehorning a fully configured workstation onto every employee's desk.

## Thin-Client/Server Hardware: Form Follows Function

In Chapter 1, I described some different types of users and the tasks they need to perform and then recommended what devices they might use. (See the table on page 9 for this description of various user scenarios.) In this section, we'll look more closely at the available devices, from Windows-based terminals and personal computers to NetPCs, network computers, and hand-held computers.

## Windows-Based Terminals

You can build a thin-client/server solution that works with almost any hardware device. However, one of the hardware devices specifically developed for this model of computing is the Windows-based terminal. The Windows-based terminal is designed to be part of a thin-client/server solution with the ICA client software built into the terminal's ROM. In addition, a Windows-based terminal has small amounts of RAM and ROM (in the 2-MB to 4-MB range for each), does not process applications locally (neither Java Virtual Machine nor browser), and can include other embedded terminal emulation (such as 3270, 5250, VT220, and so on) without local processing.

*Windows-based terminals, with no local processing, are the thinnest of thin-client/server hardware devices.*

The basic Windows-based terminal today uses the ICA client software to find a WinFrame server or servers when it boots up. It sends mouse and keyboard input to the server and displays the video output from the server. All application processing occurs on the server. Any Java applets execute in a browser on the server.

A Windows-based terminal includes the following hardware components (based on specifications for WinTerm terminals found at the Wyse Technology, Inc., Web site):

- Keyboard
- Monitor
- Serial or network interfaces
- High-speed serial ports
- Bidirectional parallel port

The Windows-based terminal connects to the network and is centrally managed. There are no options for disk storage.

Windows-based terminals are the thinnest Windows desktop and are extremely well suited to the needs of any task-based workers.

*Windows-based terminals can simplify IS functions.*

Users access only the applications for which they were granted permission by their IS department. Windows-based terminals in combination with WinFrame servers are particularly powerful solutions for organizations in which the workers depend heavily on one or two mission-critical applications, such as point-of-sale, telesales, data processing, banking, insurance, hospital, human resources management, real estate, and other such applications. The terminals are relatively simple devices with very few parts to worry about. All support is done at the server. By using terminals in a thin-client/server solution, small businesses can more easily outsource their IS functions at a reasonable cost to companies that specialize in thin-client/server solutions. The availability of outsourced IS functions enabled by thin-client/server solutions can accelerate the adoption of business solutions that boost productivity.

For more information about Windows-based terminals, refer to the Web sites listed in the following table.

**Where to Find Information About Windows-Based Terminals**

| Company | Web Address |
| --- | --- |
| Boundless Technologies | http://www.boundless.com |
| Neoware (formerly known as HDS Network Systems) | http://www.neoware.com |
| NCD | http://www.ncd.com |
| VXL | http://www.vxl.co.uk |
| Wyse Technology, Inc. | http://www.wyse.com |

### Personal Computers

How can a personal computer or a high-end workstation even be considered a thin-client device? Well, such computers are not necessarily dedicated thin-client/server hardware devices, but they can certainly run thin-client/server software such as the ICA client. You're probably familiar with these devices. They might include (but are not limited to) the following specifications:

- Intel Pentium CPU (or equivalent)
- 16 MB of RAM
- 1-GB hard drive
- 3.5-inch disk drive
- CD-ROM drive
- Sound card
- Network card
- Modem
- Monitor
- Operating system consisting of Microsoft Windows NT Workstation, Windows 95, Windows 3.*x*, or MS-DOS

The following table is a partial listing of personal computer manufacturers and their Web sites. At these sites, you can expect to find their current offerings and specifications for recent personal computers.

### Where to Find Current PC Specifications

| Company | Web Address |
| --- | --- |
| Compaq | http://www.compaq.com |
| IBM | http://www.ibm.com |
| Dell | http://www.dell.com |
| Gateway | http://www.gateway.com |
| Toshiba | http://www.toshiba.com |

By installing the ICA client on a PC, you can access applications published through a thin-client/server computing infrastructure, either by selecting the name of the published application in the WinFrame Remote Client Manager or by clicking an icon on your desktop that starts an application session on the server. In addition, PC users continue to have complete access to local system resources such as disk storage and printing. They can cut and paste between applications accessed through a thin-client/server session and a local session.

> You can cut and paste between local and thin-client/server sessions while accessing local disks and printers.

You can also activate a WinFrame session by going to a Web page and clicking on a link that activates the application server. If you choose to access WinFrame sessions through a Web browser, you'll need the ICA Web client. The ICA Web client comes with the latest version of Microsoft Internet Explorer. But even if you don't have this ActiveX control, it is automatically downloaded whenever Internet Explorer users connect to a WinFrame-enabled Web page. For Netscape Navigator users, the ICA Web client is available as a plug-in at www.citrix.com.

In addition to the methods prescribed for accessing a thin-client session via a browser or over a local area network (LAN) through your PC, you can also gain access using a modem dial-up session. The ICA thin-client/server software is optimized to run in low-bandwidth situations.

*You can conserve disk space and rapidly deploy applications by using thin-client/server solutions with PCs.*

On a personal computing device, the thin-client/server software can be used to access applications that either the users or their organizations didn't want on the local computing device—whether for disk conservation, security, application maintenance, or any number of other reasons. Published applications can include client/server applications, information applications, infrequently used applications, or even a backup set of productivity tools in case the ones on the desktop present a problem. For example, a graphic artist might keep his graphics, page layout, or multimedia tools on his local desktop but choose to have his productivity, e-mail, or corporate information applications reside on a thin-client/server system. At many large companies, it's unlikely that personal computers will be completely replaced with thin-client/server devices. However, many of the custom applications used at these companies take up significant hard disk space and would be easier to deploy and maintain if they resided on a thin-client/server system.

For mobile professionals, who may or may not have continuous access to a network and who need to preserve hard disk space and keep corporate information secure, thin-client/server solutions can help manage their applications. For example, a salesperson usually requires constantly updated information. Rather than having this dial-up user work at a snail's pace to replicate or download data, he or she could access data-intensive applications on line using the thin-client/server model. This method is secure, reliable, and optimized for low-bandwidth connections.

## NetPCs

Microsoft and Intel developed the NetPC concept and specification in response to the emergence of the network computer. The NetPC was intended to simplify and to centralize the management of Windows-based personal computing in a corporate environment, thus reducing the total cost of ownership. At the same time, it was intended to offer users the power of locally processed PC applications.

*The NetPC was intended to be a managed PC.*

The June 1997 Microsoft Windows Market Bulletin, "What Is the Net PC?" describes the NetPC configuration. The required components include these:

- Minimum 133-MHz Pentium or equivalent
- 16 MB of RAM (32 MB recommended)
- All hardware fully detectable ACPI (Advanced Configuration and Power Interface) and configurable via software
- OnNow
- Wakeup on LAN support (after January 1, 1998)
- Sealed case
- Platform instrumentation
- Internal hard drive
- Universal serial bus (USB) support
- Unique system ID structure
- Mouse and keyboard

A NetPC can also include the following optional components:

- Upgrade capabilities for RAM and CPU
- Lockable CD and floppy drives
- Audio cards

- Graphics accelerator cards
- Serial and parallel ports

*The NetPC includes a full 32-bit operating system.*

The NetPC is a personal computer that is managed centrally by an IS department. In conjunction with Microsoft's Zero Administration Initiative, the NetPC is intended to reduce the difficulty typically associated with maintaining, upgrading, and supporting personal computers on a network. Although the hardware definition of a NetPC begins to approach that of a Windows-based terminal on the low end, a NetPC runs a full 32-bit Windows operating system such as Windows 95 or Windows NT Workstation. In contrast, a Windows-based terminal runs only a very thin operating system, such as MS-DOS, from which the ICA client is launched.

You use a NetPC to access thin-client/server solutions in the same way you use a PC to access applications published through a thin-client/server solution. As with a PC, users continue to have complete access to local system resources such as disk storage and printing and can also cut and paste between applications accessed through a thin-client/server session and a local session. For example, as with a PC, you can install the ICA client on the NetPC. And as with a PC, you have the choice of deploying certain applications for use locally and other applications for use in a thin-client/server scenario. I would imagine that the NetPC would be deployed in situations where document files are centrally managed but where users prefer to have certain regularly used applications available locally. Since the NetPC might have limited hard disk space, programs such as e-mail or other mission-critical applications might be accessed from a thin-client/server solution.

For example, imagine a scenario in which the officers of a bank prefer to use locally hosted analysis tools. Word processing, calendar, e-mail, and database applications, however, can be run using a thin-client/server solution hosted on a server.

For more information about the NetPC, see the Microsoft Web site at: http://www.microsoft.com/windows/netpc.

## Network Computers

Apple, IBM, Netscape, Oracle, and Sun introduced the NC Reference Profile, or specification for the Network Computer (NC), which gained final approval by the partners in August 1996. You can find a version of this profile on Sun's Web site at:

http://www.sun.com/smi/Press/sunflash/mncrs-profile.html

The NC Reference Profile specifies a minimum set of functions that can be used over a broad range of devices. NCs are intended to attach to a network and work with other network devices and content. They will also support a Java-based programming environment, which will enable network-based or even stand-alone applications to execute on them, although they're primarily intended for use on a network.

> NCs are intended to be supported by a Java-based programming environment.

In accordance with the NC Reference Profile, the NC can include any device meeting the criteria, including a PC or a NetPC. The reference profile does not specify a particular processor. The following resource guidelines are taken directly from the NC Reference Profile:

- Minimum screen resolution of 640 x 480 (VGA) or equivalent
- Pointing device
- Text input capability
- Audio output
- Persistent local storage not required

NC devices participate in an Internet Protocol (IP)–based network and support IP as an underlying protocol. Specific hardware attachment to the network is not specified. The NC does include the following IP-based protocols:

- *TCP* The Transmission Control Protocol (TCP) creates a stream-based network above IP. If supported, secure connections are provided by the Secure Sockets Layer (SSL).

- *FTP* The File Transfer Protocol (FTP) allows NC-branded devices to exchange files. This protocol is required only for those NCs that implement either a local or a distributed file system and support file transfer.
- *Telnet* Telnet is a standard client/server protocol that enables character-based terminal emulation access to remote hosts. This protocol is required only for those NCs that support a character-based console.
- *NFS* Network File System (NFS) supports distributed file systems for NC devices. NCs that don't implement a distributed file system don't need to implement this protocol.
- *UDP* The User Datagram Protocol (UDP) is utilized by NFS and enables end-to-end application-specific communications.
- *SNMP* Simple Network Management Protocol (SNMP) enables NC devices to participate in a network-managed environment.

The NC includes the following boot and configuration options:

- *DHCP* To simplify administration and installation, Dynamic Host Configuration Protocol (DHCP) enables an NC to boot itself over the network, to dynamically acquire an IP address, and to transmit configuration information over the network.
- *BOOTP* This protocol enables an NC to boot over the network.

The following Internet standards will be included:

- *HTML* Hypertext Markup Language (HTML) is the publishing format for Internet sites, including CGI (Common Gateway Interface).
- *HTTP* Hypertext Transfer Protocol (HTTP) allows browsers to communicate with remote Web servers and allows servers to communicate with NCs.

- *Java Application Environment* This protocol utilizes the Java Virtual Machine and the run-time environment as well as the Java class libraries.

The following mail protocols are included:

- *SMTP* Simple Mail Transfer Protocol
- *IMAP4* Internet Message Access Protocol version 4
- *POP3* Post Office Protocol version 3

The NC includes the following common multimedia formats:

- JPEG
- GIF
- WAV
- AU

The NC includes security features supported through emerging APIs (application programming interfaces). Optional security standards include:

- ISO 7816 (SmartCards)
- Europay/MasterCard/Visa specifications

Additionally, the NC Reference Profile includes recommendations for printing.

Where application processing takes place is the primary difference between the Windows-based terminal presented in this book and the Java-based NC presented in the reference profile. In the thin-client/server model that uses a pure Windows-based terminal, 100 percent of the application executes on the server, with the terminal passing keyboard and mouse input to the server and receiving display. This complete application execution on the server also occurs when the client device is really a PC or workstation running an ICA client. Other than simple device booting, network connection, the display of the application user interface, and the passing of mouse and keyboard input, no execution happens on the local Windows-based terminal.

> Here's the primary difference between a Windows-based terminal and an NC: with a Windows-based terminal, 100 percent of the processing occurs on the server; with an NC, it occurs locally.

*The Citrix Java ICA client will allow NC users to use Windows applications.*

With the Windows-based terminal, 100 percent of the Web pages and Java applets are downloaded to the NC for local processing, as shown in Figure 4-2. NCs, however, can take advantage of the thin-client/server model and gain access to Windows-based applications with the Citrix Java ICA client.

The NC Reference Profile states that an NC is not a PC replacement. However, the availability of Windows applications through an NC provides many users with the applications they've grown accustomed to while they learn about Web-based computing and adopt Java applets written for their organizations. For example, travel agents might use Web-based applications through NCs to assist their customers with their travel itineraries. At the same

**FIGURE 4-2** *Thin-client/server technology makes Web pages and Java applets available to NCs.*

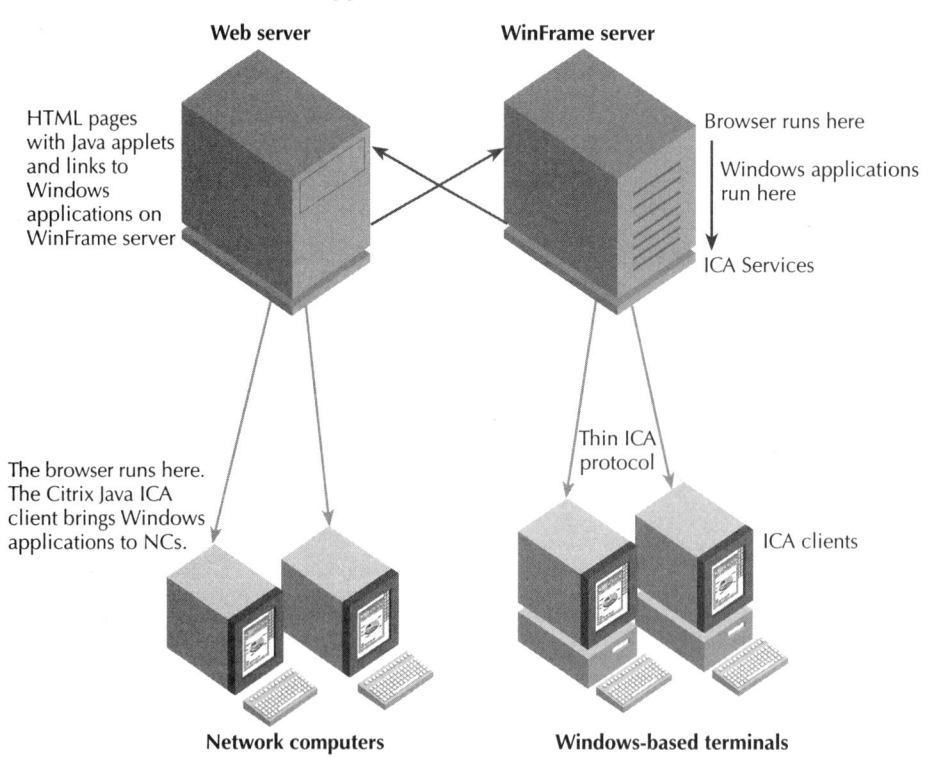

Web server — HTML pages with Java applets and links to Windows applications on WinFrame server

WinFrame server — Browser runs here; Windows applications run here; ICA Services

The browser runs here. The Citrix Java ICA client brings Windows applications to NCs.

Thin ICA protocol

ICA clients

**Network computers**  **Windows-based terminals**

time, they might call on their Windows-based applications for their own personal schedules and e-mail.

The NC, in all its forms, presents another opportunity for accessing Windows applications using thin-client/server computing in addition to the download-and-run Web-based Java computing paradigm. For the latest information on NCs, check the Web sites listed in the following table.

### Where to Find Information About Network Computers

| Company | Web Address |
|---|---|
| Sun Microsystems | http://www.sun.com |
| Oracle | http://www.oracle.com |
| IBM | http://www.ibm.com |
| Tektronix, Inc.* | http://www.tektronix.com |

\* Tektronix offers NCs that can access Windows applications using a built-in ICA client.

## Handheld Computers

Handheld computers, wireless tablets, and Personal Digital Assistants (PDAs) comprise another category of device that can be connected to a thin-client/server infrastructure. Manufacturers such as Telxon; Wyse Technology, Inc.; and Psion have signed on to add the ICA protocol to their devices. Telxon will embed ICA into wireless "ruggedized" pen-based computers. For more information about Telxon, check their Web site at:

> Thin-client/server systems allow for small, mobile form factors.

http://www.telxon.com

The Wyse WinTerm 2730 is a portable wireless terminal that works with a 2.4-GHz RF/LAN interface and a stylus. It has an 8.5-inch dual-scan color screen and is based on technology licensed from Cruise Technologies. It can be used in any number of settings for collecting and analyzing data—in schools, factories, and so on. In Chapter 8, you'll learn how this device is being used in a medical practice to access and update patient records.

*You can even access Windows applications using ICA built into the Psion 5 handheld computer.*

Psion has added the ICA thin-client/software to its EPOC32 operating system used with the Psion 5 handheld computer. This device includes a keyboard and a number of built-in applications. With access to a thin-client/server infrastructure, users of this handheld computer can check their e-mail, browse the Web, or access databases while out of the office. Visit Psion's Web site at www.psion.com.

Handheld computers and PDAs can be used in a wide variety of applications where the user is typically on the go. Imagine Telxon wireless computers being used in restaurants. A waitperson could easily check what's available and what's not, what's on special, and maybe even use the device to page security or medical personnel for an emergency. Or imagine the Psion device in the hands of a salesperson on the road. The salesperson could easily keep in touch with her central office, adding contact information and notes to a remote database.

Portable devices in combination with a thin-client/server solution can provide powerful opportunities for enhancing your business.

## Getting the Most Out of Yesterday's Computers

*ICA allows you to use 32-bit Windows applications with old PC hardware.*

All too often, deploying new software solutions requires a hardware upgrade. A strong feature of the thin-client/server infrastructure is the freedom to deploy applications regardless of available hardware. With the ICA client, you can add new life to old PC hardware with 286, 386, and 486 CPUs.

If you plan to access a thin-client/server solution over a dial-up connection, you need to make sure that the hardware has a minimum of 2 MB of RAM, a VGA card, and a network card or modem.

One ICA licensee, VXL, has created an ISA card, the EaziTC, that fits into an older PC, turning the PC into a Windows-based terminal. You install the EaziTC in lieu of a network card into your older PCs. The EaziTC has the following specifications (which can be found on the VXL Web site at http://www.vxl.co.uk/):

- The EaziTC plugs into any 16-bit ISA slot.
- Using the EaziTC, administrators can maintain a user's private data on his or her local hard disk, excluding such data from the corporate network.
- The EaziTC allows administrators, during the setup process, to prevent the transfer of corporate data to private storage.
- The independent nature of the EaziTC means that the administrator can be absolved of the responsibilities associated with the user's hard disk.
- A built-in OS and ICA engine allows Windows 3.1, Windows 95, Windows NT, and MS-DOS text applications to be delivered directly to the desktop via WinFrame application servers.
- The network interface can be programmed to be available to either PC or EaziTC or to both.
- The EaziTC uses the computer's keyboard, display, memory, and mouse.
- The EaziTC is 100 percent ICA/3 Protocol compliant.
- A built-in 10BaseT network interface is included.

Basically, you can bring old hardware up to a minimum standard for working with a thin-client/server infrastructure by adding a VGA card, 2 MB of RAM, and a network card. You can also add a card such as the EaziTC from VXL. You'll find the ability to add a thin-client/server solution extremely valuable in almost any organization.

## Other Solutions

The devices you can access are not limited to those discussed so far. You can also run thin-client/server sessions on a Macintosh computer using either the Insignia Net Client or the Citrix Java

ICA client. In addition, you can use the Citrix Java ICA client to run ICA sessions on X Windows terminals connected to UNIX servers as well as dedicated UNIX workstations connected to a network. For that matter, you can use the Java ICA client on any other hardware with a Web browser that includes a Java Virtual Machine.

*ICA clients are available for use with the Macintosh, UNIX workstations, and X terminals.*

Insignia Solutions licenses the ICA client for the NTGRIGUE Net Client for the Macintosh. For version 2.0 of this product, you need a Macintosh computer with a minimum of a 68030 processor, 8 MB of RAM, System 7.1 or 7.5.3, and either Mac TCP/IP or Open Transport. You'll need to use TCP/IP either through an Ethernet or an Appletalk connection. For more information about Insignia Solutions, go to Insignia's Web site at:

http://www.insignia.com

If you use the Citrix Java ICA client, the minimum requirements for your Macintosh computer will be those for running either Microsoft Internet Explorer or Netscape Navigator, with the appropriate Citrix add-ins. (See Chapter 7 for more information about Web computing.) For more information about the Citrix Java ICA client, go to Citrix's Web site at:

http://www.citrix.com

You can run thin-client/server sessions on X terminals with an ICA client connected to a UNIX session, or you can add the ICA client to a dedicated UNIX workstation. With any UNIX connectivity, the thin-client/server solution can be used to access productivity applications or e-mail. You might encounter scientists or engineers using high-end UNIX workstations for their research. When it comes to writing their papers, however, they would probably prefer to use Windows applications.

Several of the manufacturers that sell the dedicated Windows-based terminals also market X terminals already set up to access Windows applications through a WinFrame thin-client/server scenario. For more information, see the manufacturers listed in the "Windows-Based Terminals" section on page 76.

## In Conclusion

The thin-client/server model of computing allows you to use Windows applications with any type of client hardware, including Windows-based terminals, personal computers, NetPCs, NCs, PDAs, Macintosh computers, X terminals, and high-end UNIX workstations. With this range of hardware devices, you can rapidly deploy Windows applications where and when you need them. Among the candidates for this type of application deployment you'll find productivity applications, e-mail, and other mission-critical applications. Whether or not the hardware device has local storage, you might prefer that users maintain data such as e-mail or information applications on corporate servers rather than on local machines. At the same time, you'll want the performance that comes with a thin-client/server infrastructure.

As you decide on hardware, you'll need to decide the extent to which your users need local processing. If your users are engineers, graphic artists, scientists, or other professionals who might require local processing, you might choose to provide them with high-end workstations. If your users perform specific tasks, you might prefer to supply them with Windows-based terminals, Net PCs, or NCs. If you have a sales force that requires locally processed applications with intermittent access through dial-up connections, you might prefer to provide notebook computers.

Ultimately, you'll decide on the hardware devices to use with your thin-client/server infrastructure based on the needs of your organization and its users, the priorities you set, and your budget.

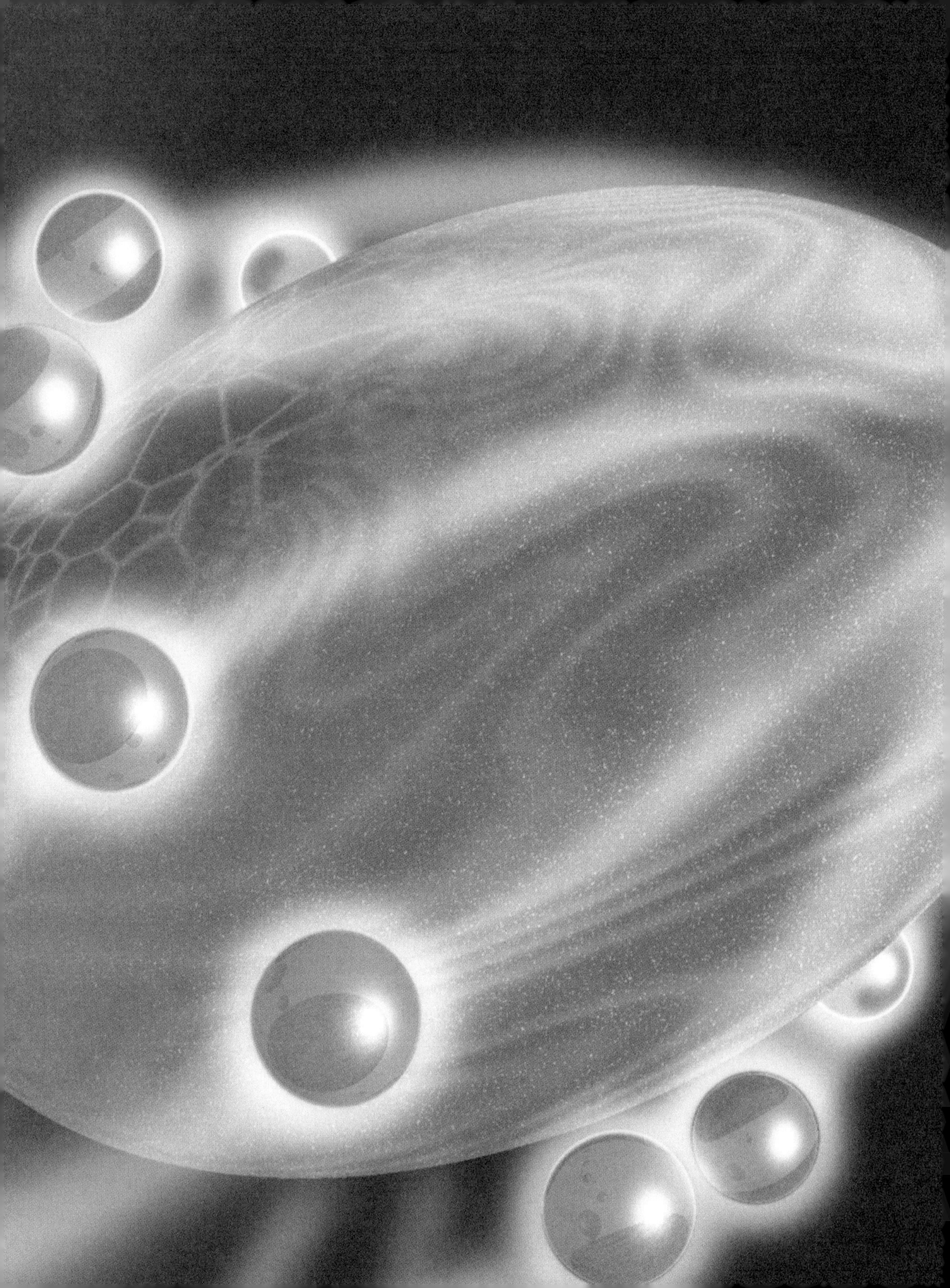

Chapter Five

# Setting Up Your Thin-Client/Server Computing Environment

In this chapter, we'll look at some of the issues you'll need to consider when implementing a thin-client/server solution within your computing environment. Among the topics covered are application licensing, application configuring and publishing, network integration, security, and accessing thin-client/server sessions.

## Licensing Considerations

Proper software licensing presents a challenge for software publishers and independent developers as well as for individual users and organizations. The licensing scheme must protect the software vendor but must not be so prohibitive that it constrains sales of the product. Users and organizations need to follow the rules of the license. Conversely, software developers need to make these rules flexible enough so that users and organizations can take advantage of the software. Organizations are responsible for ensuring that they have properly purchased and licensed the

*Software used in thin-client/server solutions must be properly licensed.*

software they intend to use. Using software in the thin-client/server model is no different than using software on a desktop computer or a file server: you must have the appropriate licenses.

*Check out the SPA Web site.*

In general, the practice of making sure that you correctly purchase and license software promotes and maintains a healthy software industry. You can find comprehensive information about software licensing on the Software Publishers Association (SPA) Web site at:

http://www.spa.org/

*Check out the Microsoft Web site for licensing information.*

At this Web site, you'll find both general information and information about specific tools and courses. Microsoft provides comprehensive guidelines for purchasing and managing Microsoft user and server software licenses on its Web site at:

http://www.microsoft.com/piracy/

When you purchase Citrix Systems' WinFrame product, you must satisfy the thin-client/server licensing requirements, which include the base-system software license and the connecting software. Because WinFrame is built on Microsoft Windows NT 3.51 under license from Microsoft, you also receive the appropriate server licenses to get started. You must also acquire the appropriate licenses for any productivity, information, or thin-client/server applications you plan to deploy. Be sure to consider all licensing issues before you implement a network installation: if you wait, the sticker shock could kill your budget.

The following sections elaborate on the licensing issues you'll need to consider when setting up your thin-client/server computing environment.

## Microsoft Licensing

Software for a network environment can typically be divided into the four categories listed at the top of the next page.

- *Server software*  Servers that contain information and provide services
- *Client access*  A client's connection to the server information and services
- *Server-based application software*  Applications that run from a server
- *Workstation-based application software*  Applications that run on the local workstation

Networking software is commonly sold in a single package that contains the server license and a fixed number of client-connection licenses. You need to plan your environment so that you'll know how many client-connection licenses you'll need to purchase. If you don't do your homework, you might end up paying for a lot of extra licenses that you don't need or purchasing too few licenses and then having a difficult time when you try to upgrade.

> You purchase networking software with a server license and a limited number of access licenses.

Microsoft allows you to purchase licenses on an as-needed basis. The server and client components must be licensed separately and are independent of the desktop operating system software you use to connect to Microsoft server products. Purchasing Microsoft Windows for Workgroups, Microsoft Windows 95, Microsoft Windows NT Workstation, or any other desktop operating system (such as Macintosh) that allows you to connect to a Microsoft server product does not constitute a legal license to connect to those products. In addition to purchasing a license for the desktop operating system, you must also purchase sufficient client-access licenses.

> Even if you have a desktop operating system, you need a client-access license.

As illustrated in Figure 5-1 on the following page, Microsoft offers two licensing schemes for its server products:

- *Per-seat licenses*  With the per-seat option, you obtain one license for each user who can log on to your network. These users access any server that might be connected to your network. Essentially, you've obtained a license for each workstation on your network.

**FIGURE 5-1**  *Per-seat and per-server client access licenses*

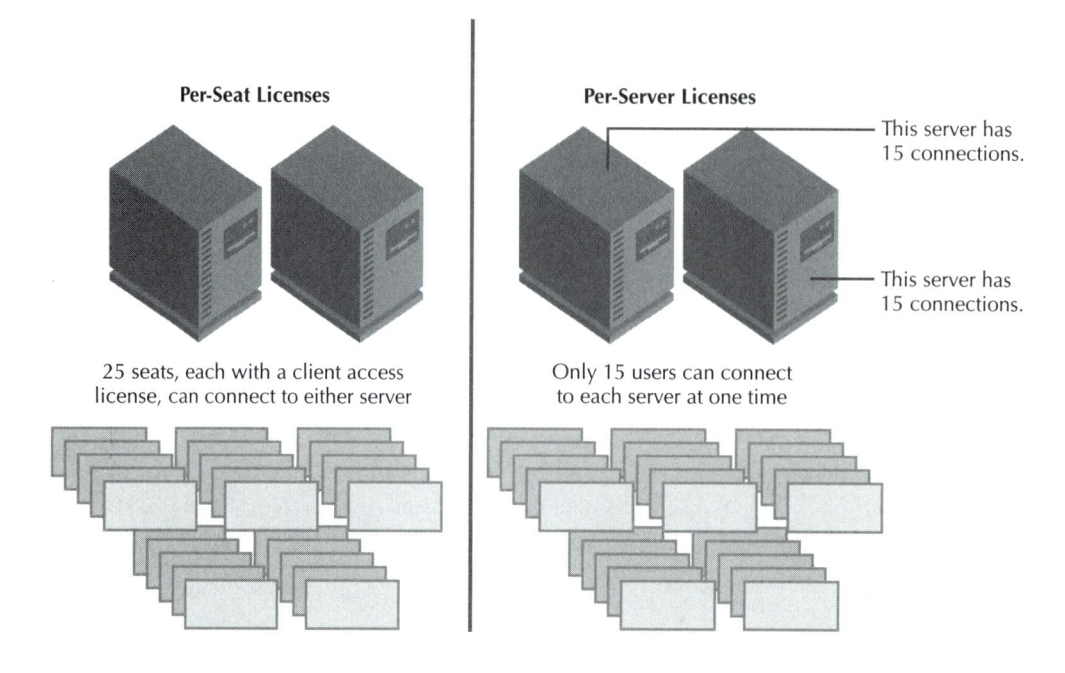

**Per-Seat Licenses**

25 seats, each with a client access license, can connect to either server

**Per-Server Licenses**

This server has 15 connections.

This server has 15 connections.

Only 15 users can connect to each server at one time

*Every server requires the maximum number of connections for per-server licensing.*

- *Per-server licenses* With per-server licenses, a maximum number of users are allowed to connect to the licensed server at a time. If you have more than one server, you must obtain connection licenses for each server. For example, if you've licensed your server for 15 concurrent connections, a maximum of 15 users can log on to that server at one time. If you purchase another server, you need to purchase another 15-user license for that server as well.

   This example of per-server licensing is in the context of a license for connecting workstations to a server. Software publishers can also use the per-server licensing model for application software.

The decision to use per-seat or per-server licensing depends on the relationship between the number of workstations and the number of servers on your network. To figure out which licensing option best suits your environment, you need to do some math. Because you must have connection licenses for each server, multiply the number of connection licenses you need for peak usage by the number of servers you have. If that number exceeds the number of workstations, you're better off using the per-seat licensing option. For example, let's assume that you have two servers, each with a different set of applications accessed by your users, with 15 connection licenses per server and 25 workstations. In this scenario, you're better off going with the per-seat option because you need only 25 licenses whereas with the per-server option you would need 30 licenses.

Microsoft permits you to convert from per-server mode to per-seat mode at no additional cost. This option is a one-time, one-way conversion, however. If you do elect to make this change, you don't need to notify Microsoft. Keep in mind that you are not legally permitted to change the licensing mode from per seat to per server.

> You can convert from per-server to per-seat licensing once legally.

### Citrix WinFrame Licensing and Activation

When you install the WinFrame software, you'll need to enter the serial number on your CD into the WinFrame Licensing manager to obtain a license number. You'll supply this license number to Citrix to receive an activation code. The following types of licenses are available for WinFrame:

- *Base license* This license lets you take advantage of the multiuser features of the WinFrame software. WinFrame Enterprise comes with 15 base licenses. You can install only one base license at a time. Additional licenses won't work without the base license. If the base license is not installed, only one concurrent logon is supported.
- *WinFrame User License Pack* The User License Pack licenses allow for additional user connections to the server. Users can log on to a WinFrame session, known as a WinStation, only if licenses are available. The number of licenses must support the number of connections;

users can't log on to a WinStation if the number of licenses has been exceeded. You can purchase User License Packs and then add WinStations later. You can also pool licenses among like servers. (See the "Citrix WinFrame License Pooling" section on the next page for more details.)

- *WinFrame Load Balancing Option Pack* This option enables the load-balancing features of WinFrame. WinFrame load-balanced farms can contain servers running WinFrame 1.7 and later; versions of WinFrame prior to 1.7 cannot participate in a load-balanced farm.

You use the WinFrame Licensing utility to add, activate, and maintain WinFrame licenses. You can enter the license information either during the install process or after installation. An administrator can always change the WinFrame licensing configuration. After installation, you'll find WinFrame Licensing in the Administrative Tools group. After you enter the serial number from the WinFrame CD, the program appends eight characters to generate a unique license number. You'll then use this license number to register the product and receive an activation code from Citrix. You'll find the information for activating your software in the *Activation Guide* that comes with your software package.

You have 35 days to register with Citrix Systems from the time you install the WinFrame software. After 35 days, you'll be able to use the server only for a single connection. If you register immediately after the install, you shouldn't experience any downtime.

### Special Multiuser Environment Application Considerations

Most applications require each concurrent user to own a legal license. Companies use different methods for enforcing licensing, such as special electronic keys, serial numbers, or just a written agreement. WinFrame has the unique advantage of allowing you to install applications for all users at one time. However, you must comply with product licensing requirements as you would if the application were installed on separate workstations.

## Citrix WinFrame License Pooling

Citrix offers license pooling as a WinFrame feature. License pooling allows an administrator to pool WinFrame sessions on the same subnet. Groups of servers that are load balanced can share registered WinFrame licenses. It doesn't matter how many licenses are on any particular machine or to which machine a user is connected. For example, if you have three WinFrame servers and each has a base license of 15, and two of the servers have User License Packs for 10 users, the three servers can support up to 65 (15 + 15 + 15 + 10 + 10) concurrent users in any combination.

You can exploit license pooling further with the WinFrame load-balancing feature, which allows for applications to be published to a server farm and for the server with the lightest load to accept the next connection. (See the "Sizing Requirements" section near the end of Chapter 6 for more information on load balancing.)

# Configuring and Publishing Applications

The enterprise-wide deployment of an application can be incredibly labor-intensive and expensive, depending on the number of desktops and the geography over which they are spread. While programs such as Microsoft's Zero Administration Initiative and other deployment methods, such as network-based applications installations and Web-based deployment and installation, make life easier for IS administrators, thin-client/server computing lends itself well to solving the application deployment problem since all users share the same source for running their applications. The IS manager installs the application once on the WinFrame server, and the application is immediately available to every user who logs on to that server.

*Install an application once; deploy it to many users.*

In this section, we'll look at how to install applications on a thin-client/server configuration using WinFrame. Then we'll go a step further and examine how to make specific applications available to a user without the user having to go through the Windows NT desktop after activating the WinFrame session.

## Installing Applications on a WinFrame Server

*You can make applications available to everyone or just to a single user.*

You can install Microsoft Windows 16-bit or 32-bit applications on a WinFrame server in one of two ways: user global, in which all users start with the same settings; or user specific, in which only one user can access the application.

**User-global installation** The user-global installation method lets you run an application's setup program once for access by all users of that server. The Change User/Install utility places the system in install mode and ensures that the appropriate files and Registry entries are copied to the WinFrame system directories. After the installation is complete, the Change User/Execute utility places the system back into the default execute mode.

You invoke the User-Global Install utility from the command prompt. You must manually place the system into install mode before installing the application and place the system back into execute mode after installation is complete.

*Using the Change User /Install and Change User /Execute commands*

1. Log on to the console as an administrator.
2. From the command prompt, type *change user /install*.
3. This command places the system in install mode and allows WinFrame to keep track of the user-specific Application Registry entries and initialization files (INI files) the application installs. WinFrame can then automatically propagate the Registry entries or INI files to each user as they are needed by the application.
4. Install the application.
5. When installation is complete, at the command prompt, type *change user /execute*.
6. This command returns the system to execute mode. To determine whether INI mapping is enabled or disabled, type *change user /query* at a command prompt.

After installing the application, log on as a user to verify that the application works correctly. Make sure that any shared resources (such as network drives or printers) are set up for each user before running the application. Check that the user's home directory is valid and that the user can access his or her \windows and \windows\system directories.

You also use the Change User command to make application upgrades or changes. By default, when a user logs on, WinFrame will remove Registry entries or INI files that WinFrame determines are out-of-date with the currently installed versions. This removal allows WinFrame to automatically update the user's application initialization data when an administrator upgrades to a newer version of an application. These out-of-date INI files are not deleted but are renamed. The file extension is changed to CTX in the user's Windows directory, so you can easily restore a file if it shouldn't have been replaced.

*Make sure to test the applications you install.*

By using the global installation tools, you eliminate the need to run setup multiple times, giving the administrator tremendous power with regard to updates and version control and saving a lot of time. Each time you want to update a software package, you install it once on WinFrame and all user desktops are updated.

**User-specific installation** You can also install an application for a specific user. The default installation process is user-specific. Any DLLs, INI files, Registry entries, or other application-specific files are installed to a particular user's home directory. To install an application for a specific user, the administrator logs on as that user and follows the regular installation procedure for the application. Of course, the user can install the application this way as well. Only the user who installed the application has access to the application, even if it is installed on a network or a shared directory. Although other users might have access to parts of the application, they generally will not have access to all that is needed to run the application and must perform their own user-specific installs. In short, a separate install must be done for each user who wants to use the application if you use the user-specific install method.

*You can do network installs to a WinFrame server.*

Because installing applications on each user's desktop can be extremely time-consuming, many applications support network installs. WinFrame permits network installs, so an administrator can install applications on the WinFrame server or on another network file server. Individual users can then connect to the server installation directory and run the application Setup or the Installation program utility, which copies the required files and Registry entries.

For more information about installing applications, refer to the documentation that comes with your software or search for application notes on the Citrix Web site at

http://www.citrix.com

## Publishing Applications on WinFrame

*You can create ICA files for distribution.*

Once you've installed applications on a WinFrame server, you can publish them to Independent Computing Architecture (ICA) clients. Publishing means that you create a preconfigured ICA file that can be sent to a user. The preconfigured file includes information used by the ICA client, running on a local device that can execute the application. You can even send one of these files to your organization through e-mail. You can use the Application Configuration utility found in the Administrative Tools group or the ICA File Editor on a Windows 95 or Windows NT desktop to create application definitions for publishing the application. Figure 5-2 shows the Application Configuration utility found in WinFrame 1.7.

As you can see in Figure 5-2, WinFrame's Application Configuration utility defines an application for running on a stand-alone WinFrame Server or any WinFrame Server in a server farm.

FIGURE 5-2  *WinFrame's Application Configuration utility*

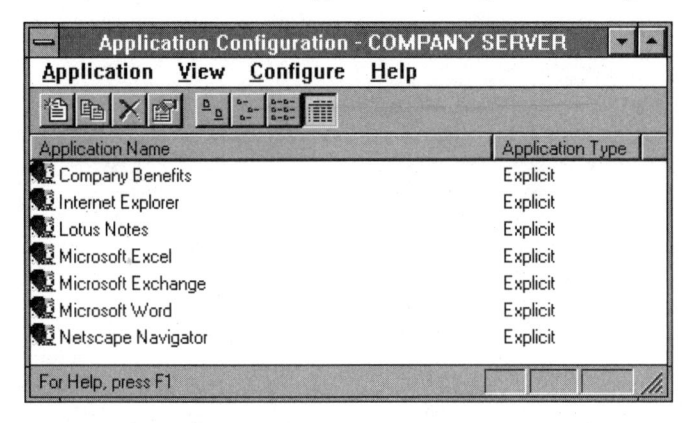

(Creating server farms is part of the WinFrame load-balancing feature, which we'll cover in Chapter 6.) Instead of choosing a server for a connection, the user chooses an application. This utility creates and maintains application definitions and stores them on the WinFrame servers in a database called the Application Registry.

*You use the Application Configuration utility to publish applications.*

I'll go into more detail about application publishing in Chapter 7 in conjunction with using thin-client/server solutions through a browser. You don't need a browser to access published applications, however; you simply need the ICA client software on your device along with the ICA file for the application, but the method for creating the ICA file is the same no matter whether you send the file to a colleague via e-mail or run it from an HTML page.

# Network Integration

People like to argue about their favorite network operating systems, especially the Novell NetWare and Windows NT devotees. This argument is like the beer commercial in which fans debate whether the beer in question "tastes great" or is "less filling." Both parties are right. Each network operating system has its advantages and disadvantages. Many people say that NetWare makes a great file server, and most won't argue with the fact that

Windows NT is a great application server. And UNIX still makes a great SQL server. The trick is to integrate them to take advantage of your existing infrastructure.

WinFrame easily integrates into most network environments. Because the underlying operating system is Windows NT Server, the system inherits all of the compatibility of Windows NT Server. Once you install WinFrame, the rest of the network sees the system as a Windows NT server.

Project leaders often deploy a WinFrame solution initially with the intention of extending the life of a legacy application. Integration in this case, at a high level, involves how compatible the application is with Windows NT and how users access the application. For example, if you use a Windows 32-bit client application to access a UNIX-based database application, with a NetWare network you would need to ensure the client ran on the WinFrame server and then answer the following questions:

- Will users access the WinFrame server using TCP/IP or IPX?
- Do you want users to log on to WinFrame separately from NetWare or autolog on to NetWare?
- Do you want users to bypass the WinFrame logon altogether?
- Do you want users to bypass the WinFrame program manager and launch the application automatically and then log off as soon as they exit the program?

Integration can be complete or partial—it's your call based on the environment you want to provide to the users.

### WinFrame Network Integration Tools

*WinFrame provides great network integration tools.*

Integrating WinFrame and Windows NT into another network operating system is done in most cases by making use of tools inherent in the Windows NT operating system. Many of these tools are automatically installed as part of your Windows NT setup, and others can be installed at another time. The following sections describe some of these tools.

**NetWare integration** Integrating a WinFrame server into a NetWare network is no different than setting up any other Windows client for NetWare. You simply install a compatible protocol stack and a client shell during the WinFrame installation. Microsoft uses NWLink to provide an IPX/SPX compatible transport and GSNW (Gateway Service for NetWare) for the NetWare client. You can add both of these after the initial installation by using the Network configuration applet in the control panel.

> NetWare integration is the same for WinFrame as for any other client for NetWare.

With GSNW, which is illustrated in Figure 5-3, you access file and print resources on NetWare servers from your Windows NT device. You also create a gateway to share NetWare resources with Microsoft networking client computers that do not have NetWare client software. You can also run NetWare utilities and NetWare-aware applications from your WinFrame session.

**FIGURE 5-3** *GSNW applet*

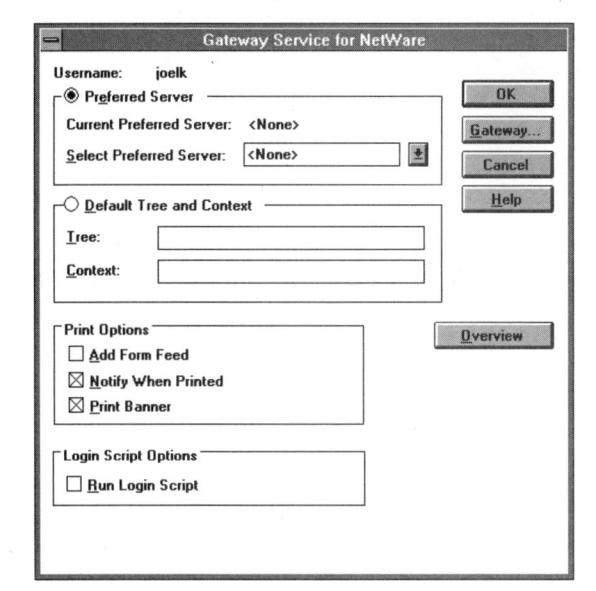

*You can connect NetWare directories to a WinFrame server.*

GSNW allows you to configure a WinFrame session to act as a NetWare client. When you log on to your WinFrame session, GSNW will log you on to a preferred server as a NetWare 3.*x* or 4.*x* bindery emulation client or to a preferred context and tree, which is the location of an object in a directory tree, as an NDS (Novell Directory Services) client. Depending on the preferences you set, you can then choose to run the appropriate NetWare login script to utilize NetWare file and print resources. You can also connect to these resources using a Microsoft tool such as File Manager or by using the Net Use command. You refer to the NetWare resources with the UNC path. For example, you can map a public directory on a NetWare volume named SYS, on a file server named FS1, by typing the following at an MS-DOS prompt:

    net use P: \\FS1\SYS\public

*You can synchronize WinFrame and NetWare accounts.*

To connect to a NetWare server from a WinFrame session, you must have an account on the WinFrame server or domain and on the NetWare server or tree and context. WinFrame supplies tools to synchronize these accounts. These tools will work only in bindery mode, however. One of these tools is the NetWare User Access for WinFrame Tool. This tool allows you to migrate NetWare accounts into your WinFrame server or Windows NT domain. The tool copies the user's name and group information. It does not copy the NetWare password. You can have WinFrame synchronize the bindery passwords by choosing the Config button in the User Manager For Domains dialog box. An administrator sets a preferred NetWare server and a Domain Admin account. This setting gives the NetWare server the ability to update the WinFrame password when a user changes his or her NetWare password.

NDS lovers, do not despair. NetWare has come to the rescue. With the IntranetWare Client for Windows NT, WinFrame version 1.7, compatibility has arrived. You can find information about this product at:

    http://www.novell.com/intranetware/

The IntranetWare Client for Windows NT is installed on the WinFrame server, not on the WinFrame clients themselves. When a WinFrame client logs on to the WinFrame server and runs a virtual session, the user is given the ability to log on to an IntranetWare Server.

Installation of the IntranetWare Client for Windows NT will not replace the WinFrame Graphical Identification and Authentication (GINA) with the IntranetWare GINA because the WinFrame GINA includes code that is necessary for proper system operation. A user is first logged on to the WinFrame server by entering his or her user credentials into the WinFrame GINA. During the initial reboot after installing the IntranetWare Client for Windows NT, the user is presented with an input screen for entering preferred/default settings. These settings include server, tree, and context. The WinFrame user credentials are then compared with the preferred IntranetWare settings for an IntranetWare credential match. If the WinFrame username and password match those for a user in the preferred tree and context, the user is automatically authenticated to IntranetWare. If the credentials do not match, the IntranetWare GUI Login Screen is displayed for login to an IntranetWare Server.

*WinFrame can synchronize with the Novell IntranetWare client for Windows NT.*

The Workstation Manager feature of IntranetWare is dependent on the IntranetWare GINA for proper operation. The Workstation Manager is not supported with WinFrame because the IntranetWare GINA is not installed on the WinFrame server.

The preferred/default settings of server, tree, and context can be entered during the initial reboot after installation of the IntranetWare Client for Windows NT or entered or changed on the Novell IntranetWare Client Service Configuration page under the Client tab. You access this page by selecting the Networking icon found in Control Panel within the Main group, selecting IntranetWare Client for Windows NT, and clicking the Config button.

These default settings are global and will be the default settings for any WinFrame client that accesses IntranetWare through the

WinFrame server. If individual IntranetWare user settings are different from the default settings, they will not be remembered for future logins by that user; therefore, users will always be presented with the preferred/default settings (server, tree, and context) of the system at login.

*OS/2 LAN servers use a domain structure similar to that of Windows NT.*

**OS/2 LAN servers** In this section, we'll cover the integration of WinFrame servers with IBM OS/2 LAN Server 4.0 servers. The information also applies to IBM LAN Manager 2.*x*. Like Microsoft Windows NT servers, IBM OS/2 LAN servers belong to logical groups called domains and the domain controller manages information about users, groups, and workstations within a domain. Unfortunately, IBM LAN Server 4.0 cannot participate in Microsoft domains or share account information with a Microsoft domain controller or a WinFrame server. You can, however, find ways to bridge these incompatibilities.

*WinFrame treats IBM LAN server domains as workgroups.*

IBM LAN server domains are viewed and treated as workgroups under WinFrame. To let users with accounts on other systems access WinFrame and Windows NT resources, you can create local accounts for those users in WinFrame domains containing those resources. You can then place those accounts in local or global groups in the domain and assign necessary permissions to those groups. Although you can give permissions directly to local accounts, I recommend that you don't. These permissions will be difficult to maintain if you later upgrade those other systems to WinFrame and no longer require the use of local accounts. Rather, if you assign the permissions to groups and you later replace other systems with WinFrame after giving those users local accounts, you can then delete the local accounts and provide those users with WinFrame accounts.

Another way to handle the integration of these environments is to configure the LAN Server as a workstation. A WinFrame server can connect to stand-alone LAN Server 4.0 servers or to LAN Server 4.0 servers participating in a LAN Server 4.0 domain. LAN Server 4.0 and WinFrame servers cooperate because they both use server message blocks (SMBs) to communicate between the redirector and the server software. The NetBEUI frame (NBF) and TCP/IP protocols used by WinFrame are also able to work with NetBEUI and TCP/IP protocols written for LAN Server 4.0. LAN Server 4.0 servers can act as backup domain controllers in a WinFrame server domain. Both local and global user accounts are replicated to LAN Server 4.0 servers acting as backup domain controllers. Because LAN Server 4.0 doesn't support trust relationships or local groups, a LAN Server 4.0 server can never be a primary domain controller.

**UNIX** You'll find many approaches to utilizing the services of a UNIX server in a WinFrame domain. WinFrame and Windows NT are naturally able to talk to a UNIX server because of the networking tools built into the operating system. By loading the TCP/IP protocol and the associated tools, such communication is very easy. Some of these tools, such as Telnet, FTP, Gopher, DNS, DHCP, TCP/IP Print services, and SNMP, allow you to connect to a server, browse and transfer files, print to and from a UNIX server, and even manage the server and its network resources.

*WinFrame communicates with UNIX through built-in networking tools.*

UNIX shines when it comes to server applications with data. Many SQL applications use a UNIX server to store the data. Most SQL engines have a compatible client for Windows NT so that the application front end can sit on a 32-bit Windows client while the data, and in some cases the logic, sit on the UNIX server. (See the "Two-tier client/server" section in Chapter 2, starting on page 30, for more information about multitiered applications.) In many cases, this works well until the company spreads out and the bandwidth is consumed, in which case the application then slows down. WinFrame has solved this problem in many instances. By placing the client on a WinFrame server, the client and the server can always be next to each other. The user logs on to the WinFrame server with a thin-client/server device or software client, and very little information traverses the thin pipe. This setup saves a lot of money that would have to be spent on either revamping the application or increasing the bandwidth.

*You can run SQL on a UNIX server with the client on a WinFrame server.*

> For databases specific to UNIX, use a terminal-emulation program on the WinFrame server.

Other UNIX applications are written to run completely within a UNIX environment. This restriction means that you need a UNIX server and workstation. To use such applications on a Windows client, you need a third-party application that will allow you to run a remote session. You can use a Windows-based Telnet application to emulate the required workstation mode, such as VT100 or X Windows. Many of these applications that are made to run on Windows NT or WinFrame, such as Hummingbird, PCXware, and JSB DeskView, let you configure the session for the needs of the UNIX application. You can also use Chameleon NFS, which gives you NFS server support for sharing and using UNIX drives. These applications also work well with a WinFrame server because they can use lots of bandwidth.

> Run login scripts to automate drive and printer mapping on a WinFrame server.

**Microsoft File Manager and Print Manager tools** WinFrame allows you to run login scripts to configure a user's environment from a Windows NT or WinFrame domain or from a NetWare server or NDS tree. These login scripts can be used to automatically map drives, configure printers, copy files, and start applications. The administrator can also choose to have users log on to a local network to set up their resource connections. When they connect to the WinFrame server, WinFrame automatically maps their Client Network drives and printers. The users, however, can control their own environments if the administrator wants them to. The two most powerful tools for exercising this control are Windows NT File Manager and Print Manager.

File Manager and Print Manager are both graphical utilities used to configure, browse, and utilize network file and print services. WinFrame comes with clients for Microsoft Networks, NetWare Networks, and Client Networks.

NetWare Networks include both 3.$x$ and 4.$x$ bindery servers and NDS trees. The client network is controlled by the Client Network Service and allows the client to map a WinFrame session to the client machine's local drives or network connections established before starting the session. Most other network resources will show up under Microsoft Networks, including Windows 95, LAN Manager and LAN Server, and Windows for Workgroups.

# Security

Building a secure network operating system is not an easy task. Security features must be built into every component of the system; and like a chain, the network is only as secure as its weakest link. Security issues you need to consider when building a secure system environment include user account storage, user authentication, file system access, memory-management integrity, environment subsystems control, and the like. The main goal of network security is to protect all of these components from unauthorized access. Many hackers have a mission of gaining unauthorized access. I'm not sure whether they are bored, greedy, or just mean—or all three—but this is the way things are. You establish security by locking components to make unauthorized access difficult. Unfortunately, such a step can also cause authorized access to be difficult. The industry has to be vigilant about staying a step ahead of hackers. A well-planned and well-implemented computer security plan can help make authorized computer use easy and make unauthorized use, intentional or accidental damage, and theft of information difficult or impossible. For more information on computer security, see:

*Stay ahead of hackers.*

http://www.radium.ncsc.mil/tpep/

WinFrame gives you new tools for limiting access to applications, system tools, and resources. The base of Windows NT Server provides the following security measures:

*WinFrame relies on Windows NT security.*

- C2-level security
- Multilevel passwords and privileges
- Roving callbacks
- Encrypted login and data
- File-level security to protect data privacy
- Network resource integrity

WinFrame goes even further by adding the following features:

*WinFrame also adds tools for security.*

- Utilities to lock down files and directories to prevent unauthorized access

- Security auditing utilities that report potential file and directory security exposures and give a detailed report of logon/logoff activity, both successful and unsuccessful
- Detailed procedures for securing trust relationships, services, and network bindings
- Utilities that allow users to execute only applications that appear on a list of approved applications
- An application execution shell that creates a secure standardized execution environment for applications
- RSA RC5 encryption of ICA data using the Citrix Secure ICA Encryption Pack

For more information on C2 security, consult:

http://www.microsoft.com/security/

### WinFrame Security

*Reinforce security by maintaining databases only on your servers.*

The WinFrame thin-client/server operating system extends the security of Windows NT by keeping vital information on a network server: data doesn't have to be downloaded to the user device. This configuration enables users worldwide to access the same centralized information, while IS managers avoid the security, cost, reliability, and management issues of widely dispersed and replicated databases. Because the applications are run 100 percent from the server, the administrator has the ability to have complete control over the workstation environment. For example, a user with a Windows-based terminal can be assigned to use specific applications. When this user logs on, he or she sees only that application—access to network resources is limited. This user will not be able to copy, ruin, or even look at anything the administrator wants to keep private or confidential. Figure 5-4 shows different types of users with various access to applications.

Because WinFrame is a multiuser operating system, additional security issues arise. You need to make sure you remove any components that a user does not need and that an abuser could

**FIGURE 5-4** *Different types of users with access to applications they need*

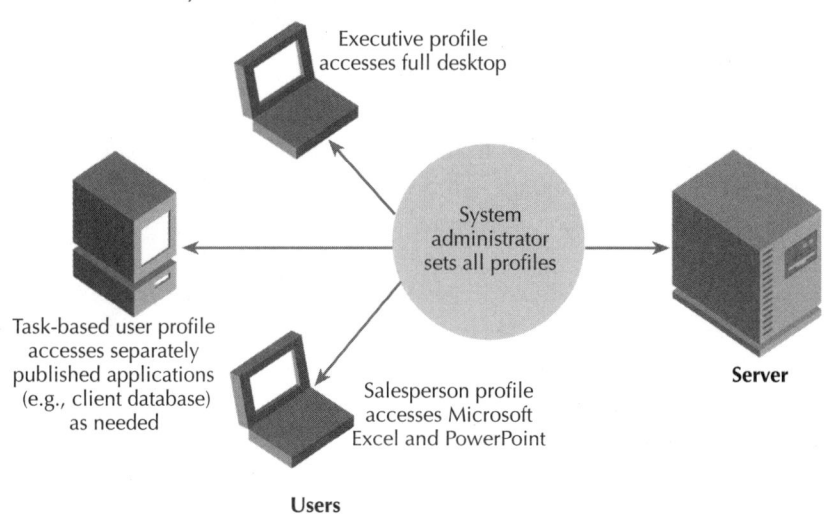

- Executive profile accesses full desktop
- Task-based user profile accesses separately published applications (e.g., client database) as needed
- System administrator sets all profiles
- Salesperson profile accesses Microsoft Excel and PowerPoint
- Server

**Users**

use to break down the system. David Carroll, the consultant you met in Chapter 2, tells a story about opening a company's Web site and finding a link to the Moody Blues at the top of the site. No, the company did not sell records. It was a simple mistake. The company had allowed FTP on the Web Server but did not secure it with a password. The culprit downloaded the HTML document and then edited and uploaded it to its original home directory. The problem could have been much worse.

*Make sure to lock down your system.*

### Another Mischievous User

I know of an administrator who hid File Manager from the users so that they couldn't map a new drive or browse the ones made available. Each user was given an MSMail mail box and a home directory with full rights. A smart user mailed File Manager to his home directory and had a field day. This problem would have been avoided if the system administrator had locked down the home directory with NTFS security.

**Use NTFS with WinFrame for security.**

Certain resources must be locked down to the general public. For example, many people who set up Windows NT servers leave themselves a FAT hard-drive partition to boot to in case of an emergency. This is fine for Windows NT because the partition can be rendered invisible to users by not making a share to it. A WinFrame server shows all to the user. Each volume on that server is seen as a local volume to the user, not a network share. So you must use NTFS only to secure a WinFrame server.

In WinFrame version 1.7, you're given a wide range of security options, including these:

- *ACLCHECK* This utility performs a security audit check on a WinFrame server. ACLCHECK reports excessive file or Registry accesses allowed by accounts other than the Administrator, administrators group, and SYSTEM.
- *ACLSET* This utility secures files and directories on a WinFrame server by setting all file and directory ACLs (Access Control Lists) to a default value.
- *Application execution shell (APP)* This shell is a script interpreter for secure application execution. APP lets you write execution scripts that copy standardized initialization files to user directories. It can also perform application-related cleanup after the application terminates. Using APP, you can simplify ICA files.
- *Application security registration utility (APPSEC)* This security utility allows the system administrator to restrict user-application access to a limited set of authorized programs. When application security is enabled, non-Administrator users are allowed to execute only the programs on the authorized application list. Attempts to execute programs not on the authorized program list are rejected.
- *AUDITLOG* This utility generates reports of logon/logoff activity for a WinFrame server based on the security event log. To use AUDITLOG, logon/logoff accounting must be enabled.

The first step in establishing security is to make an accurate assessment of your needs. Then choose the elements of security that you want and implement them. Make sure that your users know what they need to do to maintain security and that they are aware of why security is important. Finally, monitor your system and make adjustments as needed.

Why not have maximum security at all times? One reason is that the limits you set on access to computer resources make it a little harder for people to work with the protected resources. Another is that setting up and maintaining the protections you want entails extra work.

*Plan your security appropriately.*

These WinFrame tools provide a full range of security levels, from no security to a high level of security. For a description of the different levels of security possible, refer to the documentation that comes with your software.

## Accessing Thin-Client/Server Sessions

As you've seen, you use ICA client software to access WinFrame thin-client/server solutions. The following sections discuss the use of the WinFrame Remote Application Manager.

### Starting WinFrame Sessions

You use WinFrame clients, accessed through the Remote Application Manager shown in Figure 5-5 on the following page, on your local device to start and access WinFrame sessions through your local area network (LAN), wide area network (WAN), or dial-up connections.

*You access applications with the WinFrame Remote Application Manager.*

WinFrame Clients are available with your WinFrame server software or come preinstalled on a dedicated thin-client/server device such as a Windows-based terminal. You can also obtain the latest WinFrame client versions from the Citrix Web site:

http://www.citrix.com

**FIGURE 5-5** *WinFrame Remote Application Manager as seen on a Windows 95 or a Windows NT 4.0 desktop*

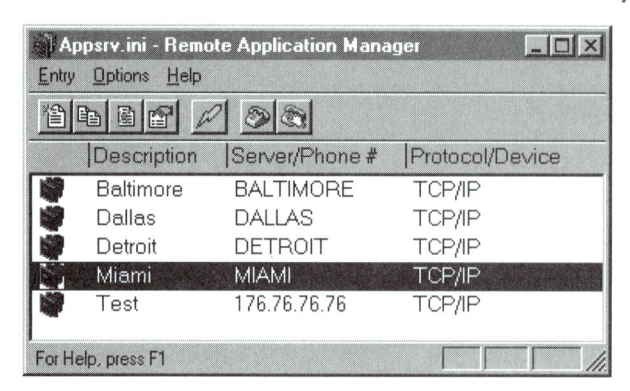

*Use WinFrame Client Creator to build disks.*

You can use WinFrame Client Creator, which is illustrated in Figure 5-6, to create disks for distributing to clients. This application is available with WinFrame version 1.7.

**FIGURE 5-6** *WinFrame Client Creator*

After users obtain and install client software on their computers, they are prompted to configure their first session. The Remote Application wizard guides the user through entering a session name, protocol for accessing the server, and a server name or an IP address or a published application, as well as an icon and a group to save it in.

WinFrame Clients are available for 16-bit and 32-bit Windows applications as well as for MS-DOS applications. You can obtain WinFrame ICA clients from third parties for UNIX and Macintosh devices. Citrix also provides Java-based clients for running WinFrame thin-client/server sessions.

## Automating Access to Thin-Client/Server Sessions

In some instances, the administrator might not want the users even to be aware of the client. It is possible to make this happen by setting up sessions and then automating their access. The Windows client comes with two executables: the application that provides the graphical tools for configuring the sessions, named WFCMGR32.EXE for the Win32 client and WFCMGR.EXE for the Win16 client; and a run-time application that actually starts the session, named WFCRUN32.EXE for the Win32 client and WFCRUN.EXE for the Win16 client. The session definitions are kept in the APPSRV.INI file. This file is laid out like most INI files, with headings and definitions. To start preconfigured sessions, the user needs only the run-time application and the APPSRV.INI file. For example, assume the following section is in a user's APPSRV.INI:

*Create ICA files for distribution.*

```
[USA]
TransportDriver=TCP/IP
Address=SERVER1CTX
Compress=On
PersistentCacheEnabled=On
IconPath=C:\Program Files\Citrix\WinFrame Client\wfcmgr32.exe
WinStationDriver=ICA 3.0
Username=user1
Domain=masterDomain
Password=0008ff990a95690b94
ProgramGroup=WinFrame Client
DesiredHRES=800
DesiredVRES=600
```

The administrator could create a desktop icon for this section with the following command line:

```
C:\Program Files\Citrix\WinFrame Client\ wfcrun32.exe "USA"
```

The user would simply click this icon, and the session would begin.

The administrator could also use the Remote Application Manager to create an APPSRV.INI file and then distribute the file along with the WinFrame client application.

As mentioned previously, the administrator could use the WinFrame Application Configuration utility to create FILENAME.ICA files for specific applications. These applications could be accessed from a desktop icon as well.

### Troubleshooting: Finding the Server

One issue that comes up when configuring clients is that the client can't always find the server. In some instances, as when the client and the server are on different segments of the same network, the client is not always able to see the server by its name. When you're in the Setup wizard for a session and you choose the server field, the client goes out over the network to look for available servers. The list you get is just what the client can see.

*You can find a WinFrame server by using an IP address instead of a server name.*

You can remedy this situation in two ways. The first is to put the physical or IP address of the server into the server field. This is the preferred way if you are connecting over the Internet or if you connect to servers on many different subnets. If you always connect to the same segment, you can permanently enter the IP or IPX address into an address list in the client.

## In Conclusion

I've covered a number of issues in this chapter—issues that will affect implementation and integration of a thin-client/server solution within your existing computing infrastructure and issues you need to be familiar with if you're building a new computing infrastructure that utilizes thin-client/server technology. These issues include application licensing, application configuring and publishing, network integration, security, and accessing thin-client/server sessions.

As you build your solutions around the application needs of your users, make sure that you're aware of all licensing issues concerning the software that you intend to use. Look at the licensing agreements and note if they allow for concurrency; find out whether you need to purchase a license for each user or for each workstation. Be sure you check out the upgrade policies so that you make purchases that will save you money later on as well as keep your users on the most current software versions if you need them.

Also, as you plan to deploy applications, determine how you want the users to see those applications. You have a choice of adding icons to the desktop for specific applications, allowing the user to see a full Windows desktop, or running applications from a Web page. If your users are doing task-specific jobs, you'll publish only the applications you want them to see for the user profile they present.

How about security? Well, you have many tools to help you with not only security through application publishing and Windows NT profiles and permissions but also tools that can lock down certain files and directories.

The thin-client/server solution using WinFrame provides the IS professional with a large number of tools for deploying applications, securing data and applications, and achieving integration within an existing computing infrastructure.

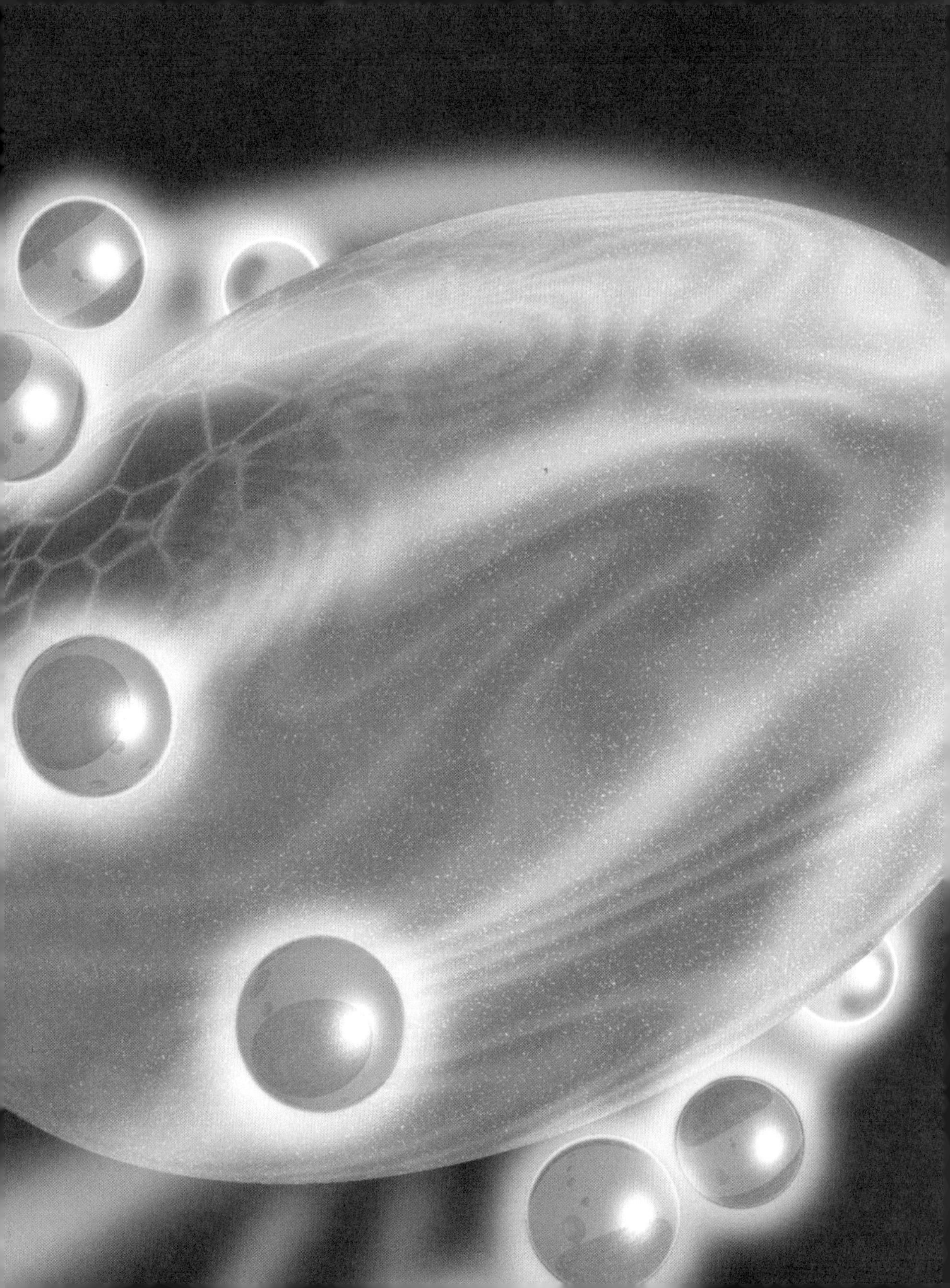

Chapter Six

# Planning Your Thin-Client/Server Environment

Because the Microsoft Windows graphical user interface (GUI) has significantly improved the usability of the PC, Windows has become the most prominent desktop operating system in use today. Although Windows has brought computing power directly to the user's desktop, using this platform can be a nightmare for the IS manager who has to manage a dozen, a few hundred, or even several thousand desktop PCs running Windows. Many IS managers pine for the good old mainframe days of centralized system management.

Employees and employers are now convinced that a computer on every desktop is an essential component for getting work done; a growing number of organizations are using networks of PCs running Windows. This growth has many implications for the IS department of any company. IS managers are now asking themselves the following questions:

> The proliferation of Windows-based PCs has created management and support challenges.

- *How do we share data across large geographic areas without overinvesting in expensive communications capacity?*

  Implementing widespread data communications systems can become very costly. Among the choices for communications systems are T-carriers such as T3 and T1, the frame relay protocol, and the ISDN (Integrated Services Digital Network). But the cheaper the media, the lower the bandwidth, and lower-bandwidth solutions can sometimes create uncomfortable situations for the user.

- *How do we control computers that are physically far away?* Remotely deploying and managing new applications over a local area network (LAN) or wide area network (WAN) can account for some serious time hits and expenses—not to mention headaches—for IS managers.

Careful planning and preparation are the key to a reliable network that supports a thin-client/server environment. In planning a successful network configuration, you must identify current needs and predict future ones and then determine the best ways to meet them. In this chapter, I'll provide information that can help you determine how you can add thin-client/server computing support and how you can optimize the computing infrastructure and resources in your existing environment.

## The Dangerous End User

Let's face it: when you give a person a tool like a pencil, he or she probably knows how to use it. A computer, however, is not so easy. The fun starts when you place a computer on someone's desk. IS consultant David Carroll describes many instances of emergency calls from users who believed that their programs had disappeared. On his way to fix a customer's system, he would wonder who could have had the kind of access that would allow tinkering with something so important. Invariably, when David arrived on the scene, he would discover that the program's icon had been moved out of sight or that the user had changed the characteristics of the window and could no longer find the application. As cases like these prove, it is often hard to control, or even understand, what a remote user has done to a network workstation.

This chapter starts with the guidelines for planning the thin-client/server environment that Citrix recommends for WinFrame. It also covers some of the hardware and software requirements and how your deployment of human resources might change based on the changes made to your computing environment.

## A Typical Planning and Deployment Scenario

Deploying a WinFrame server requires planning, preparation, and attention to detail. The Citrix WinFrame Solutions Guide (which you can download from Citrix's Web site at http://www.citrix.com) recommends a five-stage planning and deployment scenario for a typical WinFrame project:

1. Analysis
2. Evaluation
3. Capacity planning
4. System deployment
5. System maintenance

The next five sections summarize the steps involved in each stage of planning and deployment.

### Analysis

Following are some questions you can ask as you analyze your system requirements, with possible answers in parentheses:

- *What business problem are you trying to solve?* (make remote e-mail access available while traveling; grant branch-office access to large client/server applications, such as a human resources database; streamline the order-entry process; improve customer service)
- *What computing platform and applications are you using?* (NetWare, Oracle database, PowerBuilder application on Windows 3.1 desktops)

- *How many users will need access? How many are concurrent users? How long will a typical connection last?* (100 users total, 25 concurrent connections, 30 minutes)
- *How will you be connecting to the application server?* (asynchronous dial-in; remote node, such as Microsoft Remote Access Service [RAS] or third-party remote node software; LAN; WAN, such as leased line, frame relay, ISDN, ATM; Internet)
- *What client hardware and software will you be using?* (486DX/2 notebook running Windows, 12 MB of RAM, Shiva PPP dialer supporting IP and IPX)
- *What are the functional requirements for a remote user?* (interactively access Microsoft Office client/server applications; ensure 3270 connectivity to mainframe applications; print e-mail, documents, reports to client printer; transfer files between client and servers; include security protocols, such as dial-back, firewalls, third-party security hardware)
- *What are your performance requirements?* (10 seconds to look up a record; type-ahead speed limited to 23 characters for a 50-words-per-minute typist)
- *What is the time frame from the initial pilot to full deployment?* (30-day pilot, with full deployment in the following 60 days)
- *Have the resources been allocated for this project?* (budget approved, project manager and internal resources assigned, professional systems integrator/Citrix authorized reseller engaged)
- *Who are the decision makers?* (director of IS department for budget approval and overall responsibility, vice president of finance for sign-off on success criteria and final OK, project manager "owns" the project)

### Evaluation

It is essential that you establish the scope of the evaluation pilot project. The project's scope can range from demonstrating multiple concurrent users running the corporate applications to addressing issues such as optimum hardware configuration, server/application tuning, client software distribution (and automatic updates), ongoing maintenance, and disaster recovery. As you conduct an evaluation, keep the following guidelines in mind:

- Set up a test environment that emulates field conditions.
- Use the client and server hardware and software configurations that will actually be deployed.
- Agree on a prioritized set of things you want to evaluate, such as applications that need to be tested, printing requirements, authentication and security mechanisms, event logging, auditing, and reporting requirements; and set up success criteria for each, such as acceptable performance results based on clearly defined benchmarks.
- Select several users who can help you streamline the client software distribution and configuration process, and maintain a log that records common questions and problems.
- Set up a contingency plan in the event of system failure (for example, failure of server hardware, communication lines, modems, or power).
- Try to limit the scope of the evaluation to the most mission-critical applications. Once the power of WinFrame becomes apparent, you might be asked to provide support for additional applications. Evaluating these could slow down the evaluation process and move the focus away from the critical applications.

## Capacity Planning

Characterize the resource requirements of a typical user with Performance Monitor, network analyzers, or by other means. The most important resources to monitor are CPU, memory, the paging file, disk subsystems, NIC, and LAN or WAN bandwidth utilization.

Based on the above guidelines, you should be able to arrive at the optimum server configuration (CPU, RAM, disk, NICs, protocols, services), including the number of servers required, the number of users per server, and the network design considerations (backbone segments, multiple NICs/protocols).

## System Deployment

Following are a few important points to consider that can help to ensure a smooth deployment:

- Establish document server hardware and software setup procedures.
- Ensure that the staff is adequately trained to administer the system.
- Use the knowledge provided by an experienced Citrix integrator to assist in the deployment and to train key personnel. (See http://www.citrix.com/support.)
- Distribute the client software with clear documentation on setup and usage.
- Set up a help desk with trained staff to handle questions and problems.
- Establish a weekly review meeting to monitor the operation and resolve open issues.

## System Maintenance

To properly maintain your system, you should provide the following elements:

- Help desk support, problem escalation procedures, reseller or software publisher direct support
- Procedures for testing interim fixes and loading software upgrades prior to deployment
- Maintenance contracts for support, notification of fixes, and software upgrades
- Disaster recovery procedures for such issues as backup/restore and hot spares

## Reallocating Budgeting Priorities

In this section, I'll provide some assumptions and research that might help you reprioritize or reallocate your budget. Although performance issues as well as the central management of hardware and software are good reasons for deploying the thin-client/server model within your environment, it's the cost considerations that usually drive many IS professionals to look at this alternative. In his "Back to the Future..." editorial in *Windows NT Magazine*, editorial director Mark Smith states that "Industry analysts estimate that you spend more than $10,000 per year to maintain the PC you bought for $2500." In fact, comparing the setup costs of 15 thin-client Windows-based terminals to 15 PCs, the Zona Research Group calculated a 54 to 57 percent savings by using terminals. With results like this, Smith estimates that as many as 50 percent of all desktop workstations, depending on the needs of the users, could just as well be thin-client workstations.

*Performance, central management, and cost-effectiveness drive movement to thin-client/server solutions.*

Research commissioned by Citrix found that in addition to saving costs, IS managers' greatest concern was the need for rapid deployment of applications. (See Figure 6-1.) Thin-client/server computing provides IS professionals with a solution that allows them to reallocate and optimize computing infrastructure and human resources.

**FIGURE 6-1** *What's important to thin-client planners?*

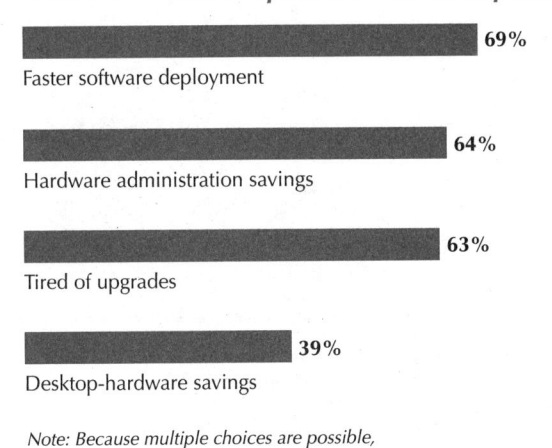

- Faster software deployment — 69%
- Hardware administration savings — 64%
- Tired of upgrades — 63%
- Desktop-hardware savings — 39%

*Note: Because multiple choices are possible, percentages total more than 100 percent.*

The following sections will look at some considerations for the capacity-planning phase of a thin-client/server rollout of WinFrame with respect to network access and bandwidth as well as hardware and software issues. Some of the efficiencies in deploying human resources to support the computing environment will also be discussed.

### Network Access and Bandwidth

*The thin-client/server model makes efficient use of a system's bandwidth.*

As companies grow, the distances between users increase and the users' needs for data expand. As people travel and satellite and regional offices are opened, users must be able to continue sharing data in a timely manner. In some cases, dial-up solutions such as RAS can meet this need. The RAS solution, however, treats a remote computer utilizing a low bandwidth modem connection as though it's part of a regular network connection. Certain applications optimized for dial-up access, such as a Web browser, might perform acceptably. However, if you need to transfer files to or from the host server or if you attempt to run an application on your remote computer that accesses a file from a host computer, RAS performance might be unacceptable. In addition, RAS can get costly if you use it to provide access for a remote office of 10 to 15 people. At that number of users, you would most likely expand your bandwidth by using ISDN, T1, or T3. The higher the bandwidth, the greater the cost, and to borrow a common phrase, "bandwidth is money." Ironically, a thin-client/server application that uses RAS for a connection runs extremely well.

*The ICA protocol is optimized for dial-ins as slow as 14.4 Kbps.*

Using a thin-client/server application, especially Citrix's Independent Computing Architecture (ICA), can reduce your costs by allowing you to utilize less bandwidth. The application and the data can both reside on the same local network. With the thin-client/server model, for which 100 percent of the processing occurs on the server, applications can run up to 10 times faster over existing remote-node servers and branch-office routers than they can using traditional methods. In fact, the ICA protocol is optimized to work well with low-bandwidth dial-up connections. This can help save on your current and future communication and expansion costs, especially for situations in which bandwidth is scarce or network traffic is heavy.

## Hardware and Software

In a speech to the 1997 National Educational Computing Conference held in Seattle, Bill Gates discussed the circular relationship that exists between software and hardware sales. Essentially, software drives the sales of hardware and hardware drives the sales of software. The hardware-software sales cycle is shown in Figure 6-2.

*You'll invest heavily in servers.*

**FIGURE 6-2** *The hardware and software sales cycle*

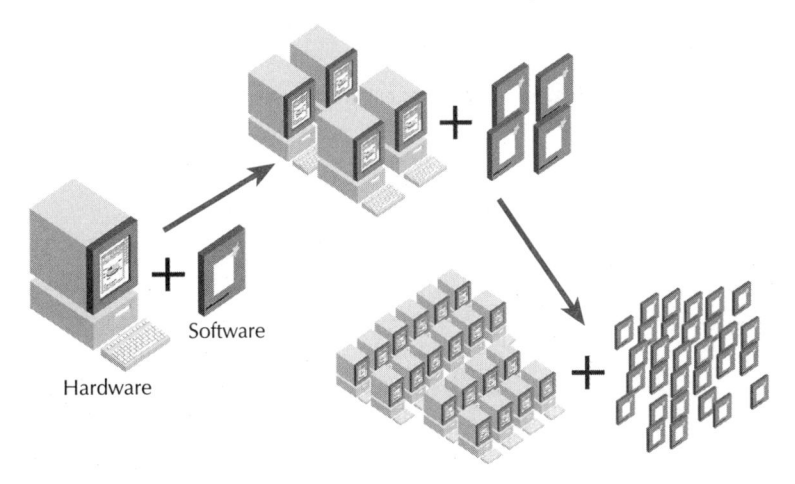

Hardware + Software

Networked computing environment issues present a variation on the theme presented in Gates's keynote. In most cases, you buy software to work with your current hardware or you buy hardware that will work with your legacy software. Upgrading an entire company to 32-bit Windows-based applications could mean upgrading the hardware at every workstation, an expense that could prevent you from using a great new software product. In the long term, you might be better off spending $25,000 to purchase a heavy-duty server with Pentium Pro 200-MHz processors that can comfortably support 40 users with thin-client/server software. Otherwise, if you purchase new equipment for 40 users' desktops, at a cost of about $2,500 per workstation for computers with the latest processor, you would be spending $100,000 or more. The cost difference between purchasing a server for a thin-client/server scenario and purchasing 40 PCs comes to about $75,000. You could use a portion of the savings to purchase Windows-based terminals, or you could opt for the NetPC platform. You could upgrade old PCs to a minimum of 2 MB of RAM and with displays and adapters capable of VGA or better. Or you could pay for the services of a planner/integrator who is conversant with installation of a thin-client/server environment. Using the thin-client/server scenario, you could deploy the latest 32-bit software for Windows, client/server applications, or any applications with a thin-client/server protocol (such as ICA) to almost any device existing on your network. (Consult the "Hardware and Software Requirements" section later in this chapter for more specific information about the type of server that is needed for a thin-client/server environment.)

> Using the thin-client/server architecture, you'll be better able to take advantage of volume licensing programs that offer concurrency.

If a savvy administrator was taking advantage of volume software license purchases, software costs for a thin-client/server solution would be similar to the costs of software licenses for every workstation, with the exception of licensing that permitted concurrency. In that case, you might think in terms of peak usage rather than number of desktops.

In short, deployment of a thin-client/server computing infrastructure allows for reallocation and optimization of funds and resources. If you use the ICA protocol, you'll make very efficient use of your system's available bandwidth. Further, ICA allows you to leverage existing hardware and offers inexpensive alternatives for new hardware.

### Human Resources

> Good people are hard to find—and hard to keep.

One of the most challenging aspects of running a computing and information services infrastructure is finding, keeping, and funding good IS professionals. Managing system and human resources from a distance presents another challenge to an IS manager. As your company grows and the geographical area served expands, you might find that you need more employees to manage the network. In general, the more centrally located your staff, the easier it will be to manage them and the network.

The thin-client/server computing model allows you to configure your network in two ways: by centrally locating all servers or by remotely connecting to and administering any server as though you were sitting right in front of it. Using either of these options, you can assign a few staff members with high skill levels to manage your client PCs from one location. In fact, if you use WinFrame for your thin-client/server solution, you'll be able to remotely perform all software configuration or administrative tasks, provided you have a connection to the server. This type of remote administration can save your organization thousands of dollars in salaries, travel, and human resource management costs. The charts in Figure 6-3 show my guesses about the relative allocations a company would make for hardware, software, and personnel for an environment in which users have the most powerful desktop PCs vs. one in which they use a thin-client/server system.

> You can maintain and support computers remotely.

**FIGURE 6-3** *Resource allocation differences*

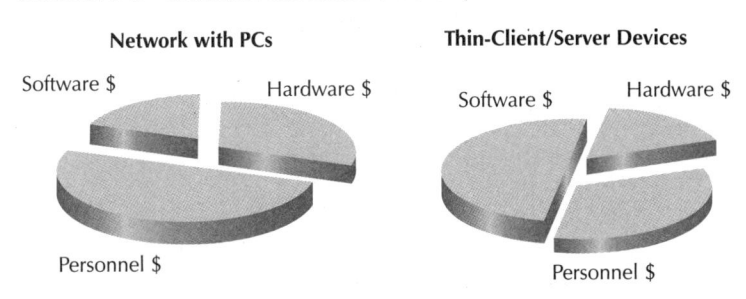

**Network with PCs**
Software $
Hardware $
Personnel $

**Thin-Client/Server Devices**
Software $
Hardware $
Personnel $

As companies plan for growth, they enable their IS administrators to respond rapidly to changing situations, deploying software and hardware where and when needed. Budgets that consider an organization's future needs allow users to access the computing power they really need, regardless of the hardware used. For example, if a powerful new workstation is required to complete a project, the funds will be available. A budget for an organization's network architecture that uses a mix of thin-client devices will require less human resources and less hardware and will allow more funds to be allocated for software. The software funding increase will occur because hardware will no longer be the critical path—or the obstacle—to software deployment. Companies will be able to quickly deploy new software when it's needed, and they'll be able to quickly take advantage of proven and reliable software innovations when the software is in sync with business development objectives.

## Hardware and Software Requirements

In this section, we'll take a closer look at hardware and software requirements for building a thin-client/server system based on Citrix WinFrame.

### Hardware Requirements

*You need a powerful server to run a multiuser environment.*

You wouldn't use a 1914 Ford Model T engine to pull a bus. Sure, using a bus to transport 50 people is more cost effective than having 50 people purchase 50 cars, but what's the purpose if the bus can't move? Thin-client/server computing offers a great deal of flexibility and savings on the client hardware and management

---

### Thin-Client/Server Requirements Differ from Those of Windows NT

A Microsoft Certified Systems Engineer (MCSE) from a Fortune 500 company once complained to David Carroll that the WinFrame servers in his test group were so slow that he couldn't justify putting them into production. After looking at the configuration, David could see that the configuration was based on the MCSE's experience with hardware used to deploy Windows NT–based servers for file and print services. No appropriate planning had been done to prepare and deploy a thin-client/server solution.

costs, but it relies heavily on a powerful server. In a thin-client/ server computing model, the server becomes the veritable engine for all of your client machines. Although you'll save money by not having to purchase new workstations for everyone, you'll need to invest in a powerful server (the engine on the bus). But with proper planning, you'll come out ahead of the game.

**Processor, storage, and memory requirements** Distributing the presentation of an application is not a new concept; it's a typical concept used in the traditional mainframe and UNIX multiuser systems. Although application distribution using the thin-client/ server model is conceptually similar to what occurs using the X Window System, the thin-client/server solution offers the following advantages:

- Transparent support for off-the-shelf applications for Windows and MS-DOS operating systems
- High performance, even over low-bandwidth connections
- Thinner client hardware and software requirements

The configuration concerns that you'd face in planning for the thin-client/server solution using WinFrame are similar to the issues you'd experience when planning for a system using the X Window System and UNIX. Before launching any of these systems, you need to project the capacity requirements for your users. You'll find that the system's performance is directly related to four critical components: CPU, memory, the paging file, and disk subsystems and storage. Each of these components must be properly configured to support a maximum number of concurrent users on a thin-client/server configuration that uses WinFrame.

Hardware requirements for multiuser servers are very different from the requirements for file servers, since multiuser servers must supply enough resources for each of many users who run applications concurrently. If bottlenecks occur, you should first examine the CPU and memory configuration.

*Hardware requirements for a multiuser server are greater than those required for a server dedicated to file and print services only.*

> Never use the minimum requirements as a guideline for a real production environment.

One of the minimum requirements for running WinFrame is a high-end 486 or Pentium-based system. However, a 486 is a bare minimum—it's not recommended for use in any kind of production environment. On the other hand, there are symmetrical multiprocessing (SMP) systems supported by WinFrame and Windows NT. The number of processors and the clock speed will help you determine the number of users your system can support. As a rule of thumb, Citrix suggests 20 users per 200-MHz Pentium Pro CPU. (See Figure 6-4.) For slower Pentium processors of 100 through 166 MHz, you might plan for 15 users per processor. Not all multiprocessor systems scale equally because of differences in bus capabilities. The bus performance will also vary based on design and type. The bus architecture in a multiprocessor system is as crucial for multiprocessor performance as the server itself. Here are my bus recommendations:

| Bus | Recommendation |
| --- | --- |
| Peripheral Component Interconnect (PCI) local bus | Best choice for high performance; lots of peripherals available |
| Extended Industry Standard Architecture (EISA) | Good choice |
| IBM's Microchannel Architecture (MCA) | Good choice, but harder to find parts |
| Industry Standard Architecture (ISA) | Not recommended because of poor performance |

As you plan for system memory requirements, you also need to consider the types of applications being used on your network. For example, 16-bit applications require about 25 percent more processing power than do 32-bit applications. Concurrent users of 16-bit applications each spawn a single application session, while concurrent users of 32-bit applications will share application components already in memory.

Generally speaking, the amount of RAM you need depends on the type of users as well as the applications that will be supported. Users generally fit one of two categories: typical users and power

**FIGURE 6-4** *Server configurations for different types of users*

**Server to support 20 concurrent *typical* users, 16-bit applications.**

Single 200-MHz Pentium Pro processor
2-GB SCSI-2 hard disk
128 MB of RAM
Single 32-bit NIC
256-MB Pagefile

Server

**Server to support 80 concurrent *power* users, 32-bit applications.**

Four 200-MHz Pentium Pro processors
4-GB RAID-5 hard-disk array
512 MB of RAM
Two 32-bit NICs
1024-MB Pagefile

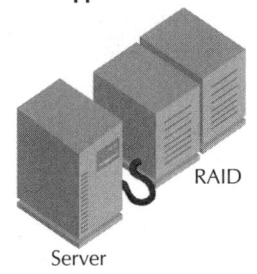

RAID
Server

users. Typical users generally run only one or two applications, but only one application is usually active at any given time. Data requirements for typical users are not complex. Power users, on the other hand, run larger applications and data files, often with three or more active applications at once. Their data requirements are more complex.

A server running mostly 32-bit Windows-based applications should be equipped with at least 16 MB of RAM for the base WinFrame operating system and 4 to 8 MB of RAM for each concurrent user: use 4 MB of RAM for each typical user and 8 MB for each power user. If you plan to deploy 16-bit applications, increase the RAM by another 25 percent.

> Allocate 16 MB of RAM for the system, and then allocate 4 MB of RAM for each typical user, 8 MB for each power user, and an additional 25 percent more RAM if you're running 16-bit applications.

The paging file (PAGEFILE.SYS) is another critical factor in providing good performance in a WinFrame multiuser system. Since all memory is treated as virtual, the memory pool consists of physical RAM plus hard disk space specifically allocated for a paging file when needed. The more RAM available, the less often the paging file is needed, but you need to create a paging file regardless of

*The PAGEFILE.SYS paging file can affect your multiuser system performance.*

RAM. Spreading out the paging file across multiple disk drives will speed things up. Conversely, performance will suffer if the paging file is not configured for enough space. For determining the minimum paging file size, use this formula:

$$\text{PAGEFILE.SYS} = (\text{Physical Memory}) \times 2$$

It's also important to locate the paging file on a hard drive (or drives) that will support the performance. Wide-SCSI drives, attached to a bus-master wide-SCSI adapter on the PCI bus, are generally the recommended approach. While a drive's "access time" should be less than 10 ms, the critical metric is "sustained data rate," and the higher the better.

### Software Requirements

Choosing the right software can be very difficult. Many times it seems that there are too many applications to choose from, and at other times nothing really seems to meet your needs. It can be hard to find the perfect match. To make matters worse, deployment of software to a heterogeneous network can be one of the worst administrative nightmares an IS professional experiences. Thin-client/server solutions, such as those using WinFrame technology, allow organizations to deploy a wide variety of client/server, productivity, and legacy applications with a single integrated software platform.

*Thin-client/server architecture using WinFrame supports Win32, Win16, MS-DOS text, OS/2 text, and POSIX text applications.*

The thin-client/server solution supports the following types of Windows-based applications:

- Win32 applications (Windows NT and Windows 95)
- Win16 applications (except applications using virtual device drivers)
- Client/server and LAN-based applications
- Database servers (Microsoft SQL Server, Oracle 7, or Lotus Notes)
- DDE and OLE support

It also supports the following MS-DOS–based applications:

- Full MS-DOS implementations
- 16-bit MS-DOS–based applications
- LIM EMS (Lotus/Intel/Microsoft Expanded Memory Specification) and extended memory specification (XMS) memory support
- DOS Protected Mode Interface (DPMI) support
- Background execution
- MS-DOS graphics and MS-DOS mouse not supported

And it supports the following types of applications:

- OS/2 text applications
- Portable Operating System Interface for UNIX (POSIX)– compliant text applications

Choosing software for the multiuser environment presents its own set of intricacies. Remember that all of the users are executing on the same server concurrently, with each user in his or her own protected space. However, an application must properly relinquish system resources when it is not actively using them. This means that not only does the application have to run on the server, but it also needs to know how to share with others.

*Applications run in their own protected space.*

As you plan your client/server environment, you should review some of the application considerations for a thin-client/server environment that are recommended by Citrix Systems. Certain application design characteristics that seem relatively benign in single-user desktop conditions might lead to decreased performance or incompatibilities in a multiuser, distributed presentation environment. Understanding these characteristics and avoiding (if possible) their negative impact will help you ensure the smooth integration of an application in a thin-client/server environment that uses the WinFrame server.

*Application design characteristics will affect performance.*

The first step is to check an application for compatibility with Microsoft Windows NT Server. For additional information regarding Windows NT Server application compatibility, please refer to these Microsoft resources:

- http://www.microsoft.com/ntserver (Keep in mind that URLs can and often do change.)
- Microsoft TechNet (For more information, see http://www.microsoft.com/technet/.)
- The Microsoft Windows NT Resource Kit for NT Workstation and NT Server version 3.51 (Microsoft Press)
- The Windows NT Server Concepts and Planning Guide (This manual is included in the Windows NT Server package.)

**General guidelines** Following are some key guidelines for when you're developing or selecting applications for a thin-client/server environment that uses the WinFrame server:

*Win32 applications are the most efficient to use in the thin-client/server environment.*

- *Win32 applications are more efficient than 16-bit Windows-based applications.* Since the WinFrame native operating system is a Win32-based system, Win32 applications are better designed for efficient use of system resources. The 16-bit Windows-based applications inherently use more overhead because they must always load the WOW.EXE subsystem for each user executing the application. An additional 25 percent performance hit is generally incurred by all 16-bit applications.
- *Accessing INI files through the proper APIs is preferred.* Although an INI file appears to be a standard text file, it's actually a database stored in a text file format. When applications access an INI file through the proper API calls, WinFrame's MultiWin technology will be able to detect changes in the file and propagate these changes to users upon login. If instead an INI file is edited in a text editor that does not use the proper APIs for reading and writing, the changes will not be proliferated by MultiWin.

- *Polling or "looping" on any device will have an adverse effect on system performance.* Polling or looping for input from a device uses an unnecessary amount of processor memory when an application is essentially inactive. Applications that yield the processor to the operating system when they are not making necessary I/O requests are preferred so that the MultiWin scheduler can best allocate higher priority requests to the processor.
- *Using standard Windows APIs instead of custom code is preferred.* Applications that are based on Windows standards are most likely to be executed properly and to exploit the advantages of the MultiWin and ICA technologies.
- *Avoid hard coding of paths and network identifiers.* The MultiWin technology of WinFrame allows for the concurrent use of a single machine by multiple users. In a MultiWin environment, it is preferred that all users have private file stores and environment settings. Applications should not require that any file or environment variable point to a single location on a given machine, since this might cause data corruption or performance problems.
- *NetWare applications must be able to run in bindery mode.* WinFrame will authenticate users in a NetWare Directory Services (NDS) environment. However, applications that make use of the NDS-specific APIs will not function properly in a WinFrame environment. Applications that are fully functional in a NetWare bindery-based environment are preferred.
- *The use of MS-DOS programs that use BIOS interrupts to generate graphics or that write directly to a video buffer is not supported on ICA Windows-based terminals.* Because ICA video data is implemented at the driver layer, any application that writes data directly to the video buffer will not be viewable over an ICA connection. Many of the older MS-DOS graphics programs write directly to the video buffer to achieve their graphic functionality. These applications will not function properly in an ICA environment.

- *Using bitmaps should be avoided; use vector-based graphics instead.* Bitmaps require more bandwidth than vector-based graphics since all of the image data for each unique bitmap must be transmitted from the server at least once.
- *Virtual device drivers (VxDs) are not supported in a WinFrame environment.* In many cases, VxDs write directly to the hardware. One of their major roles is to coordinate access to a hardware device from multiple virtual MS-DOS–based machines (VDMs) in a Windows 3.1 enhanced-mode environment. Since Microsoft NT does not allow applications to directly access hardware, these drivers are not supported. In WinFrame, the operating system already handles most of the functions that these drivers perform and, therefore, these drivers are not actually necessary.

*Use the World Wide Web to find tips, tricks, patches, and service packs.*

**Other considerations** The extra bonus to doing research is that you might get valuable tips that will save you some trouble during implementation. Most software companies, including Microsoft and Citrix, have spent a lot of time trying to make many of the most popular applications run at peak performance on their platforms. From their Web sites, these companies provide service packs, software fixes, and installation tips that can save you a lot of time and trouble. Citrix has an ongoing program of compatibility testing, and the company works closely with hardware and software vendors to make their products WinFrame compatible. For more information, use the World Wide Web to access the Citrix Web site at:

http://www.citrix.com

When you arrive at the Citrix Web site, choose the Support topic. You can also get the latest version of the *Citrix Solutions Guide,* which is updated quarterly and contains a wealth of information about installing, configuring, and using applications with WinFrame. For information about Microsoft Windows NT compatibility issues, you can check the Microsoft Web site at:

http://www.microsoft.com/ntserver

You can check out the support links and tools at this site as well.

Don't forget to look at the WinFrame Readme, an online help file supplied with the WinFrame application that contains detailed information on application tuning.

## Sizing Requirements

With PC-based architectures, adding more users to the company network generally meant new servers, additional scripts, and multiple logins for each server. With each new user, all corporate applications needed to be added to a new workstation for each new user to get to work.

Using the thin-client/server model, you can increase the number of supported users by adding another WinFrame server to your domain. Adding more machines to your infrastructure provides a greater capacity to balance loads, especially if you use the Citrix load-balancing feature. It can also improve your network's price/performance ratio.

Distributing work among several servers allows for load balancing without your having to worry about bus or device adapter bottlenecks in a heavily loaded symmetric multiprocessing (SMP) machine. The WinFrame load-balancing feature allows all WinFrame servers in a domain to share the responsibility of providing an increased level of service to all users without specifying to which server a user is connected. (See Figure 6-5 on the following page.)

You can use a global name for a server group to publish an application. Server groups configured in this manner will allow users to access all applications while maintaining personal profiles without users having to log on to a specific server. For example, suppose Domain One has 12 servers installed. The administrator publishes an application called "Domain One" and configures the application to provide complete access to all applications for all users. Each time a user connects to the Domain One application,

**FIGURE 6-5** *The WinFrame load-balancing feature allows you to distribute the processing load.*

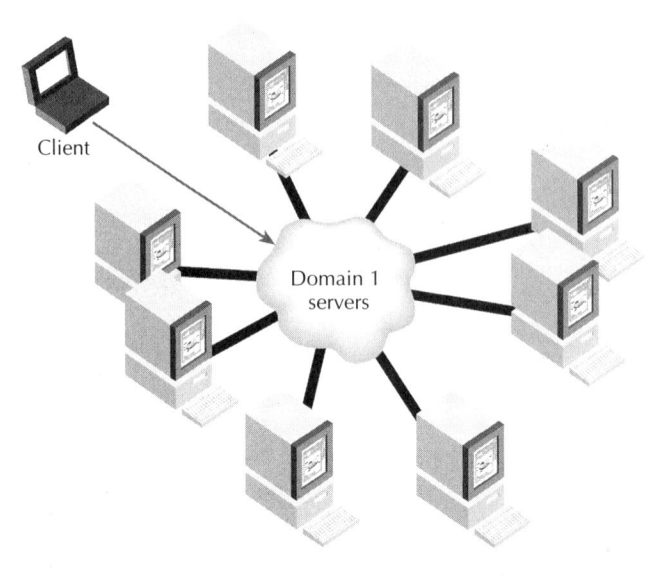

the user's PC accesses the server in the group that has the least load or is least busy. Whether or not the user accesses the same server each time he or she logs on, the user's profile and the PC screen appear the way they did the last time the user logged on. In this example, in the event of a server failure, only one-twelfth of the service is interrupted. On a system that is configured to automatically save data regularly, any affected user would simply reconnect to the application and continue working from the most recently saved data.

The load-balancing feature also allows for a greater level of scalability. When it's time to add hardware to the environment, the system administrator simply adds the server to the domain and runs the application configuration utility. Load balancing also makes expansion of services and applications transparent to the user. The system administrator adds accounts with the appropriate permissions to the server and then provides the users with the appropriate devices, such as disk drives and printers.

## In Conclusion

The thin-client/server model requires some planning and research before its implementation to help IS departments better allocate funds and resources within their organizations. In implementing a thin-client/server solution, you need to examine your hardware, network bandwidth, and application platforms. When purchasing servers, you need to consider the power, speed, and number of processors as well as hard disk space and RAM. You also need to examine the types of applications that will be used and their level of use in your environment.

In this chapter, we covered the software requirements for applications that will run in a thin-client/server environment based on WinFrame. As you test applications that you plan to run, you should refer to this list.

You also saw what sizing considerations are necessary within the environment and how easy it is to add a server to a thin-client/server environment. Essentially, the Citrix load-balancing feature can provide a high level of performance to the users on your network by locating the least-used server when a user logs on to the network.

With effective planning, the thin-client/server architecture can certainly complement your computing infrastructure and assist with the rapid deployment of applications in your environment. It can also reduce and consolidate support resources in a central location, or it can allow centrally located administrators to troubleshoot and maintain a server remotely.

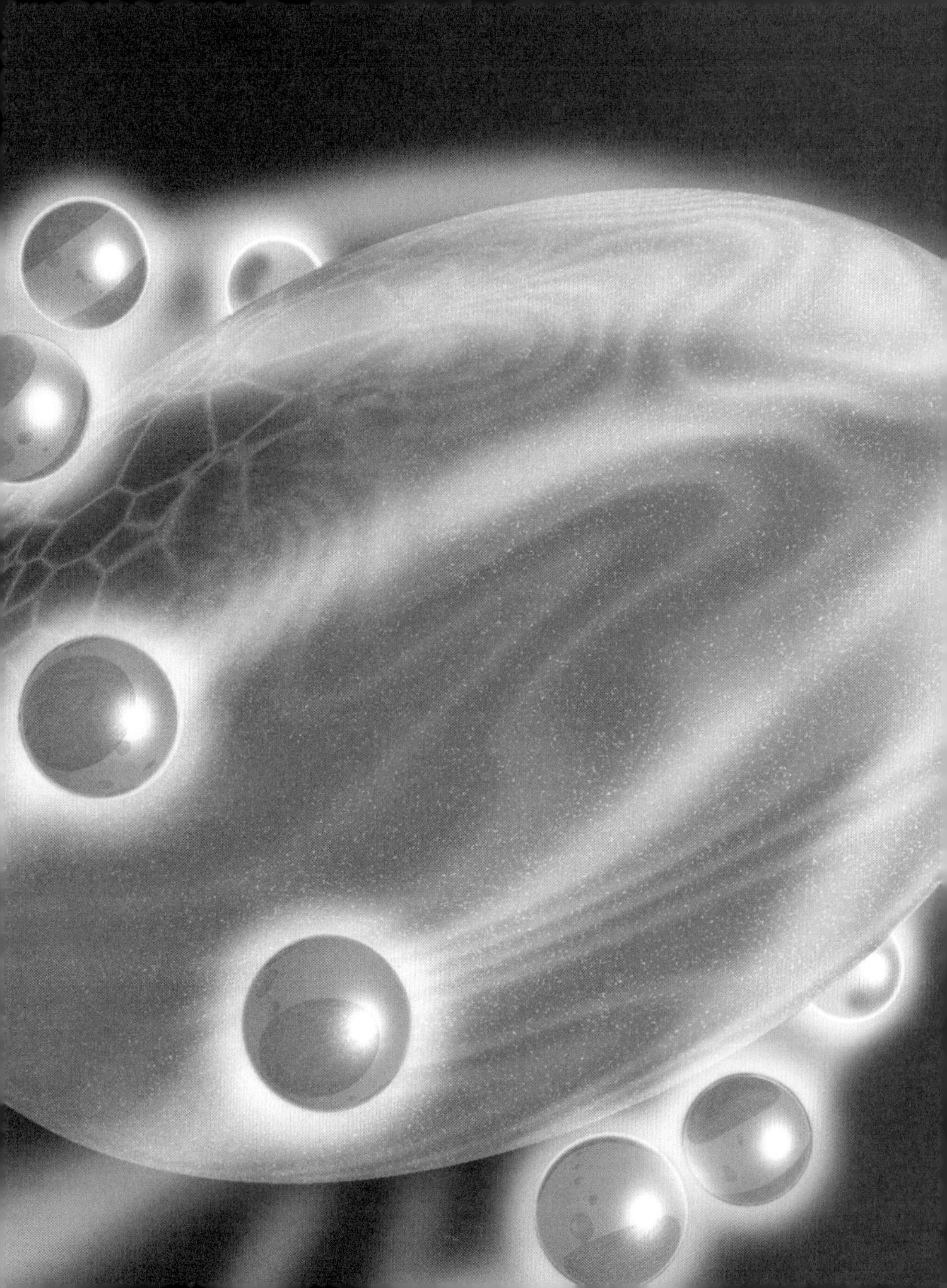

Chapter Seven

# Thin-Client/Server Computing on the Web

As discussed in Chapter 2, the thin-client/server architecture works with and enhances access to client/server and Web-based computing models. You can use the Internet, intranets, or extranets to deploy information and applications to groups that require different levels of security.

You can also combine a thin-client/server solution with Web architecture to provide some very intriguing possibilities. For example, you can extend the typical "download-and-run" Java paradigm of delivering application applets to a browser by adding a thin-client/server client to your browser with application activation from a Web page. To do this, you first create a Web page with an intuitive user interface that is customized specifically for your organization. You can then publish any type of application on your Web site—whether it's an information application, a productivity application, or a mission-critical application.

*Combine the Internet, intranets, and extranets with thin-client/server computing for a powerful solution.*

Users can run applications from customized Web pages instead of from their desktops. Or, to take this example further, a browser can automatically display your organization's home page whenever a user starts his or her desktop computer, as shown in Figure 7-1.

**FIGURE 7-1**  *Simple customized home page for deploying typical applications and information*

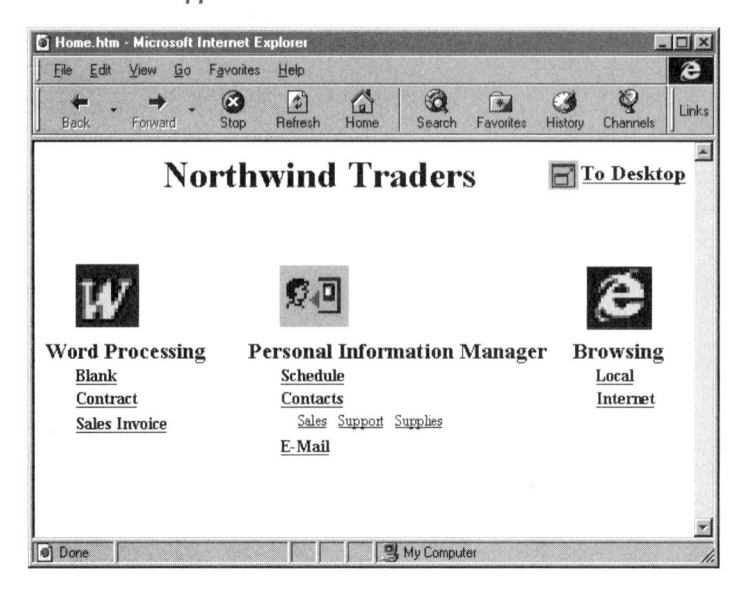

Figure 7-1 shows the home page for an administrative assistant at the fictitious company Northwind Traders. Across the top of the page, application icons, paired with the most common templates for creating documents, appear for starting the most frequently used tasks and applications. Each user has a stored set of custom settings for creating a startup home page with a limited set of choices. Because the home page, the Web browser, and the applications are stored and executed on the server, the IS department can easily maintain all of them.

*You can embed an application in a Web page or run it from a separate window.*

As another option, you can have an Independent Computing Architecture (ICA)–enabled Web browser that resides on either a network computer or a personal computer, with the applications accessible from the HTML Web pages and executing on the server. The terms "launching" and "embedding" describe the ways that you can use HTML Web pages for starting applications. *Launching* simply refers to starting an application in a new window from a link on the Web page, as illustrated in Figure 7-2. *Embedding* takes that a step further: the application is executed and then runs in a defined space within a Web page, as illustrated in Figure 7-2.

FIGURE 7-2   *Application launching and embedding from an HTML page*

Launching                                    Embedding

Launch application in separate window        View embedded application

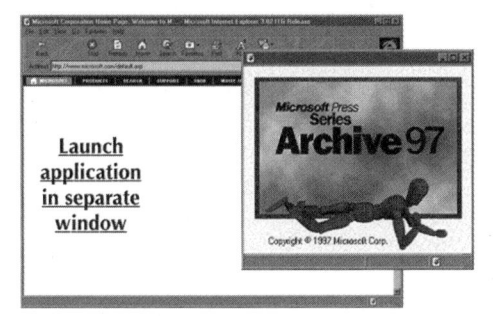

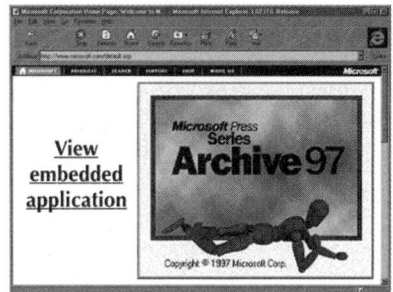

Application launching and embedding (ALE) allows your organization to customize its intranets and extranets by "publishing" any applications without having to adapt the application to some standardized, predetermined user interface. These embedded applications can then be accessed via the World Wide Web, as well as via the organization's local area network (LAN) or intranet.

*Web computing and thin-client/server technology combine to deliver all types of applications.*

In this chapter, you'll learn how to combine thin-client/server solutions and Web-based technology to create applications that are accessible over the Web. You'll see how an organization can use HTML-based browsers to launch and embed applications with the WinFrame application server accessed by ICA for Web-based computing.

In Chapter 8, you'll read some case studies about companies and organizations that are successfully using thin-client/server architecture. One company, Claimsnet.com, uses the World Wide Web for processing its subscribers' health claims. Other companies are looking at expanding their thin-client/server solutions to work with Web servers that take advantage of HTML. Of particular interest is the combination of Web-based computing and thin-client/server solutions for educational institutions at which a lack of funds, use of old equipment, and a lack of IS support prohibit effective use of the latest technology.

## Overview of WinFrame Web Computing

Web Computing consists of three components:

- The WinFrame application server.
- A Web server, such as Microsoft Internet Information Server.
- The WinFrame Web client modules (WFICA*x*.EXE, NPICA*x*.DLL, and WFICA.OCX), which need to be installed on each PC that has a Web browser. Some Web browsers come with the Citrix ICA extensions already installed, some can be ICA-enabled by clicking on a Web page hot link to install the ICA extensions, and some require that a user perform several steps to become ICA-enabled. (These features are covered later in this chapter.)

One important distinction that sets WinFrame Web Computing apart from the traditional Common Gateway Interface (CGI) and newer Java and JavaScript models is that the Web server does not execute any additional software to support WinFrame Web Computing. The Web server contains files (HTML scripts or Web pages that can incorporate ICA hot links in the form of ICA file references) that can be downloaded to the Web browser for processing. The Web browser downloads and executes the Web page HTML script, which might contain references to ICA files.

If an embedded ICA file reference is encountered, the Web browser downloads and passes the ICA file to WFICA.OCX (Microsoft Internet Explorer) or NPICA*x*.DLL (Netscape Navigator), which in turn passes the ICA file to WFICA*x*.EXE. The WFICA*x*.EXE application then initiates a session on the WinFrame server using the information contained in the ICA file and the application definition to launch the desired application. The application can pass video, keyboard, and mouse data between the session on the WinFrame server and the Web browser.

ICA files can be generated on the WinFrame server by using the Write ICA File option from the Application Configuration utility or, in Microsoft Windows 95 or Microsoft Windows NT version

4.0, by using the ICA File Editor utility supplied with your WinFrame server for use with these platforms. For more information about the ICA File Editor utility, see your WinFrame documentation.

## The Server Side: WinFrame for Web Computing Support

WinFrame Web Computing support is automatically loaded during installation of the WinFrame server for thin-client/server computing. This section describes some of the features of WinFrame Web Computing support for your thin-client/server infrastructure. These features include the following:

- The ability to allow anonymous users as well as explicit users to access your applications
- ALE
- Security

These features are covered in depth later in this chapter.

### Configuring User Privileges: Anonymous vs. Explicit Users

WinFrame for Web Computing supports two types of users: anonymous users and explicit users. An *anonymous user* is a special type of user unique to WinFrame Web Computing. By default, anonymous users have guest user privileges and belong to both the Anonymous and Guest user groups. If an application published on the WinFrame server can be accessed by guest users, the application can be configured (using the Application Configuration utility) to allow access to anonymous users. When a user starts an application that allows access to anonymous users, the WinFrame server does not require an explicit username and password. Instead, WinFrame selects an anonymous username (one that isn't currently being used) from a pool of anonymous usernames, and it logs on using that name. During WinFrame installation, an Anonymous user group is created and anonymous usernames are created. (WinFrame creates as many anonymous

> An anonymous user has guest access privileges.

usernames as are allowed according to the product's licensed user count.) These usernames have the form Anon*x*, where *x* is a number in the series 000, 001, 002, and so on.

Anonymous users are given minimal privileges, which differ from the default user (explicit user) configuration in the following ways:

- After 10 minutes of idle time (no user activity), the connection times out.
- The user is logged off on a broken connection or a time-out.
- No password is required.
- The user cannot change his or her password.

These configuration options can be manually changed by using User Manager For Domains utility.

> An explicit user must supply a username and a password.

An *explicit user* is a conventional WinFrame user who must supply a username and a password (in most cases). Explicit users are created and maintained by the system administrator using the User Manager For Domains utility. The main difference between explicit users and anonymous users, from a system administration standpoint, is that each explicit user must be individually created and configured using User Manager For Domains. This method gives an explicit user account the most versatility and configurability but requires additional maintenance by the system administrator.

### Configuring Your Web Server and Setting Up Web Pages for WinFrame Web Computing

In this section, we'll talk about configuring the Web server and setting up your Web pages for launching applications. You start with a Web server such as Microsoft Internet Information Server or the equivalent for WinFrame Web computing. Your Web server can be running on the same machine as the WinFrame application server, or you can run your Web server on another local machine or a remote machine. For security or performance reasons, you might decide to install the Web server and the WinFrame application server on separate machines.

WinFrame Web Computing has been tested for compatibility with Microsoft Internet Information Server, Netscape Communications Server, Netscape FastTrack Server, and Apache Web server for UNIX. Because the WinFrame application launching capability uses standard HTML features, the WinFrame functionality will work with almost any Web server software.

*WinFrame Web computing works with a number of Web server applications.*

Two steps are required to configure your Web server for application launching: you must register the ICA MIME type with the server, and you need to create and add ICA hot links to your HTML pages. The next section discusses how to register the ICA MIME type. After I explain a few concepts about ALE, I'll tell you how to create ICA-launchable applications and how to add hot links to these applications to your HTML Web pages.

**Registering the ICA MIME type** First you need to register the ICA MIME type with the server. Procedures for doing this vary according to the particular Web server used. Refer to the section entitled "Installing the WinFrame Client for Web Computing" later in this chapter for information on how to set up ICA MIME support for your Web server software, or consult the documentation that's provided with your Web server.

For more information about setting up a supported Web server, see the documentation shipped with your version of WinFrame.

**Application launching and embedding** Before you learn about adding hot links to Web pages, you need to understand the basics of ALE. When a user connects to a Web page with an ICA-enabled browser and clicks on an application hot link, the user actually launches the application from a WinFrame server running in the background. ALE enables users to run applications remotely from a Web page via its launching and embedding capabilities.

- Launching an application from a Web page means that the application will start from the Web page and run in a window on your local desktop. To launch an application, you click on a hot link, or hyperlink, that's "embedded" on the Web page and the application "launches," or starts, and appears to run locally on your machine.

- Embedding means that the application appears to run in a window within a Web document (much like a picture) on your local machine. In reality, the application is hyperlinked to the application that is running on the server.

Most browsers available today support application launching; however, only Microsoft Internet Explorer version 3.0 or greater and Netscape Navigator version 2.0 or greater support application embedding. If you use Internet Explorer, Microsoft ActiveX control technology will be used to display the embedded application. Netscape Navigator uses a plug-in to access and execute embedded HTML documents.

*Hot links are embedded on the Web page.*

**How hot links work** When a user clicks on an ICA hot link, the Web server sends an ICA file to the user's Web browser. The ICA-enabled browser recognizes the ICA file extension and invokes the WinFrame client helper application, a very small ICA client, to handle the ICA file. The ICA file contains information that tells the client which WinFrame server to connect to and which application to launch on the server.

*ICA files help define hot links.*

**Creating an ICA file** Before you can create an ICA file and subsequent hot links, you must first install the application to be launched on the WinFrame server. After installing the hot-linked application, you use the Application Configuration utility found on the WinFrame server to write the ICA file. You can also use the ICA Editor, which runs on either Windows 95 or Windows NT 4.0, to create the ICA file. The following information is included in the ICA file:

- The full path of the program to be run
- The working directory (optional)
- The logon username and password (optional)
- The Internet Protocol (IP) address or Domain Name System (DNS) name of the WinFrame server

**Creating ICA-launchable applications** Hot links allow you to launch an application from a Web page. You can create your own hot links with a hyperlink to a valid ICA file located in a public HTML directory on a Web server, as shown here:

`<A HREF="word.ica">Microsoft Word</A>`

When this ICA hot link is clicked by a user, it downloads the file WORD.ICA to the client machine and runs the WinFrame Client for Web Computing program ICA32.EXE (for 32-bit systems), using WORD.ICA to define the connection parameters.

To embed a working hot link on a Web page, you must create two files on your Web server: an HTML document and an ICA file. The HTML document is, of course, the actual Web page that contains the hot link. The ICA file contains the information that the WinFrame Client for Web Computing helper application needs to locate the Win-Frame server and launch the application. The ICA file is referenced in your HTML document just like an image or another Web page would be referenced, using the <A HREF> tag.

Here's some sample HTML code with an ICA-launchable hot link for an HTML page. The Citrix-specific fields are shown in boldface type:

```
<HTML>
<HEAD>
    <TITLE>NORTHWIND TRADERS ONLINE INTRANET</TITLE>
</HEAD>
<BODY>
<CENTER>
<IMG SRC="head.gif" ALIGN=CENTER VSPACE=2 BORDER=0><BR>
<IMG SRC="light.gif" ALIGN=CENTER HEIGHT=200 BORDER=0>
</CENTER>
<H1 ALIGN=CENTER>NorthWind Traders Employee Intranet
</H1>
<H2 ALIGN=CENTER>Company News</H2>
<font size=2>As a member of the Northwind Traders
outside sales team, you can now log in and update
your customer records - remotely - wherever you are.
```

*(continued)*

```
whenever you wish.</font>
<P>
<!--NOTE: The ICA file below starts the database
application. It is accessed via a hyperlink just like
any other file. -->
    <CENTER>
    <A HREF="customer.ica"><IMG SRC="database.gif"
    BORDER=0 VSPACE=6></A>
</CENTER>
<BR>
<HR>
</BODY>
</HTML>
```

Embedding Windows-based applications into a Web page can prove a challenging or confusing undertaking because of the various methods used by Netscape and Internet Explorer browsers to handle embedded files. For example, 32-bit Internet Explorer works with both ActiveX controls (represented by the HTML <OBJECT> tag) and 32-bit Netscape plug-ins (represented by the HTML <EMBED> tag) to access embedded files. However, 16-bit Internet Explorer works only with 16-bit Netscape plug-ins. Netscape Navigator 2.0 and 3.0 work only with the plug-ins, while Netscape Communicator stalls when it encounters an <OBJECT> tag. All in all, it might be difficult for you to create Web pages with embedded applications that work for all of these types of browsers.

The following is a workable example of a script written in JavaScript/JScript to create a Web page that will work with both Netscape Navigator and Internet Explorer. Copy these lines of code to your Web page where you'd normally put your <OBJECT> and <EMBED> tags. Change the first set of *var* definitions to specify your ICA file, embedded window height and width, and other information.

```
<SCRIPT language="JavaScript">
<!-- Author: Thomas Pierce.
// YOU SHOULD NEED TO CHANGE ONLY THE VARIABLES BELOW.
//
// icaFile: location of the .ICA file for
// both the OBJECT and EMBED.
```

```
var icaFile = "/bin/ica/solg.ica";
// width and height: pixel-size of the
// embedded application.
var width = "440";
var height = "438";
// start attribute: if Auto, app fires up upon pageload.
// If Manual, app waits to be clicked by user.
var start = "Auto";
// border attribute: On/Off, to specify border around
// app window.
var border = "On";
// Want vertical/horizontal space around the app? Set
// these just like for the <IMG> tag.
var hspace = "2";
var vspace = "2";
// Where is the ActiveX CAB file located? It's probably
// best to leave this set to Citrix:
var cabLoc = "http://www.citrix.com/bin/cab/wfica.cab#
    Version=4,2,274,317";
// Where is the Plug-ins Reference page located? It's
// probably best to leave this set to Citrix:
var plugRefLoc =
    "http://www.citrix.com/demoroom/plugin.htm";
// The following is the ActiveX tag:
var activeXHTML = '<OBJECT classid=
    "clsid:238f6f83-b8b4-11cf-8771-00a024541ee3"
    data="' + icaFile + '" CODEBASE="' + cabLoc +
    '" width=' + width + ' height=' + height +
    ' hspace=' + hspace + ' vspace=' + vspace +
    '> <param name="Start" value="' + start +
    '"><param name="Border" value="' + border +
    '"></OBJECT>';

// And the Plug-in tag:
var plugInHTML = '<EMBED SRC="' + icaFile +
    '" pluginspage="' + plugRefLoc + '" width=' +
    width + ' height=' + height + ' start=' + start +
    ' border=' + border + ' hspace=' + hspace +
    ' vspace=' + vspace + '>';

var userAgent = navigator.userAgent;
if (userAgent.indexOf("Mozilla") != -1) {
    if (userAgent.indexOf("MSIE") != -1) {
        if (userAgent.indexOf("Windows 3") > 0) {
            document.write(plugInHTML);
        } else {
```

*(continued)*

```
                document.write(activeXHTML);
            }
        } else {
            if (userAgent.indexOf("Win16") > 0) {
                document.write(plugInHTML);
            } else {
                document.write(plugInHTML);
            }
        }
    }
//-->
</SCRIPT>
```

If you want to include some kind of content for nonembeddable browsers, include the following at the end (after the </SCRIPT> tag):

```
<NOSCRIPT>
<A HREF="URL of ICA file">
Click here to launch the application!
</A>
</NOSCRIPT>
```

This additional code provides an option for users whose browsers can't handle an embed—it allows users the choice of launching the application instead.

### Setting Up System Security

*Place Web servers outside the firewall.*

Citrix Systems and most Web professionals recommend that you either disassociate your Web site from your production system or rigorously restrict external access to your system. Any system accessible over the Internet is by definition a security risk. Because you don't want to permit unauthorized access to your production site through the Web, unless you have very robust security and plan to use this with an intranet, you should keep your Web server on a separate network loop outside your firewall. Citrix strongly recommends that you read the security information that comes with your software to assist you in formulating a security plan for your installation.

In addition to the standard Windows NT and WinFrame security features, access to the WinFrame server can be restricted in several ways:

- WinFrame supports Internet firewalls that can be used to restrict Internet access to the WinFrame server.
- You can require that a username and a password be entered before a user can execute an application (explicit user access only).
- You can restrict an application to specific users or groups of users via the Application Configuration utility.
- You can use the AUDITLOG utility to generate reports of logon and logoff activity for a WinFrame server based on the security event log. To use AUDITLOG, logon/logoff accounting must be enabled.
- For added security, you can use the Restricted Application List (APPSEC) utility to restrict user program access to a list of authorized applications.
- The ACLCHECK utility examines the security ACLs associated with your hard disk directories and reports on any potential security exposures.
- The Application Execution Shell (APP) lets you write execution scripts that you can use to set up an application before executing it and to perform cleanup after the application terminates.
- The C2 Security Manager helps you configure the level of system security you want.

## The Client Side: The ICA Web Client

The Citrix WinFrame Web Client, available in a 16-bit version for Windows 3.x users and a 32-bit version for Windows 95 and Windows NT users, automatically configures most browsers when it's installed. The WinFrame Web Client is smaller than the standard WinFrame Client, which is about 250 KB. After downloading the client, you must exit from your browser; otherwise, the installation process will not complete properly. When you restart the Web browser, the WinFrame Web Client extensions are fully integrated into the Web browser and available for use.

### Internet Browsers Supported by the WinFrame Client for Web Computing

*The WinFrame Client for Web Computing supports a number of browsers.*

The Web browsers that have been tested with the WinFrame Client for Web Computing include the following Win32-based browsers:

- Attachmate Emissary Desktop Edition 1.1
- Enhanced Mosaic from Spyglass 2.11
- Frontier SuperHighway Browser 2.0.1
- Microsoft Internet Explorer 1.5, 2.0, 3.0
- NCSA Mosaic 2.11
- NetManage WebSurfer 5.0
- Netscape Navigator 2.0, 3.0
- QuarterDeck Mosaic 2.0

The compatible 16-bit browsers include:

- Frontier SuperHighway Browser 2.0.1
- Microsoft Internet Explorer 1.5, 2.0
- Netscape Navigator 2.0, 3.0
- SpryNet

Because new Web browsers and newer versions of existing Web browsers are continually appearing in the marketplace, I'll offer only general instructions for installing the WinFrame Client for Web Computing in the following sections.

### Installing the WinFrame Client for Web Computing

Web browsers typically support configurable MIME types, giving you the ability to define how the browser reacts when it receives a file with a certain file extension (the characters that appear after the dot in the filename). Typically, the browser defines helper or viewer applications for the different MIME types it encounters. To enable your browser to support ICA extensions, you need to configure the ICA MIME type and associated file extension as follows:

```
MIME type/subtype: application/x-ica
File Extension: .ICA
Viewer program: WFICA32.EXE (32-bit) or WFICA16.EXE
    (16-bit)
```

When you install the WinFrame Client for Web Computing software, all of the browsers listed in the preceding section are automatically configured for ICA file support to both launch and embed applications. You can install the WinFrame Client from a diskette or by downloading it via the Internet or your intranet. You can include installation files on diskettes by using the WinFrame Client Creator, which is available with WinFrame Enterprise version 1.7.

*Create installation disks, or download the install files from the Web.*

If your browser is not automatically configured for ICA file support after you install the WinFrame Client for Web Computing software, you can manually configure the MIME type, file extension, and viewer program name using the configuration information provided above.

To create installation diskettes with the WinFrame Client Creator, follow these steps:

1. From the Administrative Tools program group, double-click WinFrame Client Disk Creator.
2. Select WinFrame for Web Computing Client from the list.
3. Follow the displayed directions.

To install the WinFrame Client for Web Computing from a diskette, follow these steps:

1. Exit any active Web browsers before installing the WinFrame Web Client.
2. Insert the WinFrame Web Client diskette in drive A (or another appropriate drive) of the client PC.

3. In a Windows 3.x environment, execute *a:setup* using the Run option of the Program Manager pull-down menu or the File Manager. In Windows 95 or Windows NT, select Run from the Start menu, enter *a:setup*, and then click OK. The first installation screen appears.

4. Click Yes to continue. A status window appears, showing the progress of the installation. When the installation is complete, a completion message window appears.

5. Click OK.

The WinFrame Client for Web Computing is now installed.

To download and install the WinFrame Client for Web Computing from a Web, follow these instructions:

1. Start your Web browser.
2. Access a Web page (on your local intranet or Internet site, such as http://www.citrix.com) containing a hot link to install the WinFrame Client for Web Computing.
3. Click the hot link, and follow the displayed directions.

## Running an Internet Browser on a Thin-Client/Server System

*You can run Internet browsers on a server and view them from a thin-client machine.*

The last part of this chapter is devoted to running an Internet browser, such as Microsoft Internet Explorer or Netscape Navigator, from the WinFrame server. After installing Internet Explorer or Netscape Navigator on a WinFrame server, users can run the browser by starting an ICA thin-client/server session on their local devices. They can access the browser from a desktop displayed in the ICA session, or they can access an ICA session in which the browser is the published application.

When the browser is executed on the server, it takes advantage of the server's power, speed, and connection to the Web. Browsers also seem to download Web pages very quickly when run on a server. Another advantage of running the browser on the server is that a single IP address is shared.

On a user's desktop, you can set up an icon to an ICA session that starts a browser. The browser session would appear in a separate window, and it would look like any other application running on the computer. Currently the only reason that you wouldn't want to run a browser in an ICA session is the lack of sound and video support. However, Java applets and animation, as well as GIF, JPEG, and bitmap graphics, would work just fine. I'm sure that you'll be seeing support for streaming sound and video in the near future.

The implications for publishing Internet browser applications are tremendous. You will be able to use the thinnest possible client hardware, such as Windows-based terminals, older PCs, or simply an alternative to a desktop. As an alternative to a desktop, as mentioned at the beginning of this chapter, applications can be launched from a Web page.

Using the ICA client to run an Internet browser over a dial-up session provides a very efficient way to browse the Internet or an intranet. You can take advantage of the server's connections and speed while leveraging the performance of the ICA client.

## In Conclusion

You'll find that using WinFrame thin-client/server solutions in conjunction with Web computing will help you deploy applications rapidly throughout your enterprise or organization. You'll also find it easier to supply information and sales applications for your customers to access. You could also provide application access to your sales force or to traveling employees. You might even prefer to use Web pages as an alternative for accessing the most commonly used applications, document templates, e-mail, and other programs.

Supplementing Web computing with thin-client/server solutions can really help to optimize your computing environment by getting your users what they need while maximizing the resources in your IS department.

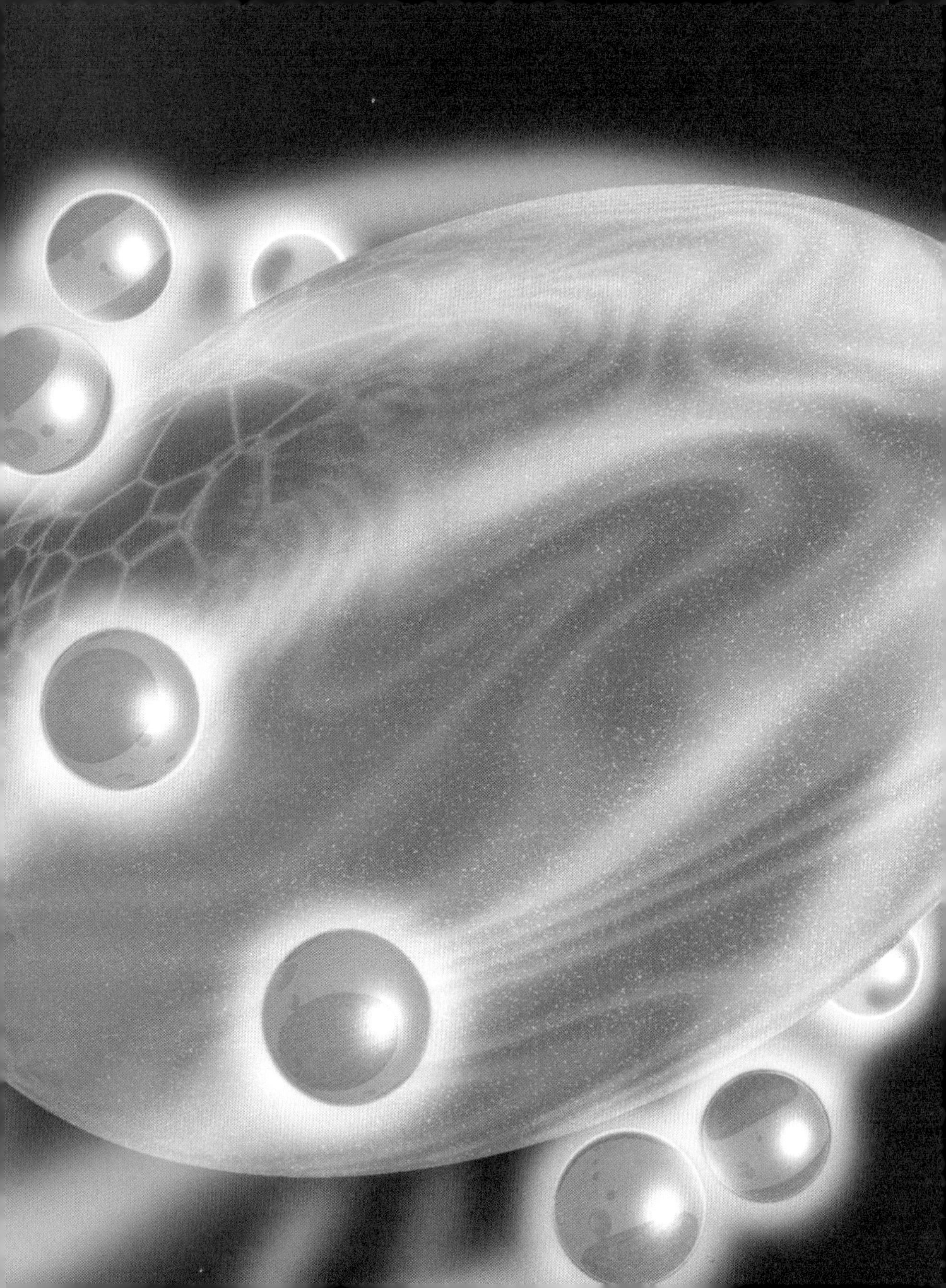

Chapter Eight

# Case Studies

The best way to fully understand where and how the thin-client/server computing model can fit within your company or organization is to see where and how the technology has already been applied. Companies currently taking advantage of thin-client/server computing using Citrix technology include LaSalle Partners, Omnes, Honeywell Europe S.A., Pyramid Breweries, Standard Forms, Anne E. Biedel & Associates, Clarion Health, Mecon, Claimsnet.com, Pro Staff, ReloAction, Bell Mobility, and Vodac. Thin-client/server technology is also used in such organizations as the Orange County Public Defender's Office, Florida Water Services, and Goodwill Industries of Southern Arizona, at the Tulsa City-County Library, and at educational institutions such as Idaho State University.

In this chapter, we'll examine how each of these companies, organizations, and schools uses the thin-client/server model. As you'll see, the thin-client/server technology is versatile and is useful in a broad range of situations. The case studies in this chapter are drawn from the following general areas:

- Accounting and financial reporting
- Sales automation
- Health care services
- Thin-client/server use on the Web
- Human resources management
- Communications and remote computing

- Legal services
- The public and nonprofit sectors
- Education

*This chapter examines solutions using Citrix WinFrame.*

So read on for a closer look at some of the innovative ways in which thin-client/server computing with Citrix WinFrame is currently being used. Each case study is set up in a similar manner: first, the presenting problems are introduced; second, the software and hardware used to solve the problems are listed; and finally, the overall solution is described and its results are assessed. The cases are presented in terms of the vertical problem that was addressed.

## Accounting and Financial Reporting

Thin-client/server computing works extremely well for accounting and financial reporting functions within a company. Accounting and financial reporting systems require information from all areas of the company. Managers analyze this information and take action based on it. The smoother the data collection systems run, the quicker information can be consolidated, reports can be created, and the results can be distributed for management action. Although accounting is the common denominator for the companies in the case studies in this section, some of the companies also deploy applications not strictly related to accounting. For example, Lasalle Partners, the subject of the first case study, also deploys real estate management software.

### LaSalle Partners

LaSalle Partners provides commercial real estate, investment management, occupancy, and property services to U.S. and international markets. The company sought a high-performance solution to give its regional offices access to centralized accounting and property management applications over dial-up and wide area network (WAN) connections.

LaSalle Partners implemented a thin-client/server solution using WinFrame multiuser application server software. This solution improved remote application performance while consolidating mission-critical accounting and property management information into a single, centrally administered, and manageable system.

**Presenting problem** Since its founding in 1968, LaSalle Partners has provided its services to 212 domestic markets and eight foreign countries. It has corporate offices in major metropolitan cities and satellite offices all over the United States. This geographic dispersion was one of the factors that made it difficult for LaSalle to manage its accounting and management functions.

*The challenge: Consolidate the accounting system without sacrificing performance.*

In an effort to streamline its property management functions, LaSalle Partners created a centralized property management "data warehouse" that its 80 property management offices across the United States could share. In searching for an efficient way to centralize its accounting functions, LaSalle Partners discovered WinFrame multiuser application server software from Citrix Systems.

LaSalle Partners realized that a remote computing solution could satisfy its needs and save time and money. The company also felt that such a solution would prepare it for a technologically sound future.

Before deciding to implement a thin-client/server solution using WinFrame, LaSalle Partners deliberated the pros and cons of alternative solutions, including remote-control software and remote-node hardware. Remote-control software allows a remote PC to capture a networked PC and control it remotely. This type of solution requires a dedicated PC for every dial-in line supported. The IS group at LaSalle Partners quickly realized this method of remote access would be prohibitively expensive and that it would involve high maintenance. LaSalle Partners also evaluated remote-node servers. Under this approach, all application processing occurs on the remote workstation, with the data transmitted over the telephone line. If large amounts of networked data—such as

*LaSalle evaluated and rejected remote-control and remote-node solutions.*

database information—require access over low-bandwidth connections, remote-node solutions can suffer performance problems.

**Hardware and software** The LaSalle Partners thin-client/server networking environment includes:

- Compaq DeskPro 100-MHz Pentium server with 144 MB of RAM
- Microsoft Windows NT file servers
- Digital Pathway Defender 5000 security authentication system

LaSalle Partners uses WinFrame Enterprise to deploy MRI and Skyline property management databases and Dun & Bradstreet payroll software across its frame relay WAN to branch offices.

**Solution and results** LaSalle Partners installed nine WinFrame application servers to deploy its mission-critical applications over its frame relay WAN. The strategic implementation of a thin-client/server architecture resulted in greater efficiency, consistency, and accuracy in gathering and analyzing financial and accounting data for the company's property management business. Implementing this system also significantly reduced system administration and maintenance, since remote users were able to access and share a single accounting database, located at the company's headquarters in Chicago, Illinois.

Although initially evaluated and purchased as an application deployment platform for extending the reach of mission-critical applications to remote offices, the thin-client/server solution positively impacted LaSalle Partners in many other ways. The company is now using WinFrame to provide its approximately 150 mobile professionals and telecommuters with dial-up access to Lotus Notes, cc:Mail, and other corporate applications.

LaSalle Partners is also taking advantage of the WinFrame server's multiuser capabilities by employing it as an Internet gateway for approximately 400 employees. As an Internet gateway, the

WinFrame server allows multiple users to share a single IP address, maximizing the investment in an Internet connection while providing performance that rivals dedicated IP addresses. The company has also deployed Netscape Navigator as its Internet browser via WinFrame.

By equipping remote offices and employees with a thin-client/server solution based on WinFrame, LaSalle Partners is succeeding in managing its accounting and management functions efficiently. But more than that, LaSalle Partners is now able to respond more quickly and more accurately to its customers' requirements, a bonus that differentiates the company in the highly competitive commercial real estate management business.

## Omnes

Omnes specializes in delivering global communication solutions to multinational companies, particularly in developing countries. Omnes sought a high-performance dial-up solution for quick, easy, and cost-effective deployment of its Great Plains Dynamics C/S+ financial application to regional offices that would allow it to maintain centralized administration.

Omnes implemented a thin-client/server solution with WinFrame, improving remote application performance by 80 percent while consolidating mission-critical financial information into a single, centrally administered system.

**Presenting problem** Omnes was formed in 1994 as the result of a joint venture between Schlumberger, the world's leading oil field service company, and Cable & Wireless Company, a telecommunications firm based in the United Kingdom. Initially, Schlumberger handled the financial processing for the entire organization. Total integration of Omnes' financial processing was impractical for Schlumberger, however, and the need for an independent financial system became apparent.

The challenge: Deploy mission-critical financial and information applications across a wide geographic area.

The Omnes Houston office originally selected Great Plains Dynamics local area network (LAN) and later upgraded to Dynamics C/S+ for its basic accounting functions, which included accounts payable, accounts receivable, general ledger, and fixed assets. The Schlumberger accounting centers in London, The Hague, and Paris maintained books on their local systems. Data was input, and summaries of the financial results were sent via e-mail to Omnes in Houston; the Houston office then entered the information into a management ledger to perform a worldwide financial consolidation.

Omnes approached Great Plains Software for assistance in improving worldwide WAN access to its financial system. Great Plains Software recommended WinFrame Enterprise as the preferred application deployment platform for its Dynamics C/S+ financial management software over remote dial-up and WAN connections.

*Omnes deploys financial management software across a WAN.*

**Hardware and software** The Omnes thin-client/server networking environment includes:

- Compaq DeskPro 100-MHz Pentium server with 64 MB of RAM
- Microsoft Windows NT file servers

Omnes uses WinFrame Enterprise to deploy Great Plains Dynamics C/S+ client/server financial management software across its global WAN to branch offices.

**Solution and results** Creating an efficient, worldwide financial system has been no small task for Omnes. Like most companies today, Omnes has a growing number of telecommuters and branch offices, making worldwide access to mission-critical applications and information a necessity for the efficiency of even its most remote operations. By using a thin-client/server solution, Omnes has extended the reach of its Great Plains Dynamics C/S+ client/server financial management software across its expansive global network to regional offices in London and Caracas via modem and WAN connections, respectively.

Omnes installed WinFrame at its Houston office and began initial testing from its London office. After testing Great Plains Dynamics C/S+ and WinFrame over its WAN, Omnes discovered that the thin-client/server solution improved remote application performance by as much as 80 percent. With WinFrame, all of Omnes' application processing occurs in Houston rather than being pulled down across the network to remote desktops. As a result, far less data is moved back and forth across the network, and application response times improve substantially. Omnes reports that with Dynamics C/S+ running by itself over its WAN, it took about 4 to 5 seconds to tab from field to field. With WinFrame, it takes only 1 second.

Omnes' strategic implementation of this technology resulted in a number of improvements for its financial organization, including allowing remote offices worldwide to simultaneously access and work with one consolidated financial database. This benefit alone offered greater overall efficiency, consistency, and accuracy in the gathering and analyzing of financial results. Implementing the thin-client/server solution also significantly reduced system administration and maintenance for each office, since remote users could access and share a single Great Plains Dynamics C/S+ database located at the Houston office.

## Honeywell Europe S.A.

Honeywell is a global controls company providing products, systems, and services that enhance comfort, protect the environment, conserve energy, and increase productivity and safety in homes, buildings, industry, aviation, and the field of space exploration and research. In 1995, Honeywell reported sales of $6.7 billion.

Honeywell wanted a high-performance remote computing solution for quick, easy, and cost-effective deployment of its Hyperion Enterprise financial application to affiliate offices worldwide. At the same time, Honeywell needed to maintain centralized administration and support.

Honeywell's implementation of a thin-client/server solution using the WinFrame server has helped the company to consolidate mission-critical financial information into a single, centrally administered system.

*The challenge: Apply a single downsized solution to global financial reporting.*

**Presenting problem**  Honeywell employs 50,000 people in 95 countries on 6 continents. When a company this size wants to consolidate monthly financial results from subsidiaries around the world, it faces a serious challenge.

Honeywell's European operation is headquartered in Brussels, Belgium, and encompasses 65 reporting units and 12,000 employees in 24 different countries, including eastern Europe, South Africa, and the Arab states. In 1995, Honeywell Europe S. A. reported sales of $1.9 billion.

Collating financial results from such geographically separated locations presented Honeywell with an administrative nightmare. Just compiling the data took days—analyzing it and consolidating it into informative reports took even longer.

For the past 15 years, Honeywell's corporate headquarters in Minneapolis, Minnesota, and its European headquarters in Brussels had used separate mainframe computer and minicomputer systems for financial planning and reporting. Early in 1995, however, the company decided to move away from these proprietary systems to a single packaged solution based on less expensive PC technology.

Having experienced previous success using Hyperion's Micro Control product to assist in the reporting process, Honeywell's U.S. corporate headquarters selected Hyperion Enterprise for its financial reporting system as it downsized to a PC-based platform. Hyperion Enterprise controls the reporting and consolidation of financial information at the U.S. and European corporate headquarters, which are directly linked.

**Hardware and software** The networking environment at Honeywell includes:

- Compaq ProLiant 4-way 166-MHz Pentium server with 300 MB of RAM
- Microsoft Windows NT file servers

Honeywell uses WinFrame Enterprise to deploy Hyperion Enterprise financial software to its remote affiliates over dial-up and WAN connections.

*Honeywell deploys financial software through a WAN.*

**Solution and results** The company faced the challenge of having insufficient bandwidth for remote locations to access Hyperion Enterprise from a single, consolidated platform over its existing WAN and dial-up connections.

Honeywell's solution was to deploy the Hyperion financial application to remote users using a thin-client/server model. By using the WinFrame server's thin-client network-centric architecture, Honeywell affiliates were able to connect to U.S. and European headquarters and gain LAN-like access to mission-critical applications, such as Hyperion Enterprise, and to use them to report monthly financial results.

Honeywell's strategic implementation of WinFrame resulted in a number of improvements for its financial organization, including allowing remote offices worldwide to simultaneously access and work with one consolidated financial database. This capability alone offered greater overall efficiency, consistency, and accuracy in gathering and analyzing financial results. Since each remote user could access and share a single financial database system, administration and maintenance costs were significantly reduced for each office.

*Honeywell's thin-client/server implementation significantly improved the quality of financial information.*

Currently, Honeywell has four WinFrame application servers in Brussels and one in Minneapolis. Each Honeywell sales office and factory also connects to WinFrame via WAN or dial-up connections at the end of every month to access the Hyperion database and input financial results for global consolidation.

According to IS managers at Honeywell, WinFrame has equipped them with a unique way of entering large amounts of data into a Windows-based system without having to upgrade the existing communications infrastructure. Previous reporting systems had involved developing and maintaining a mainframe consolidation application, a costly venture. With WinFrame, costs were dramatically reduced. Honeywell also realized significant savings by running the application with network-centric PC-based technology provided by a thin-client/server solution using WinFrame, as opposed to using two different mainframe systems.

The thin-client/server solution gave Honeywell employees—regardless of their location—global access to consolidated financial figures. Within just a few days of implementing the solution, Honeywell was able to consolidate its affiliates' data to produce a global picture that reflected overall monthly performance.

Through the use of WinFrame and the Hyperion database, Honeywell developed strategies and plans for the future by facilitating regular, up-to-date reports. The solution also offered quick and painless implementation to remote staff. The WinFrame/Hyperion project leader at Honeywell also lauded the capability of "shadowing" a user with WinFrame. Shadowing allows one user to follow another user's WinFrame session. Using shadowing, an administrator can literally take over the screen, keyboard, and mouse of a remote user in order to troubleshoot problems.

The ability to shadow a user in Johannesburg from a desk in Brussels allowed administrators to give instant advice and to take corrective action in order to keep everyone using the system correctly. The WinFrame shadowing feature is equally useful for remote training, helping trainers to avoid costly travel expenses and time on the road.

# Pyramid Breweries, Inc.

Pyramid Breweries, Inc., is one of the leading craft brewers in the rapidly expanding market for fresh, flavorful beers. It was founded in 1984 in Kalama, Washington, a small logging town in the foothills of Mount St. Helens. The company brews two brands of beer: Pyramid Ales and Thomas Kemper Lagers. Pyramid's main brewery is now located in Seattle, Washington; the company has another brewery close to Portland, Oregon, and recently opened a $14.5 million facility in Berkeley, California. Besides strong market coverage in the western states, Pyramid Breweries' beer is distributed across the United States. The company sought a high-performance dial-up solution that would enable it to quickly, easily, and cost-effectively deploy its integrated accounting application to regional breweries yet maintain centralized administration.

Pyramid Breweries recently embarked on an expansion strategy, building breweries in major metropolitan areas across the United States. A thin-client/server solution that employed WinFrame complemented this strategic expansion by helping the company deploy mission-critical applications to new and emerging brewery sites efficiently and economically.

**Presenting problem** Pyramid Breweries' rapid expansion strategy presented a complex set of challenges: How was the company to both manage growth and maintain tight control of its corporate computing environment? An added complication was the fact that the IS "department" consisted of just one person, the IS director, who had to support more than 350 employees and a growing base of regional microbreweries.

*The challenge: Manage growth and maintain tight control of the computing environment.*

The IS director sought a thin-client/server solution that would centralize application execution and consolidate mission-critical information at headquarters while providing remote users with high-performance access over low-bandwidth modem connections. In the midst of tremendous growth, Pyramid needed an efficient way to deploy its data-intensive integrated accounting application, named Speed, to regional microbreweries. Consolidating information and applications was critical in order to avoid duplication of efforts and to ensure the security of sensitive corporate data.

Prior to using WinFrame, Pyramid Breweries had tried using single-user remote-control software but had not been satisfied with the results.

*Pyramid Breweries deploys its accounting application to regional sites and to its sales force.*

**Hardware and software** The Pyramid Breweries thin-client/server networking environment includes a Compaq ProSignia 500 P5 150 with 64 MB of RAM and a 1-GB hard drive.

Pyramid Breweries used WinFrame to deploy Speed to its regional microbreweries and to its mobile sales force over low-bandwidth modem connections.

**Solution and results** The strategic implementation of a thin-client/server solution has allowed Pyramid's remote breweries throughout the United States to simultaneously access one consolidated accounting database. Pyramid can now gather and analyze its finances more efficiently and more accurately. Implementing WinFrame has also significantly reduced system administration and maintenance for each brewery location, since users now have a single, consolidated base of financial information, centrally located and managed at headquarters.

Employees can now dial in from other breweries to access and update centralized shipment, inventory, and order information. Pyramid's sales force and external consultants can also dial in to headquarters to access other mission-critical applications.

In addition to the successful deployment of Speed, Pyramid Breweries' mobile sales force enjoys dial-in access to e-mail from home or when on the road. External consultants can also dial in to update and refer to information they need on Microsoft Access databases.

WinFrame's single-point application management is also reducing Pyramid Breweries' cost of application ownership, since all application additions, updates, user configuration, and support occur centrally from the WinFrame application server.

*Remote training and support tools helped the IS department solve problems from a central location.*

As with Honeywell, the Pyramid staff takes advantage of the remote training and support tools that come with WinFrame, including the shadowing feature that allows the monitoring of remote users. The remote support tools also allow the IS director to spend less time troubleshooting and traveling to remote sites and to devote more time to planning and rapidly implementing solutions.

Pyramid Breweries is already exploring other enterprise application deployment possibilities. The company plans to deploy corporate applications to Web users through a Web-based thin-client/server scenario. This particular implementation takes advantage of WinFrame's application launching and embedding (ALE) capabilities. ALE allows existing Windows, client/server, or legacy applications to be embedded in HTML Web pages and viewed from a Web browser. WinFrame's Windows ALE capabilities enable companies to extend existing Windows applications to the Web environment without having to rewrite any application code.

*Pyramid Breweries extended the reach of its existing applications to Web users.*

## Sales Automation

Many sales automation applications are mission-critical; they need to be secure, and they require some form of version control. Client/server applications with high-powered hardware and bandwidth requirements can be expensive to implement and often provide a less than optimal solution, especially if data is replicated all over the world. Many companies still use legacy mainframe applications. A thin-client/server solution using WinFrame provides the requisite security and reliability for sales automation applications. Client/server or mainframe applications that use a thin-client/server solution for interfacing with the user solve a number of deployment problems. In addition to taking care of the problem of replicated data, the thin-client/server solution makes the best use of existing user hardware as well as system administration and support resources.

The next case study shows how a thin-client/server solution can be used in sales automation. The Standard Forms company built a thin-client/server solution using WinFrame that leveraged its legacy mainframe applications and allowed the company to make its product catalog available on line.

## Standard Forms

Standard Forms is one of the largest manufacturers and distributors of standard and custom-printed business forms in the United States. The company maintains warehouse operations across the United States and has more than 20,000 active customers.

The company sought a cost-effective and manageable way to deploy legacy order-entry and product-catalog applications to employees and remote customers over low-bandwidth dial-up and Internet connections. WinFrame has enabled Standard Forms to deploy its CD-ROM–based order-entry and product-catalog applications to customers over the Internet. The immediate availability of up-to-date product-catalog information and the option of ordering on line have improved the speed with which orders are processed and shipped, which has helped Standard Forms gain a competitive advantage.

*The challenge: Find a cost-effective, easily managed way of deploying mainframe terminal-emulation software.*

**Presenting problem** All of Standard Forms' business applications, including its order-entry program, were developed in legacy RPG code to run on an IBM AS/400 system. To access these applications, employees needed to run Reflection, a 5250 terminal-emulation software package made by WRQ, Inc., on their PCs. The company faced the challenge of finding a cost-effective, easy-to-manage way of deploying the Reflection software so that employees and customers could access its order-entry and other legacy applications over low-bandwidth dial-up and Internet connections.

The terminal-emulation package needed to be installed at each remote location. Users were required to build specialized overlay settings to define the files required for the Reflection session. The user intervention normally required several hours of technical support for a step-by-step setup of a host file for the Reflection 5250 emulation. As a result, installation took several months and hundreds of hours.

Standard Forms also looked into deploying the legacy applications to users through a distributed client/server system. To Standard Forms, however, this proposition was an overwhelming prospect because the company had not yet moved to an intelligent client model. Five gigabytes of business applications requiring four years of work would need to be rewritten for a distributed client/server system, and therefore this approach was not considered an option.

Standard Forms also considered extending the network's arm to the remote users' sites. This step would have entailed placing a 5250 terminal at each site and running an SNA protocol through a dedicated 9600-baud or higher link 24 hours a day. At 9600 baud, Standard Forms would have had to absorb the monthly expense of a dedicated line for each remote site, the 5250 terminals, a router, and a "pearl box," which converts lower-level IBM protocols to a higher-level IBM protocol. This initial setup expense could have run up to $16,000 per site, which was a costly and unacceptable option for Standard Forms.

**Hardware and software** The Standard Forms thin-client/server networking environment includes:

- Dell Optiplex dual Pentium 90-MHz server with 2-GB Fast-Wide SCSI disks and 64 MB of RAM
- Compaq ProLiant 1500 Pentium 100-MHz server with 4-GB Fast SCSI-2 disks and 92 MB of RAM
- Microsoft Windows NT file servers

Standard Forms deploys legacy mainframe applications for order entry.

Standard Forms is using WinFrame to deploy mission-critical legacy applications for order entry and product catalogs to 125 employees and over 15 remote customers.

**Solution and results** In the days before WinFrame, Standard Forms took 24 hours to process customer orders through its electronic data interchange. With the new thin-client/server system maintaining the company's distribution system, customers can look at inventory in real time. Items are now allocated from inventory the instant a customer places an order. Within one minute of a customer printing a copy of the shipping document, the original is printing in the warehouse.

Standard Forms currently has 125 internal users and about 15 remote customers accessing its WinFrame application servers. The remote users access WinFrame through a TCP/IP connection via a network card or through a dial-up Point-to-Point Protocol (PPP) account.

> Prospective customers can now browse CD-ROM–based catalogs.

Using this thin-client/server solution, Standard Forms' customers and prospective customers can browse the company's CD-ROM–based product catalogs over the Internet. The company's proprietary CD-ROM catalog resides and executes on the WinFrame server, and only the graphical user interface displays on client PCs.

Once customers know which products they want to order, they can check inventory availability as well as their own billing and account information on line by launching Reflection from the WinFrame application server. WinFrame acts as a gateway to the company's AS/400 system, on which the order-entry and inventory-control applications reside.

The thin-client/server solution using WinFrame allows Standard Forms to quickly, easily, and cost-effectively deploy its mission-critical legacy applications to remote users by issuing a single setup disk that contains the WinFrame thin-client software and a special customized script with all the settings already built into the installation cell. Users only need to install the WinFrame client software and create an icon on their desktops. Standard Forms builds one Reflection session file on the WinFrame server, which multiple concurrent users can then access.

When the customer double-clicks the WinFrame icon, a WinFrame session is started and the customer is given a predefined application profile. The customer can then log on to an AS/400 session and access the CD-ROM–based product catalog and order-entry applications.

Standard Forms is exploring other enterprise application deployment possibilities. One such use the company is considering is to extend the reach of its product catalogs and order-entry applications to the Web through WinFrame's ALE. This capability allows existing applications to be embedded in or linked to HTML Web pages and viewed from a Web browser. Standard Forms can offer its product catalog this way. Customers will not only be able to look up product information but can also place orders directly from the catalog.

*Standard Forms is currently expanding its applications to World Wide Web implementations.*

## Health Care Services

As in other industries, the ability to deploy and manage applications from a central location, to access applications from any type of connection, to ensure rapid and efficient performance, and to maintain security have proven to be common denominators for success in the health care industry. The three case studies in this section demonstrate different ways in which the thin-client/server model has been implemented in this field.

### Anne E. Biedel & Associates

Anne E. Biedel & Associates is a medical practice located in Port Townsend, Washington. Dr. Biedel needed a high-performance, secure dial-up solution to deploy the electronic medical records (EMRs) and Microsoft BackOffice applications used in her private practice quickly, easily, and cost-effectively to medical and administrative staff.

The thin-client/server solution has helped Dr. Biedel, who is chief of staff at Jefferson General Hospital as well as head of her own private clinic, to run a more efficient practice without increasing costs or compromising patient care. In fact, she has noticed overall improvements in her medical practice since implementing WinFrame thin-client/server software.

*The challenge: Allow access to mission-critical information anywhere, any time.*

**Presenting problem** In the medical profession, stringent insurance requirements are driving many practitioners to cut costs, work more hours, and find new ways of becoming more efficient in order to stay in business. A key factor in remaining viable is to create a fast, accurate information-retrieval system without increasing expenditures.

Known for their paper-intensive nature, medical practices often seem to be bogged down by insurance forms, patient records, and accounting invoices. Dr. Biedel knew that paper-based systems were too cumbersome and hard to keep current. Her husband Jim, the systems administrator for the practice, researched different options when he heard that several HMOs were switching from paper-based systems to EMRs.

In creating the information system, the Biedels didn't want to use proprietary software or hardware. They were concerned that proprietary products were too expensive and didn't give the widest range of options. Furthermore, the data had to be secure.

*Anne E. Biedel & Associates deploys applications to its professional and administrative staff.*

**Hardware and software** The thin-client/server networking environment at Anne E. Biedel & Associates includes:

- Dual Pentium Pro 200 server with192 MB of RAM, Ultra-wide SCSI drives, Proxim Range LAN
- Wyse Winterm Windows terminals
- Wyse Wireless 2930 handheld unit

Anne E. Biedel & Associates is using WinFrame to deploy several applications to its professional and administrative staff, including an EMR program named Patient Education, Optus Facsys, Microsoft Exchange, and several Microsoft BackOffice applications.

**Solution and results** Dr. Biedel's practice implemented a thin-client/server solution using the WinFrame server along with Wyse Winterm terminals and wireless tablets. This solution worked as the practice's approach to accessing information and communicating with each other. The practice now has five different applications, many of which are graphics-intensive, running concurrently. One of the most frequently used applications is the Patient Education program, which is an EMR designed by Metaphor.

The thin-client/server solution has improved the ability of Dr. Biedel's medical and administrative staff to retrieve patient medical record information remotely and to keep patient records current and secure. System administration is also easier. As a result of this increased efficiency, Anne E. Biedel & Associates has met insurance industry requirements and is being reimbursed regularly.

Being paperless has several advantages: doctors can easily and quickly access patient information while on call or working off-site; employees can update patient records more easily while ensuring accuracy and security; system administration can be performed remotely; and the practice is better prepared to meet insurance requirements. Anne E. Biedel & Associates is enjoying all these benefits, in addition to the benefits of savings on both up-front acquisition and overall application ownership.

WinFrame's remote-access capability gives Dr. Biedel and her staff fast, secure retrieval of patient information when they are away from the clinic. In an emergency situation, the on-call doctor can become familiar with a patient's history by accessing the patient's EMR via the wireless tablet and thin-client/server software. Jim Biedel says that the remote-access capability goes straight to the heart of patient care by allowing the doctors to access a patient's files from any location at any time. He also says that the server's speed is key in a time-critical situation such as a medical emergency and that the application response time is so short that it feels like using an online system rather than dialing in from a laptop.

*Eyes-only security ensures patient confidentiality.*

With WinFrame, patient records are easier to keep secure, accurate, and up-to-date because only one set of data is manipulated. Although WinFrame allows more than one user to access the EMRs at a time, all changes to the records are kept on the server, thereby maintaining the data's integrity. In contrast, paper-based systems are harder to keep current, especially if more than one doctor sees the same patient.

Dr. Biedel and her staff are also using WinFrame to handle a variety of other tasks while away from the clinic, such as responding to e-mail, reviewing accounting ledgers, entering checks, and issuing invoices. Many tasks that used to take up valuable clinic time are now being done from home—the data doesn't have to be transported between locations nor does a copy of the software have to be maintained on a laptop since all the information resides on WinFrame and can be accessed within seconds.

According to Jim Biedel, system administration has become much easier too. For example, when he needs to deploy new software, Jim has to load the software only once on the WinFrame server and it is instantly available to all users. Jim can easily troubleshoot a user's problem by dialing up WinFrame from any device anywhere and shadowing the user's session.

Better managed patient records and system administration have helped Dr. Biedel's practice keep its costs under control, which is the primary requirement of the insurance industry. Because the practice is so efficient, it is able to submit charges to insurance companies more regularly, which in turn results in the doctors being reimbursed more regularly.

Dr. Biedel views WinFrame thin-client/server system software as a way to protect the well-being of her medical practice and her patients while meeting the challenges posed by the insurance industry. At a time when many physicians are scrambling for ways to remain in business, this practice is thriving.

# Clarion Health

Clarion Health, located in Indianapolis, Indiana, is the result of a recent merger among Methodist Hospital, Indiana University, and Riley Hospital. It is the second-largest and seventh-busiest private hospital in the United States. Clarion Health houses a large network of primary care physicians, specialty physicians, outpatient centers, and affiliates throughout the state of Indiana who treat more than 45,000 admissions a year.

**Presenting problem** Clarion Health sought a high-performance, cost-effective, and secure way to deploy mission-critical Electronic Signature and SoftMed applications to approximately 500 physicians and staff members in area locations over low-bandwidth dial-up connections. These applications enable physicians to sign for patient medical records remotely. Since the applications contain confidential patient information, they require central management and deployment to ensure the highest security.

Before implementing the thin-client/server solution, Clarion Health accessed mission-critical applications over remote-node connections. Under this approach, application processing occurs on the remote workstation, and actual files are transmitted over telephone lines. Remote-node solutions tend to suffer performance problems when large amounts of data, such as database information, must be accessed over low-bandwidth connections.

The remote-node solution also required one dedicated PC for every dial-in line supported. The IS director quickly realized that this method of remote access would be prohibitively expensive and would require heavy maintenance. The IS director also found the clustered-CPU alternative too costly. (Clustered-CPU products provide a hardware platform for stand-alone remote-control software.)

The challenge: Deploy mission-critical applications to physicians and other health care providers.

*Clarion Health deploys Electronic Signature and SoftMed applications.*

**Hardware and software** The Clarion Health thin-client/server networking environment includes:

- Compaq ProLiant 4500 4-way Pentium 166-MHz server with 128 MB of RAM
- Microsoft Windows NT 3.51 and Novell NetWare 3.*x* file servers

The Clarion Health thin-client/server solution uses the WinFrame server to deploy its Electronic Signature and SoftMed applications.

**Solution and results** Clarion Health installed several WinFrame application servers to deploy its mission-critical applications to approximately 500 physicians and staff members in area locations over low-bandwidth dial-up connections.

*Clarion Health now has greater physician efficiency through 24-hour access to patient information.*

The strategic implementation of this thin-client/server solution has resulted in greater physician efficiency and productivity by arming doctors with 24-hour access to patient information. Busy physicians and staff employees now have secure, real-time access to mission-critical information, regardless of whether they're located in an office that's part of the LAN or if they're out and accessing the software through a low-bandwidth connection.

The Clarion Health Information Technology (IT) group reported that the thin-client/server solution using WinFrame exceeded their response-time criteria for dial-up connections. The solution also allowed them to leverage Clarion's existing technology by working with the available remote access and communications infrastructure. And finally, it offered the centralized support, security, and application management for remote users so valued by many of the other companies you've read about in this chapter.

Clarion Health employees dial into the network through its NetBlazer remote-node server. The WinFrame server back-ends the remote-node server to execute applications on the high-bandwidth LAN. Only the user interface is sent across the wire, significantly enhancing remote application performance.

Because of its highly confidential medical environment, Clarion Health added an additional layer of security to WinFrame's stringent Microsoft Windows NT Server–based system through the use of Security Dynamics' ACE/Server and SecurID identification and authentication software. SecurID provides dynamic, two-factor authentication that combines a personal identification number (PIN) with a randomly generated access code that changes every 60 seconds. To access a SecurID-protected WinFrame server, users are challenged by both WinFrame security and the SecurID token passcode security. Once authenticated, users can log on to a WinFrame application server.

The thin-client/server solution using WinFrame has simplified system administration and maintenance for Clarion's IT organization, enabling the IT staff to solve system administration issues remotely as well as to support remote users conveniently from a central location—the WinFrame application server.

Initial deployment of the thin-client/server solution improved the outpatient center's response time tremendously. Following this initial success, other departments in the hospital plan to use WinFrame to deploy mission-critical applications, such as financial and human resources applications.

## Mecon

Mecon, located in San Ramon, California, has offered consulting services to hospitals across the United States for over 13 years. As insurance companies gained greater influence over the health care industry during the late 1980s, Mecon recognized the need for hospital information systems (HIS's) that could help hospitals compete more effectively without sacrificing quality of care. The company began developing and marketing an HIS that enabled hospital units to compare their practices against industry benchmarks and then make adjustments as needed. By using these systems, many Mecon customers have reduced their annual expenses by 10 to 15 percent, saving millions of dollars annually.

At the same time, Mecon sought a high-performance, cost-effective way to deploy business-critical applications to its remote work force nationwide without sacrificing data security.

*The challenge: Deliver secure access to information to off-site workers.*

**Presenting problem** Mecon supports its customers with a network of consultants, account executives, and field service personnel who need fast, easy, and secure access to information when they are working off-site. Like many companies today, one of the biggest challenges for Mecon is information access for these employees. Until recently, field workers had to use an unreliable, time-consuming remote access system.

Drawbacks to the existing remote access system were so severe that people avoided using it. According to one of the senior members of Mecon's IS department, users dreaded dealing with the remote access system because it took several minutes just to download a 5-MB to 6-MB client file. This lag time severely restricted customer support efforts. Data sent to the field as hard copy wasn't nearly as up-to-date as online information, but no one had the patience to access the online information.

Prior to implementing the thin-client/server solution using WinFrame in mid-1996, Mecon (as did several companies in the preceding case studies) also evaluated and rejected several remote-control software packages.

*Mecon deploys proprietary medical products and productivity applications.*

**Hardware and software** The thin-client/server networking environment at Mecon includes:

- Digital Prioris 133-MHz Pentium server with 296 MB of RAM and a 2-GB hard drive
- Oracle database
- Frame relay WAN
- Internet

Mecon uses WinFrame to deploy its HIS products, including PeerView, Action Point, and Optimis, as well as its office software, such as Lotus' cc:Mail, to its field employees. WinFrame also provides access to the Internet via Netscape Navigator 3.0.

**Solution and results** Mecon implemented its thin-client/server solution using WinFrame. The solution provided Mecon employees with quick, efficient, and secure access to a wide range of business-critical applications, regardless of the user's location or available bandwidth.

Using this solution, Mecon's sales, marketing, and field service employees obtain client data, access e-mail, and use PeerView, Action Point, and Optimis. Remote workers in search of competitive information or industry news also use WinFrame to access the Internet via Netscape Navigator 3.0.

The thin-client/server solution also gives Mecon's software developers and system administrators the flexibility to work from home. For software developers, this means fast access to Oracle development tools that reside on the WinFrame server or connection to the Internet to conduct research. For system administrators, it means the ability to upgrade applications easily or to handle network problems during off-peak hours.

Mecon employees find the WinFrame thin-client/server solution extremely easy to use because of the Windows interface, which is ideal for less technical users. Additionally, the company has greatly benefited from WinFrame's Internet support, since Mecon depends heavily on the Internet as a source of research information. The reliability of the connection between users and WinFrame has also been a big improvement.

Since WinFrame's implementation, Mecon has increased user productivity significantly because field workers can more easily and quickly access a wide range of information. They use laptops to dial in to the WinFrame server via a frame relay WAN and access client databases, e-mail, the company's bulletin boards, or the Internet. They say that WinFrame is so fast that it feels like an actual node on the Mecon network. The field employees can download large client files and receive up-to-the-minute status reports in just a few seconds.

*Mecon's solution has significantly improved productivity.*

The WinFrame implementation significantly simplifies system administration and user support. Administrators can now easily and economically deploy new applications and software updates or troubleshoot problems in the field from the WinFrame server. With only two administrators supporting over 150 people, WinFrame's single-point management has been especially beneficial.

The increased productivity of Mecon's employees using the thin-client/server solution has enhanced the company's overall competitiveness. In fact, Mecon sees so much potential in the thin-client/server solution that it has established several business objectives for the future—such as an intranet with Web-enabled applications and human resources information—that will be dependent on these capabilities.

## Thin-Client/Server on the Web

The next case study is also about a company that serves the health care community. What makes Claimsnet.com remarkable is that it combines thin-client/server technology and an extranet on the Internet.

### Claimsnet.com

Claimsnet.com supplies health care providers with complete, reliable electronic claims processing through a secure Internet connection and private extranet technology. The company sought a solution that would allow it to distribute its mission-critical application, CyberClaim, to its customers quickly and reliably over the Internet. It also wanted a solution that was easy to use and manage. Without the thin-client/server solution that used WinFrame, Claimsnet.com would not have been able to process medical claims over the Internet.

*The challenge: Make information available through the use of secure Internet technology.*

**Presenting problem** Several years ago, the founders of Claimsnet.com had the idea that electronic claims processing could be made available and affordable to all medical practitioners through the use of a secure Internet connection. Currently, of more than

4 billion claims submitted annually to payers by physicians and dentists, only about 35 percent of all medical and 10 percent of all dental claims are submitted electronically. Nearly all these submissions are by high-volume claims producers, such as hospitals and specialty clinics, which can afford the high setup costs of electronic claims processing. With fewer resources, small medical and dental offices—which account for about 2 billion claims a year—were being shut out of the opportunity to file electronically.

To extend electronic claims filing to smaller customers, Claimsnet.com developed CyberClaim, a robust, 32-bit Windows NT–based application that enables confidential, easy-to-use claims processing and editing through the Internet. The company then turned its attention to finding a solution that could deploy CyberClaim quickly and reliably.

To this end, Claimsnet.com first attempted to create a bulletin board service through the Internet using a Novell NetWare–based server. Despite a lengthy development effort, that plan was abandoned because the server downloaded the application's executable code to the client desktop, which slowed the system down considerably. Just to log on, a user was forced to wait seven minutes or more—an unacceptable waste of time. The users needed a solution that would allow them to log on quickly and create a file that the payers would accept electronically.

After abandoning the bulletin board, Claimsnet.com began its search for a thin-client/server solution that would allow application processing to occur not at the customer site but at Claimsnet.com's central server site. As a result, users would gain LAN-like access to the application over the Internet.

**Hardware and software** The Claimsnet.com thin-client/server networking environment includes:

- Compaq ProSignia Pentium Server with 64 MB of RAM
- Microsoft Windows NT and Novell NetWare file servers
- Dual T-3 connections to the Internet

Claimsnet.com deploys its claims processing application to offices around the country.

Claimsnet.com uses Citrix WinFrame, in conjunction with proprietary client application software, to deploy its mission-critical CyberClaim claims processing application across the Internet to medical, dental, and outpatient offices throughout the United States.

**Solution and results** Citrix WinFrame provides Claimsnet.com with the high performance and universal application access its users need.

*Enables smaller organizations to process claims on line.*

Claimsnet.com now affords thousands of medical practitioners, dentists, and outpatient clinics easy, low-cost electronic processing and rapid turnaround for their claims. Claimsnet.com has been able to provide this service while holding down its own costs and retaining centralized control over its widely distributed customer base.

Once logged on to the system, users direct CyberClaim to access claims from existing medical or dental accounting applications, so the claims don't have to be rekeyed into the Claimsnet.com processing system. The system then automatically checks the claims for errors, a frequent—and often inadvertent—occurrence that can delay payment considerably. Errors are highlighted, and once corrected on line, the claims are transmitted to the insurance company for payment. Along the way, multiple levels of security, including firewalls and encryption, are used to ensure that the claims information remains confidential. Another benefit is the ability to print locally; users can print claims reports in hard copy if needed. The WinFrame server implementation also allows for remote training on claims filing. As a result of Claimsnet.com's thin-client/server implementation, health care professionals are getting paid more promptly than before, and just as important, they no longer have to commit large amounts of resources to filing, editing, tracking, and—when errors occur—refiling claims.

Although the Claimsnet.com service is still young, the company sees a huge market opportunity and room for rapid growth. Even as it expands, the company expects few growing pains with its thin-client/server solution. The solution will scale easily to meet the claims processing needs of Claimsnet.com's increasing client base. Moreover, by using a thin-client/server architecture, Claimsnet.com expects to be able to keep employee growth to a minimum, thereby retaining firm control over personnel costs. This technology will also eliminate the need for Claimsnet.com to create a large communications and support center for reporting and correcting network systems problems. In the meantime, servers are located and managed from a central location, giving the company maximum control over its service.

## Human Resources Management Applications

The human resources field requires information systems that can provide maximum security for sensitive data and wants information infrastructures that can be maintained and supported centrally. In this section, we'll look at two companies that focus on different aspects of human resources management. The first, Pro Staff, provides staffing services. The second, ReloAction, provides relocation assistance. Both companies use thin-client/server solutions to deploy legacy applications over a WAN.

### Pro Staff

Pro Staff is a national staffing services company specializing in placing accounting, clerical, administration, information technology, creative services, and technical personnel. The company has more than 130 branch offices across the United States supported by a staff of 700. In 1996, Pro Staff placed more than 60,000 professionals. By the year 2001, Pro Staff expects to triple its size.

Pro Staff believes it can accomplish its aggressive 2001 growth initiative with minimal capital outlay and a flat, centralized IS support staff by using a thin-client/server solution based on WinFrame Enterprise. By placing Wyse Winterm terminals on the desktops, Pro Staff can further simplify user management while providing 32-bit Windows application support to low-cost terminals.

**Presenting problem** Pro Staff's operating philosophy is that of a "regional company with a national presence." The company gives its branch offices complete autonomy to react to local market conditions and their particular needs for custom client reporting. Pro Staff knows that in today's competitive job market, information is power. That's why the company is pushing mission-critical PeopleSoft HRMS, for human resources management, and Windows staffing applications out to employees in branch offices over its AT&T-managed frame relay WAN.

*The challenge: Provide branch offices with timely information.*

Pro Staff's lean IS staff needed to provide branch offices with online, real-time access to business-critical applications from a centrally managed, consolidated base of information. As an additional complication, the IS staff had to address the complex set of challenges related to growth management and control that resulted from Pro Staff's tripling in size in five years.

Rather than give all the offices separate information systems and then try to consolidate the data, the IS staff decided to consolidate the data first and then give the offices high-performance, remote access to mission-critical information and the freedom to customize it through WinFrame. The IS department also based its decision on Pro Staff's expected growth over the next five years—with plans to add more than one new branch office every month, it would be nearly impossible to set up and support a LAN in each office.

*Pro Staff deploys human resources management, payroll, e-mail, and productivity applications over a WAN.*

**Hardware and software** The Pro Staff thin-client/server networking environment includes:

- Digital Prioris 4-way 133 MHz
- Pentium server with 512 MB of RAM
- Microsoft Windows NT file servers
- Oracle database

- Frame relay WAN
- Wyse Winterm Windows terminals

Pro Staff uses WinFrame to deploy PeopleSoft HRMS, payroll, and financial client/server applications, Microsoft Exchange Server, Microsoft Office, and a 32-bit Windows staffing application over its WAN.

**Solution and results** Using a thin-client/server solution with the WinFrame application server software and Wyse Winterm terminals, Pro Staff has been able to bring a new branch office on line within a week. When setting up a new office, Pro Staff ships Wyse Winterm terminals to the branch office and then plugs them into the WAN. Business-critical applications are instantly available from the WinFrame server—which resides centrally and is managed from headquarters.

Pro Staff effectively uses Windows-based terminals.

To date, Pro Staff has implemented seven WinFrame Enterprise application servers to deploy PeopleSoft HRMS, payroll, and financial client/server applications, Microsoft Exchange Server, Microsoft Office, and a 32-bit Windows staffing database to its branch office employees. Their goal was to have all 130 offices running applications centrally on the WinFrame servers by mid-1997. Instead of putting a fully equipped PC on each employee's desk, Pro Staff realized the up-front acquisition and overall application ownership savings of putting thin ICA-based Winterm Windows terminals on the desktops instead.

Over the long term, Pro Staff expects to reduce the annual cost of application ownership dramatically, since all application deployment, user configuration, and support occur centrally from WinFrame servers located at the corporate headquarters. WinFrame Enterprise has satisfied the management, support, and budget requirements of Pro Staff's IS department while providing its branch office workers with fast, real-time access to business-critical Windows information.

The IS director at Pro Staff credits the thin-client/server WinFrame/Winterm solution with providing his organization with several competitive advantages. First it provides the flexibility to enter data at the staffing offices level; so the people who know most about their market information are entering it, ensuring greater detail and accuracy. This information can then be consolidated and centrally managed. Second, WinFrame and Winterm enable rapid implementation, so Pro Staff can add new offices within a week. Finally, WinFrame empowers branch offices with real-time access to information, helping them retain autonomy and better respond to local market needs with customized information.

WinFrame will carry Pro Staff well into the next century, enabling the company to extend the reach of its mission-critical applications to the Internet as well as on its corporate intranet. The company plans to use WinFrame's Windows ALE capabilities to integrate Windows applications into its Web site so that applicants can register on line, query databases for job listings, and so on.

## ReloAction

ReloAction, an employee-owned business, has been providing corporate relocation services for three decades. Its corporate clients highly value the company's experience, expertise, and dedication.

The relocation industry has been changing rapidly, making it more challenging for smaller relocation companies to compete with the giant national firms. Increasingly, corporations no longer want to do business with a large number of regional vendors. They want to work with fewer vendors, ones who can handle their needs across multiple locations.

This shift in corporate preferences meant that ReloAction needed to efficiently extend its IS services to branch offices. Previously, Microsoft FoxPro files were manually uploaded and downloaded between locations. Not only was this method clumsy and slow, but it was a tremendous waste of employee time.

**Presenting problem** ReloAction spent years developing and fine-tuning a custom FoxPro database that served as an extremely effective tool for its relocation consultants. Because of the expense required to implement a WAN with speeds high enough to provide reasonable access to the information from one source, the database was isolated at each of the company's branch offices, located in California, Arizona, Oregon, and Washington. Interoffice access of common data was becoming more and more essential to providing the complete breadth of service ReloAction's clients were demanding. For example, without this access to common data, consultants in Portland and San Francisco could be working independently on relocating the same person without knowing it.

ReloAction also evaluated other options besides a high-speed WAN. In particular, the company considered rewriting the FoxPro program using Lotus Notes to take advantage of replication between offices. But such an endeavor would have entailed a very costly—and worse, a very lengthy—conversion period to rewrite the software to run within the Lotus Notes environment. If ReloAction had chosen to implement the Lotus Notes environment outside a thin-client/server solution, it would have needed to upgrade many employees' PCs to more expensive units capable of running Windows 95.

**Hardware and software** The ReloAction thin-client/server networking environment includes:

- Hewlett-Packard NetServer LS server with dual Pentium 166-MHz processors and 256 MB of RAM
- Novell NetWare file servers

ReloAction is using WinFrame to deploy its mission-critical FoxPro for MS-DOS database, Goldmine Contact Management application, and cc:Mail over low-bandwidth frame relay WAN connections.

> The challenge: Share information among branch offices working with the same client.

> ReloAction deploys custom database, contact management, and e-mail applications over low-bandwidth connections.

**Solution and results** ReloAction's IS department deploys a single WinFrame application server at its headquarters. This server has enabled employees in remote offices to access the FoxPro, Goldmine, and other mission-critical applications across inexpensive, low-bandwidth frame relay WAN connections. The consultants can access the same consolidated base of information, which is managed, backed up, and administered by the IS department at headquarters.

*ReloAction's solution allowed the company to deploy applications and updates rapidly.*

The thin-client/server single-point application management is reducing ReloAction's cost of application ownership, since all application additions, updates, user configuration, and support occur on the centrally located WinFrame server. Remote performance accessing FoxPro for MS-DOS and other Windows applications over frame relay WAN connections has been excellent. Consolidating all mission-critical applications and information at headquarters has made it much easier for ReloAction's managers to receive timely reports or run ad hoc queries on the activities of remote offices. In turn, managers at headquarters now find it easier to share relevant general statistics with the remote users.

The IS department at ReloAction, like the IS departments in the other case studies, has been able to take advantage of the training and support tools provided with the WinFrame server, which include the ability to shadow branch office users. Session shadowing has significantly improved the ability of ReloAction's IS organization to provide both training and troubleshooting to remote users.

WinFrame has enabled ReloAction to provide its branch office with services on a par with the nation's largest relocation companies. Managers at ReloAction intend to use thin-client/server solutions with WinFrame to boost the company's competitive advantage even further. They plan to extend the reach of ReloAction's services directly to clients via the Internet. They also plan to upgrade their FoxPro application to a Windows version and allow clients to access the database through the familiar HTML interface of the Web. Clients will be able to make direct requests for services as well as track their relocation status.

# Communications and Remote Computing

The case studies in this section are about two communications companies, Bell Mobility of Canada and Vodac in the United Kingdom. Both companies provide wireless services to their customers. Bell Mobility deploys activation and customer service applications internally; Vodac deploys applications through its reseller network, over varying platforms and hardware.

## Bell Mobility

Bell Mobility is Canada's leading provider of wireless communications. Operating in Ontario and Quebec, Bell Mobility provides nearly 1.8 million customers with cellular, paging, mobile radio, air-to-ground, wireless data, and mobile satellite services. The company sought a fast, easy, and manageable way to deploy mission-critical applications to employees in its activation and customer service call centers while ensuring maximum system uptime. The company developed a thin-client/server solution to support its mission-critical call activation and customer support centers. The solution, built on WinFrame, has increased LAN-based application performance, reduced the cost of application ownership, and enhanced IS productivity through single-point application management and control.

**Presenting problem** Bell Mobility needed to deploy mission-critical applications to employees in its call activation and customer service call centers in Montreal and Toronto. The company's call activation and customer service applications are based on PowerBuilder. Running these powerful applications on employee desktop PCs would have required high system overhead and intensive IS support. Bell Mobility also faced the potential effort and expense associated with upgrading employee desktops to optimize application performance on the LAN.

The challenge: Deploy call activation and customer service applications.

The potential expense, however, did not begin to account for the staff time and expense associated with actually upgrading hundreds of individual desktop systems. One of the company's senior

LAN specialists commented, "I'd much rather upgrade multiple WinFrame servers than hundreds of desktops any day."

A progressive technology company, Bell Mobility also needed to deliver "anytime, anywhere" computing capabilities to its employees. Although the company had tried several remote-computing alternatives, including remote-control software and remote-node hardware, management wanted improvements to support the corporate ethos of flexible schedules and a flexible workplace.

*Bell Mobility deploys customer service databases across a LAN.*

**Hardware and software** Bell Mobility's thin-client/server networking environment includes:

- Dell Optiplex GXpro and Hewlett-Packard Vectra XU 200-MHz dual Pentium Pro processors with 256 MB of RAM and 2-GB and 4-GB disk drives
- NetWare and Windows NT file servers
- IBM 9672/R3 mainframe

Bell Mobility uses WinFrame Enterprise to deploy customer service databases developed by PowerBuilder to its employees across the LAN.

**Solution and results** Bell Mobility chose to implement WinFrame as its standard application deployment platform for its call activation and customer service centers because of WinFrame's fast application performance over any type of network connection. The product has proven reliable, helping the company to realize its goal of maximum system uptime. The fact that WinFrame is based on Windows NT Server was another big advantage to Bell Mobility.

Bell Mobility has experienced significant performance gains in its call activation centers by accessing PowerBuilder applications via WinFrame. Support representatives verify addresses and driver's license numbers in only a few seconds with WinFrame over LAN-based connections. As a result, the company activates more phones faster with fewer staff. In addition, several hundred mobile professionals and telecommuters can dial into WinFrame and get the same desktop and access the same set of applications as they can at the office, regardless of their location.

The WinFrame server's single-point application management also reduces Bell Mobility's total cost of ownership since all application additions, updates, user configuration, and support occur centrally at the WinFrame application server. The centralized support tools, including the ability to assist remote users, have resulted in a steep drop in visits to individual desktops. Bell Mobility is also experiencing a significant increase in first-call help desk resolution with WinFrame.

*Bell Mobility's solution enables telecommuting.*

Additional IS benefits for Bell Mobility include accelerated application deployment through WinFrame's standard Windows-based production and development environment. The company can now develop in the same environment it's going to produce in—Windows—saving a great deal of development time. Bell Mobility is also able to deploy new applications to employees across its entire enterprise in less than one minute.

As Bell Mobility's standard deployment platform for the company's call centers, WinFrame is beginning to play an increasing role throughout the organization.

## Vodac

It would be an understatement to call today's mobile phone market volatile; it seems as if a new technology battles its way into the market every day. As a leading service provider, Vodac recognizes the dynamics involved in meeting customer needs and sees its role of supporting its growing network of phone dealers as crucial to staying at the forefront of the market. As a key player in the communications business, streamlining its own internal and external communication links is critical.

Vodac is a subsidiary of the Vodafone Group, the U.K. market leader in mobile communications that has over 2.8 million subscribers. Vodafone has been operating in the United Kingdom since 1985, when the company launched the United Kingdom's first cellular telephone network. Vodac was created to handle Vodafone's sales operation. In addition to a national direct sales force operating from nine regional offices, Vodac has an extensive network of independent dealers across the United Kingdom and a specialist chain of Vodastore Communication Centres.

Part of Vodac's mission is to make sure that phone dealers have all the information they need to provide quick and courteous service to their customers. A clean and efficient transfer of the user details from the dealer to the service provider is imperative in order to service the customer well after the initial sell.

This flow of information seems like a simple transaction, but Vodac was faced with a dealer network that used a wide variety of desktop platforms, with devices of varying specifications. Implementing a common computing system to deploy mission-critical applications and information was challenging. Vodac's challenge was further fueled by the pace of the market it serves. In addition, the mobile phone market tends to experience a large turnover of resellers and is made up of small businesses that don't have the resources to buy expensive, state-of-the-art computer hardware.

Vodac wanted to connect phone dealers across the United Kingdom to its own computer system, leveraging the existing systems at its dealer locations. Connections had to be simple and easy to use. To achieve these goals, Vodac used a thin-client/server solution built on the WinFrame server.

Since implementing this solution, dealer access to mission-critical applications has increased 500 percent. Vodac has maximized its return on investment and has centralized its application deployment and management.

**Presenting problem** Vodac sought an easy, economical solution that would allow its network of phone dealers to access mission-critical applications for forwarding customer information requisite to connecting phone service. Since the phone dealers were supplying their own computer systems, the sheer diversity of the client base only exacerbated Vodac's search for a single application-deployment solution.

Originally, Vodac's dealer system ran on a mainframe provided by a service bureau. At the other end, the dealers had a terminal-emulation system running on a PC. Although the system was reasonably stable, Vodac experienced gateway problems that affected the service's reliability. And because of the complexity and size of the investment involved to set it up, the system didn't have many users. At the time the system was replaced, very few dealers were connected.

Vodac decided to run a new system in-house and selected Gemini, a customer administration and billing system. The company believed that the Gemini system would give it a competitive edge because this system offered more flexible billing, quicker connection, and much better service to customers. The Gemini system deals with the entire customer life cycle, performing the credit vetting, taking the name and address details of customers, and effecting the connection of the new phone to the network.

Having downsized from its mainframe system, Vodac faced the challenge of deploying mission-critical applications to its geographically dispersed dealer network across the United Kingdom while keeping total cost of ownership low and application and user support manageable. The company still needed a cost-effective solution that would be easy to implement. With the advent of Gemini, the PC client running at the dealer end required a powerful PC on which to run. The IS department was concerned about the problems of putting higher specification machines out with dealers and of maintaining both the software and the machines. So Vodac began investigating other ways of getting the Gemini PC client out to the dealers.

*The challenge: Deploy applications to resellers who have diverse computer systems.*

*Vodac deploys a customer administration and billing system to its network of dealers.*

**Hardware and software** Vodac's thin-client/server networking environment includes:

- P133 dual Pentium with 128 MB of RAM
- P166 dual Pentium with 384 MB of RAM
- Microsoft Windows NT Server 3.51

Vodac uses the WinFrame server to deploy the mission-critical Gemini customer administration and billing system to its phone dealer network across the United Kingdom. Dealers connect to the server via leased lines, ISDN, and V.34 dial-up connections.

*Vodac's solution significantly increased the number of dealers that were able to connect to the system.*

**Solution and results** Vodac initially piloted a thin-client/server solution using the WinFrame server. During the pilot phase, Vodac found that this solution proved flexible and scalable and that it could be launched to a limited number of existing dealers inexpensively. It was also easy to set up.

WinFrame's thin-client/server approach to enterprise computing enabled Vodac's dealers to use any PC they wanted on the desktop, as long as the PC could handle the native system's graphics (in effect, running a minimum of VGA graphics). The dealers could use whatever machines they had on hand, including machines running Windows NT, Windows 95, Windows 3.*x*, MS-DOS, UNIX, or the Macintosh OS.

Since going live, the number of Vodac dealers connected via WinFrame has increased by almost 500 percent. They have spread out too: there are now dealers on line as far north as Glasgow, Scotland, and as far south as southern England. More dealers come on line as they are brought on board.

## Legal Services

For all the same reasons as those you've read about in the preceding case studies, thin-client/server computing holds a great deal of promise for users in the legal field. In the next case study, we'll look at a legal services organization with a need to share information. The Orange County Public Defender's office was driven directly to a thin-client/server solution solely because of cost—once again, the cost not only for hardware but also for maintenance and support.

## Orange County Public Defender's Office

In the wake of bankruptcy and frozen budgets, the Public Defender's Office in California's Orange County is meeting its challenges head-on while contributing to the county's financial recovery. To date, the Public Defender's Office has saved Orange County an estimated $6 million in legal costs—thanks in part to a thin-client/server solution. The solution maximizes the office's return on technology investments by allowing older hardware to deploy for CD-ROM legal libraries.

**Presenting problem** Following the bankruptcy of Orange County, the already underbudgeted Public Defender's Office had to deal with problems arising from both monetary and staffing limitations. For example, the Public Defender's Office was rebuilding older 286 computers handed down from other departments just to get enough word processing power for attorneys to prepare their own legal briefs.

*The challenge: Leverage older hardware for legal research applications.*

The underlying technology problem facing the Public Defender's Office was the need to deploy its mission-critical 14-bay CD-ROM legal libraries to attorneys and investigators. The CD-ROM libraries would facilitate faster, easier legal research from home or the field to improve productivity. Since the county couldn't afford to hire a larger secretarial staff, attorneys were preparing their own legal briefs using systems that ranged from older 286 and 386 PCs to powerful Pentiums. The diversity of the Public Defender's user base coupled with its economic hardships exacerbated the search for a remote-computing solution that could address all the office's needs. The question of the hour was this: How was the Public Defender's Office to offer greater remote access to legal information during a time when capital budgets were constrained by the county's fiscal problems?

**Hardware and software**  The thin-client/server networking environment for the Orange County Public Defender's Office includes:

- Compaq ProLiant 1500 Pentium 166-MHz server with 128 MB of RAM
- NetWare 3.11 and 3.12 file servers
- Meridian CD Net for NetWare
- CD-ROM server
- 286, 386, 486, and Pentium PCs

The Public Defender's Office uses a thin-client/server solution based on WinFrame multiuser application server software to deploy its 14-bay CD-ROM legal libraries to attorneys at home, investigators in the field, and emerging branch offices over standard telephone lines.

**Solution and results**  Since implementing the thin-client/server solution using WinFrame as an application server, user productivity in the Public Defender's Office has increased significantly because attorneys can access the CD-ROM law library from home and other remote locations. In fact, the access provided at remote locations facilitated the opening of more offices without the need to buy expensive, duplicate CD-ROM libraries. At the same time, lawyers at any location can share the legal research done by co-workers, saving time and effort. These changes allowed a complete restructuring of the Public Defender's Office.

The thin-client/server solution allowed the county to open two new offices and hire more attorneys without adding to the system administration staff. This savings allowed them to start taking the second and third defendants in multidefendant cases at about one-fifth the cost of what private attorneys were billing the county. When the numbers started coming in, it turned out that the implementation of the thin-client/server solution paved the

*The Orange County Public Defender's Office deploys CD-ROM legal libraries to branch offices over telephone lines.*

*The efficiency of the solution saved about $6 million in private attorney fees.*

way for almost $6 million in savings and allowed the Public Defender's Office to do more with less resources.

The Orange County Public Defender's Office has continued to grow, adding more offices and attorneys—all without increases in IS staff. To date, the office is supporting 165 attorneys in 10 locations with an IS staff of only three, thanks to the efficiencies of the thin-client/server solution. Using WinFrame Enterprise as the software, the Public Defender's Office was able to meet increased demand for dial-up access from home or from its numerous emerging branch offices. WinFrame also allowed the older 16-bit machines to access the same information as the latest 32-bit Windows-based PCs owned by some private attorneys.

The solution continues to save Orange County money by providing Internet access to county investigators in the field. Instead of placing long-distance calls to a branch office, roaming investigators can connect to the WinFrame server via the Internet to access attorney assignments and to download information from their notebook computers. The WinFrame server provides the Public Defender's Office with an Internet gateway, allowing multiple investigators to share a single IP address.

The Public Defender's Office is exploring other uses for this thin-client/server solution. They're considering extending the reach of their mission-critical legal libraries to the Internet and to their intranet. The office plans to use WinFrame's Windows ALE capabilities, which will allow 16-bit and 32-bit Windows, client/server, or legacy applications to be embedded in or linked to HTML Web pages and viewed from a Web browser.

*The Public Defender's Office is currently exploring Web-based applications.*

## The Public and Nonprofit Sectors

IS departments in public sector and nonprofit organizations face the same issues as corporations do, only more so. Lack of funding, diminishing resources, and aging equipment plague these organizations. They truly need to be creative about doing more with less. Thin-client/server solutions enable these organizations

*Public and nonprofit sectors have the same IS issues as large corporations do.*

to obtain and share information and thus to function much more efficiently. The case studies presented in this section include Florida Water Services, Goodwill Industries of Southern Arizona, and the Tulsa City-County Library. As with the previous case studies, thin-client/server solutions using WinFrame as an application server allowed these organizations to deploy applications that would otherwise have been out of their reach.

## Florida Water Services

For many people, the mere mention of Florida brings to mind visions of sandy beaches and sparkling water. Florida Water Services is a company that works to preserve and conserve these natural resources.

Owned by the MP Water Resources Group, a subsidiary of Minnesota Power Corporation, Florida Water Services is the largest investor-owned water and wastewater services company in Florida. Servicing more than 170,000 people in 120 communities, the company's services include the treatment and distribution of potable drinking water, the reclamation and treatment of wastewater, and the contract management of stand-alone community water systems throughout Florida.

Florida Water Services has approximately 500 employees at its headquarters in Orlando and in four customer service offices located across the state. Although the company's business is mainly in Florida, it maintains daily interactions with its predictive maintenance company, Instrumentation Services, Inc., of Charlotte, North Carolina.

*The challenge: Share financial database information over a low-bandwidth connection.*

**Presenting problem** Florida Water Services faced three major challenges. First, it had to devise an economical way for Instrumentation Services to remotely access Florida Water Services' consolidated financial database, which resides in Orlando, over a low-bandwidth frame relay WAN connection. Second, the IS team required an efficient method of administering and assisting users in geographically dispersed regional offices around Florida.

Finally, Florida Water Services wanted to provide high-performance dial-up access to Datastream's MP2 maintenance management database.

Without a thin-client/server solution, Florida Water Services would have had to install the MP2 maintenance management and financial applications at all its remote sites. The LAN in Orlando is linked through a frame relay WAN to the company's regional customer service sites. Additionally, some sites connect to the main facility in Orlando to access MP2 over 28.8-Kbps modems.

At the time, Florida Water Services was using single-user remote-control software for its remote application access needs.(Single-user remote-control software has been defined in earlier case studies.)

**Hardware and software** The thin-client/server networking environment at the Florida Water Services includes:

- Compaq ProLiant 1500 dual processor 166-MHz Pentium server
- Oracle databases
- Frame relay WAN

> Florida Water Services deploys a maintenance management database through dial-up and frame relay WAN.

Florida Water Services is using WinFrame to deploy Datastream's MP2 maintenance management and financial applications to branch offices over dial-up and frame relay WAN connections.

**Solution and results** Florida Water Services relies on the Citrix WinFrame thin-client/server solution to extend the reach of its business-critical financial application to both local users and branch office workers across its frame relay WAN. WinFrame is also enabling the company to cost-effectively deploy MP2.

> Florida Water Services' solution allowed for management of employees across the state.

The thin-client/server implementation using WinFrame is helping Florida Water Services to reduce its total cost of application ownership. The solution is cutting maintenance expenditures in half while providing branch office workers high-performance access to centrally located mission-critical information. It has enabled the IS staff in the main office to remotely manage applications and employees across the state.

With all application processing occurring on the server, the thin-client/server solution using WinFrame better utilizes network bandwidth. Application response times have improved substantially, and operating costs for remote application deployment have been reduced.

### Bandwidth Usage

The Tolly Group—an independent consulting, testing, and industry analyst organization—recently benchmarked the average throughput between the WinFrame server and its thin client using Citrix's ICA thin-client/server technology. The Tolly Group deemed ICA "bandwidth-efficient," determining that it uses an average bandwidth of only 12.9 Kbps between the WinFrame server and the ICA thin client.

### Goodwill Industries of Southern Arizona

Adhering to its mission of supporting people who are disabled and disadvantaged, Goodwill Industries is one of the world's largest and most successful providers of employment and training services for people with barriers to employment. Revenues from donated goods sold in Goodwill retail stores, funds from industrial and contract services performed by Goodwill workers, and proceeds from other public and private sources combine to fuel a business that, for nearly 100 years, has been bringing people into the mainstream of society. The organization provides a range of vocational training and employment support programs, including competitive manufacturing services for hire, that increase participants' self-reliance while using employment to decrease dependence on private and public support systems.

In southern Arizona, Goodwill is in the vanguard of charitable organizations in its commitment to using advanced computer solutions not only to support its administrative operations in five separate locations but also to provide its clients with advanced computer skill training. In making the transition from typing and filing paper-based reports and documents to using computerized inventory, telemarketing, and accounting, Goodwill Industries of Southern Arizona sought a thin-client server solution.

**Presenting problem** In 1995, Goodwill Industries of Southern Arizona was very much behind the technology curve. Only a few staff members had computers. Managers wrote case notes by hand that were retyped and filed by administrators. Even though its five southern Arizona offices were within one square mile, the physical separation was a barrier to communication. Collaboration with other Goodwill agencies around the country was limited to occasional phone calls. Goodwill Industries of Southern Arizona was determined to adopt computers throughout its organization so that it could work more efficiently despite its well-founded concerns about costs, upgrades, and flexibility.

The challenge: Bring a nonprofit organization up to current technology standards.

The landscape for nonprofit organizations is remarkably different now than it was even a decade ago. The same trends affecting other businesses are influencing Goodwill. The days of charities that rolled along without technology plans, options, and alternatives are gone. It is becoming necessary for nonprofit organizations to operate as businesses—that is, paying attention to the bottom line—in order to provide enhanced services. The more efficient they are, the better they are at saving the community money. And efficiencies determine more than the quality and quantity of services—they determine whether the services can be offered at all. Because of its mission to support its clients, Goodwill Industries of Southern Arizona didn't just need to keep pace with for-profit competitors—it wanted to surpass them in efficiency in order to have more money to spend on its services.

Currently, Goodwill staffers in different offices can collaborate by connecting to WinFrame servers over ordinary telephone lines to remotely access Windows-based applications. WinFrame's thin-client/server approach to enterprise computing enables Goodwill to operate much more efficiently and cost-effectively. As a result, the organization can reinvest the savings into its human services programs.

*Goodwill deploys contract proposal tracking, accounting, telemarketing, and personnel management software.*

**Hardware and software**  The thin-client/server networking environment at Goodwill Industries of Southern Arizona includes:

- IBM ValuePoint Pentium and 486 servers running Ethernet and Microsoft Windows NT
- Wyse Winterm terminals
- PCs ranging from 386 to Pentium-class machines

Goodwill Industries of Southern Arizona uses WinFrame to deploy BidRight contract proposal tracking, MIP accounting, and Telemagic telemarketing applications as well as ADP personnel management software.

**Solution and results**  The thin-client/server solution has allowed Goodwill Industries of Southern Arizona to maximize its investments in lower-end PCs. The organization has been able to use WinFrame not only with its Pentium PCs but also with its 386s, 486s, and Wyse Winterm Windows terminals. In addition, the single-point management of the thin-client/server solution has saved a considerable amount of money in IS resources while providing consistent control over the technical environment.

Today, Goodwill Industries of Southern Arizona supports 30 concurrent users who connect to four separate WinFrame servers via Ethernet connections. Managers can remotely access ADP personnel management and MIP accounting programs. The Industrial Services division uses a sophisticated inventory management package to keep its operations streamlined and efficient. In addition, the organization uses the BidRight application to track contract proposals for its industrial customers, and Telemagic, a telemarketing program, to solicit donations of cash and goods.

Making computers and WinFrame-enabled applications available to clients for training is as important to Goodwill as all of its management capabilities. People who have disabilities or who are disadvantaged need computer access. The thin-client/server solution has allowed Goodwill to offer rehabilitation and training programs that provide computer training to people with disabilities, helping them to obtain jobs that are a cut above minimum wage. For example, Goodwill received an Arizona State grant to train clients on the Telemagic application. The organization was able to use 10 inexpensive Winterm Windows terminals connected to WinFrame, which enabled them to train more people at less cost.

Goodwill's solution also delivers computing power to people in need.

Moving forward, Goodwill Industries of Southern Arizona plans to add retail point-of-sale terminals in each of its four stores in the Tucson area. Plans are also in place to provide laptop computers to caseworkers, which will help Goodwill to extend its mission to outlying communities.

Suzanne Lawder, president and CEO of Goodwill Industries of Southern Arizona, said, "WinFrame has made a difference. We've become more efficient, which will be critical in moving forward. Plus, we're helping more people get better jobs, and that makes all the difference in their expectations for the future. Our bottom line is this: WinFrame is good for our company, our community, our employees, and the clients we serve. We have to be good stewards of our community's resources, and WinFrame is key to helping us do that."

## Tulsa City-County Library

The Tulsa City-County Library System (TCCL) is composed of 22 public libraries serving the greater metropolitan area of Tulsa, Oklahoma. The library system provides wide-ranging services, including support of educational and business-related research. The library system defies a lingering public misconception of the library as an old-fashioned institution with dimly lit aisles lined with dusty old tomes. Truly in step with the information age, TCCL serves more than 300,000 library cardholders, who are reaping the benefits of a technology-driven enterprise.

TCCL's network of 22 branch locations linked to a central library makes more than 1.7 million volumes and a wide range of services available to the public. Chief among these services is the support of educational and business-related research conducted daily by patrons of varying ages and interests.

Around the globe, libraries are turning to high technology to reinvent themselves for enduring community value in the information age. For TCCL, the desire to satisfy patrons' research requirements through access to enterprise and Internet information resources was the catalyst for implementing an enterprise-wide thin-client/server computing system.

*The challenge: Migrate 22 branch libraries from print to CD-ROM–based research products.*

**Presenting problem** Anticipating the increasing volume and sophistication of the research requirements of its patrons, library officials opted to migrate from print to CD-ROM–based research products. These products include Newsbank Newsfiles, Current Biography, and Social Issues Resources Series (SIRS), three well-known research tools.

TCCL knew that a switch to CD-ROM products would have tremendous advantages over the printed products traditionally provided. CDs are less expensive to produce than printed products, which means big savings in annual subscription fees. CDs have a shorter production cycle, which often means that CD content is more timely and relevant than its print counterpart. When distributed across a network, a single CD program is simultaneously accessible by many patrons visiting various branch libraries. In addition, CDs enable more refined searching and better-quality research results in less time than is possible with printed research tools.

But TCCL was also aware of a crucial drawback. Library officials knew that it would be prohibitively expensive, both in terms of dollars and IS resources, to put stand-alone PCs fully loaded with CD players, hardware and software for dial-up, WAN, and Internet access, and all the necessary research software in each of TCCL's 22 branches.

**Hardware and software** The thin-client/server networking environment at TCCL includes:

- Polywell dual processor P6 200 with 256 MB of RAM
- Windows NT file server
- U.S. Robotics 28.8-Kbps modems
- TCP/IP WAN with 3COM LinkBuilder FMSII Bridge module and NetBuilder router
- 22 Pentium 133-MHz PCs with 16 MB of RAM and Microsoft Windows 95

TCCL deploys CD-ROM–based research databases over its TCP/IP WAN to 22 branch locations using WinFrame.

**Solution and results** To deploy the new products from its central library across a TCP/IP WAN to PCs installed at its 22 branch libraries, TCCL implemented a thin-client/server solution that uses the WinFrame application server. This solution helps the library to deploy new software-based research applications quickly, easily, and cost-effectively, while maximizing the library system's return on technology investment.

By centralizing enterprise application deployment on the WinFrame server, TCCL can deliver fast, targeted, and controlled access to relevant research information to all its branch libraries from one central location. WinFrame's single-point, end-to-end application management means the entire library system saves on acquisition, maintenance, and support costs for its important research tools. Within three months, the CD-ROM research tools had been deployed throughout the entire library system.

Each TCCL branch library has a Pentium 133-MHz PC running Windows 95 that can dial up over regular telephone lines to one of three U.S. Robotics access servers at the central library. The access servers route communications via TCP/IP from branch PCs to the WinFrame server or to a 3COM NetBuilder router for Internet access. ICA thin-client software existing on each of the PCs at the library connects to a session on the servers at the

> TCCL deploys new software-based CD-ROM research products through WAN to 22 branch libraries.

central library, making it appear as if the information is housed locally on the PC.

Branch library staff and patrons needed little time to acquaint themselves with the new PC-based research tools. The overall library system and its inner workings were completely transparent to the user, who dealt with only a simple database or browser interface that's as comfortable as Windows. This familiarity helped people to focus on the research goal instead of the research process and made them noticeably more productive.

*TCCL can now upgrade software easily and offer more access devices.*

TCCL staff are also able to shadow users from a central location. (You've read about WinFrame's useful shadowing feature throughout this chapter.) Staff can provide remote support and training without leaving the main library. Using WinFrame application server software in its new thin-client/server computing environment, the Tulsa City-County Library System can continue to expand its suite of research tools, increase communications and connectivity power, and add more network access points quickly, easily, and cost-effectively. New access devices can be plugged into the WAN with minimal involvement from branch library staff, and new research products can be made instantly available from the WinFrame application server at the central library.

## Education

Educational institutions stand to benefit greatly by putting thin-client/server technology to use in almost all areas and at all levels. From the administration of local school districts to the instructional labs of universities, students, teachers, and administrators alike can deploy and use state-of-the-art applications. In my previous position as a product manager at Microsoft, I was given a server by Zenith Data Systems for use in demonstrating developer tools running on a WinFrame server. I was able to install WinFrame, Microsoft Office, Microsoft Visual Basic, and Microsoft Visual C++. The Microsoft Internet Information Server was installed and the applications made available on the Microsoft intranet via an ICA file that was e-mailed to my colleagues.

Those who saw the demo were amazed at how easy it was to create Visual Basic or Visual C++ applications.

After I left Microsoft, the server was sent to Idaho State University, Pocatello, Idaho, for use in its instructional lab to teach information systems classes that required Visual Basic as a programming language.

## Idaho State University

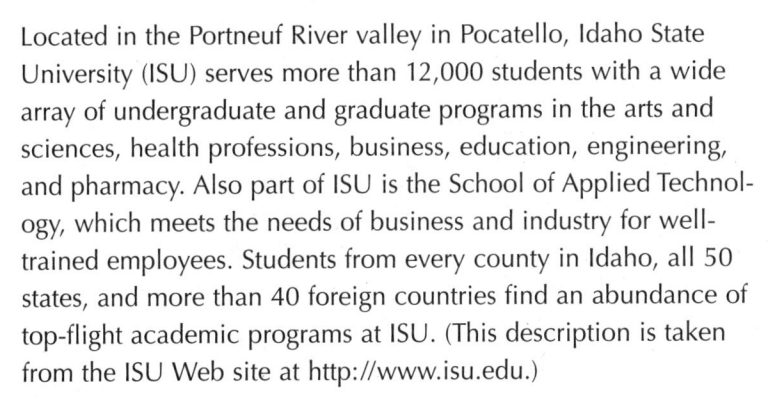

Located in the Portneuf River valley in Pocatello, Idaho State University (ISU) serves more than 12,000 students with a wide array of undergraduate and graduate programs in the arts and sciences, health professions, business, education, engineering, and pharmacy. Also part of ISU is the School of Applied Technology, which meets the needs of business and industry for well-trained employees. Students from every county in Idaho, all 50 states, and more than 40 foreign countries find an abundance of top-flight academic programs at ISU. (This description is taken from the ISU Web site at http://www.isu.edu.)

On the Web site at ISU, you can also find information about the College of Business, which offers a curriculum in computer information systems. The curriculum is designed specifically to prepare students to design and manage computer-based information systems.

As with almost every other school and college in the country, ISU must find ways to keep its courses as current as possible to ensure the competitiveness of its students. To do so, the university must find ways to use the limited funds allocated by the state and small supplements from lab fees to acquire rapidly changing hardware and software.

**Presenting problem** The Computer Information Systems (CIS) department at ISU resides within the College of Business (http://cob.isu.edu). Because the College of Business is fully AACSB accredited at both the undergraduate and graduate level,

The challenge: Rapidly deploy tools to support courses with current technology.

an emphasis on quality programs and current technology is imperative. The CIS curriculum supports students from four academic groups:

- Campuswide students in a computer literacy course
- Accounting majors who are required to take CIS courses in analysis and design, Visual Basic, and database
- Computer science majors who take courses in analysis and design, database, and systems implementation, among others
- CIS majors who take a year of courses in Visual Basic, database design (Microsoft Access and Microsoft SQL Server), software engineering, human interface design, systems implementation, and networking

In addition, the CIS department reaches out to several regional high schools to provide access to programming resources. The WinFrame server allows students to sample modern programming technology without having to come to the ISU campus.

This broad spectrum of users provides a diverse population of instructional opportunities. Each semester, 800 ISU students have access to the system, with over 200 students using elements of the two Citrix WinFrame servers daily.

*ISU deploys Visual Basic and Microsoft Office to an instructional lab.*

**Hardware and software** The thin-client/server networking environment at ISU includes:

- Micron P200 with 64 MB of RAM and a 9-GB disk as a Windows NT domain controller
- NEC/Zenith dual P-200 with 128 MB of RAM and a 9-GB disk
- Micron dual P-200 with 128 MB of RAM and 18 GB of hard disk space
- Hewlett-Packard LH series server with a 40-GB disk array in a RAID 5 configuration and a CD-ROM tower
- Diskless 80386-25 workstations with 8 MB of RAM, a VGA card, and a 10-base T network card

The CIS program in the College of Business at ISU uses the WinFrame server for deploying Visual Basic version 5.0, Visual C++, Microsoft Visual J++, Microsoft Access, and Microsoft Office.

**Solution and results** The networking solution at ISU addresses diverse computing needs. (See Figure 8-1.) The Computer Center provides central access to a PPP dial-up pool, the Internet, and backbone support for the entire campus. The College of Business supports a large connected network for both faculty and student use. Since College of Business students need to be familiar with the most current hardware and software, the college has focused its efforts on Microsoft Windows NT enterprise solutions including Microsoft Exchange and SQL Server. Citrix WinFrame plays a critical role in making current technology available to the students.

FIGURE 8-1   *The networking environment at ISU*

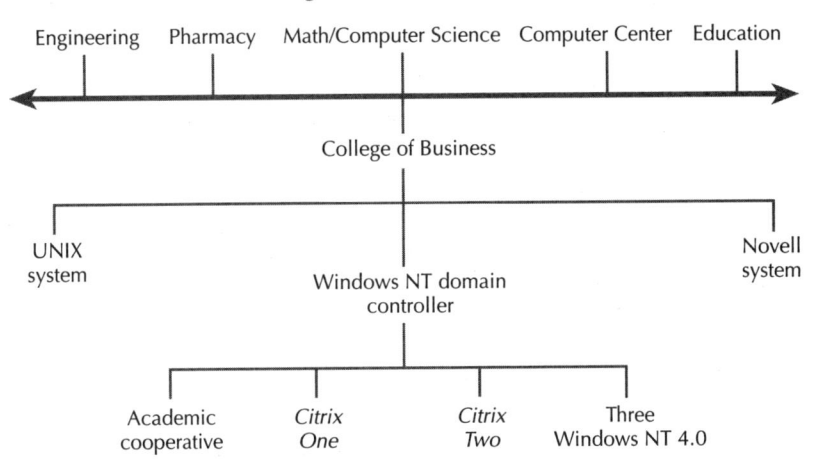

To simplify access control to all systems, ISU has devoted a Micron P200 with 64 MB of RAM and 9 GB of disk space as a Windows NT domain controller. This system validates access to all computing assets, including both WinFrame servers. The server *Citrix One* supports an instructional laboratory as well as students from other colleges, and the *Citrix Two* supports an instructional laboratory in the College of Business.

In the past, providing this level of support to the College of Business has proven expensive. Normally, to support a 16-station laboratory, at least a P-200 with 16 MB of RAM and a 1-GB hard disk would be needed. These systems would have to be replaced annually. WinFrame provides the college with an affordable solution to the problem of access to technology.

Each student station is a diskless 80386-25 station with 8 MB of RAM, a 10-base T card, and a VGA card. (See Figure 8-2.) The workstations in the laboratory were built from the scraps of an earlier system upgrade. These stations provide seamless access to all the university's computing assets. For example, students in introductory courses can write applications in Visual Basic or Visual C++ using ancient MS-DOS hardware systems while more advanced students can write Microsoft Access programs or SQL Server applications using advanced software technology. All students are able to develop reports and presentations using Microsoft Office 97. The WinFrame systems have allowed the College of Business to expand its enrollment by 29 percent while holding the hardware budget constant.

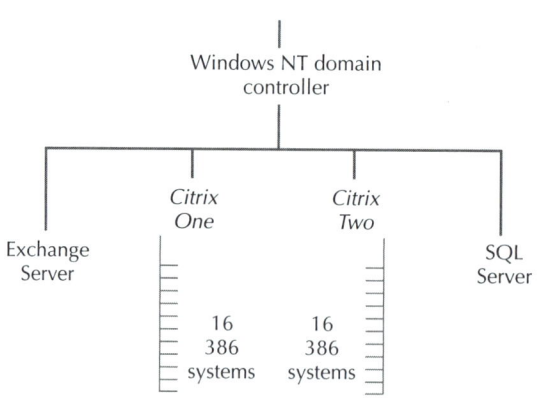

**FIGURE 8-2** *Instructional lab configuration at ISU*

```
                    Windows NT domain
                        controller
        ┌──────────┬──────────┬──────────┐
                Citrix      Citrix
                 One         Two
     Exchange                              SQL
      Server                              Server
                  16          16
                 386         386
               systems     systems
```

The *Citrix One* server is a NEC/Zenith dual P-200 with 128 MB of RAM and a 9-GB disk; the *Citrix Two* server is a Micron dual P-200 server with 128 MB of RAM and 18 GB of hard disk space. Via the domain controller, the two Citrix systems have access to a Hewlett-Packard LH series server with a 40-GB disk array in a RAID 5 configuration and a CD-ROM tower. The two Citrix servers are configured to provide redundant service in the event that one hardware suite crashes.

Student evaluations of the thin-client/server system are positive. Students appreciate the increased access to modern systems and languages such as Visual Basic version 5.0 and SQL Server.

Generally speaking, thin-client/server access to the latest software can revitalize academic coursework, allowing instructors to teach students the latest programming tools and computing concepts and making the students more marketable after they complete their courses of study. This knowledge will also reduce the training time required by an employer to get students up-to-date on the latest tools and techniques.

## In Conclusion

In this chapter, you've seen how a broad range of companies and organizations have successfully implemented thin-client/server solutions. Each case study has presented similar themes: the need for simplified management, uniform access to applications regardless of hardware platform, uniform performance regardless of available bandwidth, and security—and all of this on a budget.

Each case study in this chapter presented an organization that had a vision of something it wanted to accomplish. Deployment of software solutions across hardware of varying age, power, and platform; through available bandwidth and geography; and with limited funding presented challenges to the implementation of each vision. In each case, a solution built on a thin-client/server architecture implemented with WinFrame helped to remove those barriers. Even better, the thin-client/server architecture further enabled client/server and Web-based models of computing.

In this chapter, you've seen how the thin-client/server architecture can help turn a company's vision into reality.

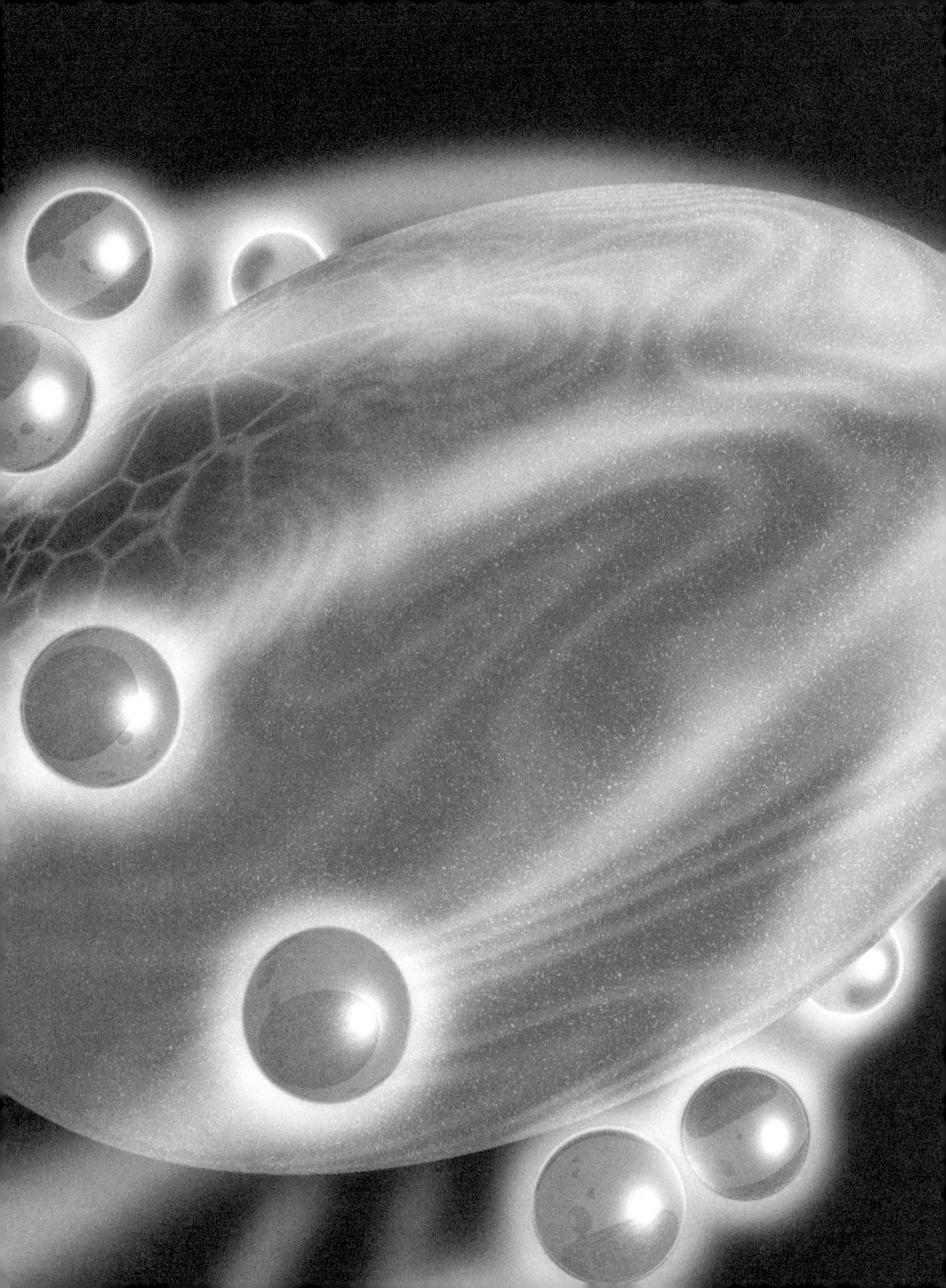

Chapter Nine

# The Future of Thin-Client/Server Computing

"A truly enabling technology" summarizes my thoughts about thin-client/server computing, a computing model that allows information to be available anywhere at any time, regardless of computing device or connection. Thin-client/server computing will significantly impact the ability of businesses, small and large, to implement new computing solutions at a rapid pace and at lower costs than ever before.

Nevertheless, this implementation can pose some challenges. All organizations experience variations of the same implementation problems. These problems can be categorized into management, access, performance, and security issues. For example, let's look at a hypothetical small business—Adventure Works—that has about 20 employees. The business decision makers see Adventure Works as too small to need an IS department. The organization purchased computers when such purchases seemed necessary, along with off-the-shelf software, which nobody learned to use to its fullest potential. Recently business has taken off, and Adventure Works' employees barely have time to keep the products flowing to customers, let alone update their computing systems. New computers were purchased as they were needed, without following any cohesive plan. Furthermore, Adventure Works'

*Thin-client/server computing can accelerate access to computer solutions.*

remote sales force, consisting of 10 people located in different parts of the United States, can barely get access to the information they need because downloads are too slow and the system wasn't designed for the workload.

Adventure Works would greatly benefit from implementing a thin-client/server solution. With such a solution, the organization could leverage its existing hardware, bring its implementations of business software solutions up-to-date, and make information readily available to its sales force as well as to its customers. Rather than invest in an IS department, Adventure Works would be wise to save costs and outsource its IS function to another organization that would effectively provide remote administration, support, and training. The thin-client/server solution would allow the original small (and growing) company to comfortably accelerate its growth.

Larger companies face similar issues—on a grander scale—to those mentioned in the above scenario. They need solutions that can facilitate business growth. Thin-client/server solutions can help large companies achieve these solutions by addressing the management, access, performance, and security aspects of computing while conserving resources. (See Figure 9-1.)

**FIGURE 9-1** *With thin-client/server technology, management, access, performance, and security barriers will crumble and allow businesses access to solutions.*

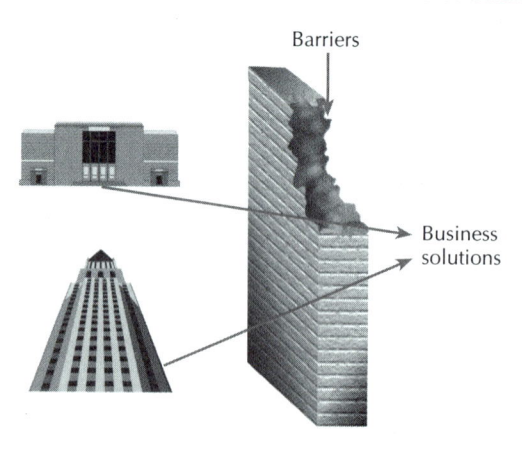

220  Chapter Nine

Government, nonprofit, health, and educational institutions can also benefit tremendously from thin-client/server technology. (Refer to the case studies in Chapter 8 to see how thin-client/server technology has helped companies, organizations, and educational institutions revitalize their ways of doing business.) Computing issues of management, access, performance, and security are as pervasive to these organizations as they are to any large or small business. In some ways, because of constantly constrained and changing budgets, institutional hardware and personnel issues can more intensely impact these types of organizations than they affect typical small businesses. Sooner or later, every organization that uses computers bumps up against the same software issues, not to mention the complexity issues that are created by adding the newest hardware and software to the equation.

In this chapter, I'll briefly discuss some of the products that are currently being developed by Microsoft Corporation and Citrix Systems. I'll also talk about the potential impact of thin-client/server solutions on today's computing world. In the last part of the chapter, I'll stretch your imagination even further and look at how this technology might bring computing resources to new markets that, while ready and willing, were previously unable to use such solutions.

## Changes to the Thin-Client/Server Landscape

In this section, I'll focus on Microsoft's and Citrix Systems' current products and coming attractions with regard to thin-client/server computing solutions built on Microsoft Windows NT Server. (Keep in mind that the following information was current at the time this book was being written and is therefore subject to change.)

*Citrix and Microsoft will be working together on thin-client/server system software.*

As you'll recall from previous chapters, Citrix built WinFrame as a licensed extension to Windows NT Server version 3.51. The innovative WinFrame technology was recognized and licensed by

Microsoft for use with its forthcoming multiuser version of Windows NT, code-named Hydra. The most current version of the WinFrame product released by Citrix, version 1.7, was released in September 1997.

Under an agreement reached between Citrix and Microsoft, Citrix engineers are building the multiuser component of Hydra. The technology will be made available in a forthcoming release of a multiuser version of Windows NT Server version 4. Citrix Systems will continue to do the development work for Microsoft on future versions of the technology.

*Citrix pICAsso will significantly enhance Microsoft multiuser products.*

Citrix will continue to develop, enhance, and market its thin-client/server software, code-named pICAsso, for use with multiuser versions of Windows NT Server. Citrix pICAsso will continue to provide all of the necessary management, security, and performance enhancements for a robust thin-client/server environment. You'll be able to use this ICA-based thin-client/server software natively with many devices as well as with any device that runs a Java-enabled browser. ICA is optimized for both low-bandwidth and high-bandwidth situations and allows access to applications on a wide range of devices, regardless of operating system. ICA clients can be used with new and/or old PCs running any version of Micro-soft Windows or MS-DOS, Windows-based terminals, Apple Macintosh computers, network computers, UNIX workstations, and handheld devices such as cellular phones, personal digital assistants (PDAs), and handheld PCs based on the Psion EPOC32 operating system.

Microsoft will ship its Hydra client with a rudimentary client protocol called T-Share that works only for devices built around a version of the Windows operating system, which could include either Microsoft Windows CE, Microsoft Windows 95, Microsoft Windows NT Workstation, or some variation thereof. (See Figure 9-2.) Microsoft also plans to make a 16-bit version of the Windows 3.*x* client available. The Hydra beta product's ship date is undetermined as of this writing.

FIGURE 9-2  *Thin-client/server products from Microsoft and Citrix*

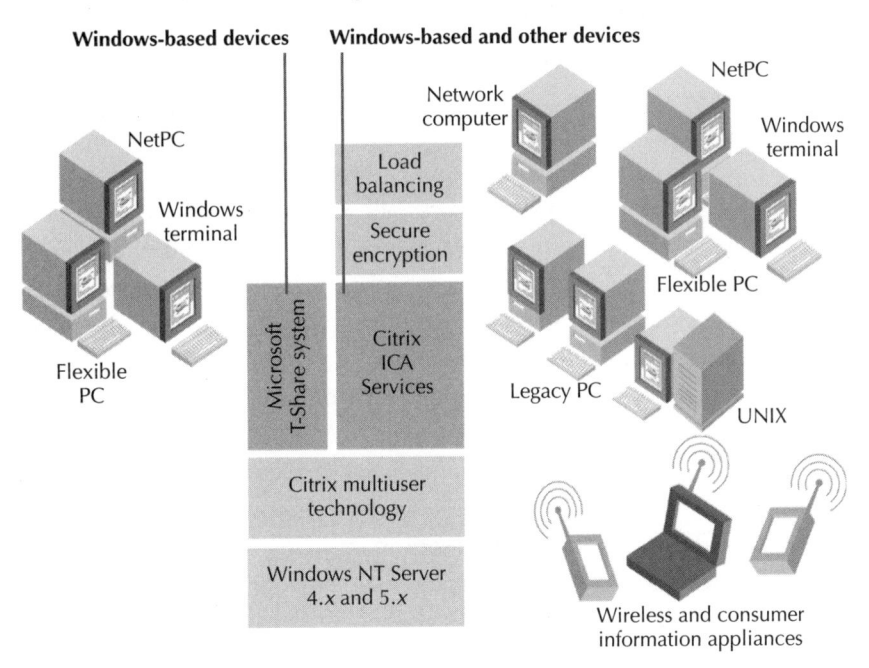

In addition to the client software, pICAsso will include a valuable set of additional system services and tools for use with ICA thin-client/server devices. Citrix will continue to sell products that enhance the services available with either WinFrame or future versions of pICAsso, adding additional security and encryption as well as load balancing.

# The Future of Thin-Client/Server Computing

In the near future, thin-client/server computing will impact all kinds of organizations, with sophisticated computing solutions that were previously out of reach. These computing solutions will be quick to deploy because of the removal of human resource and hardware barriers in existing computing environments.

With the availability of thin-client/server solutions, organizations will be better able to match the most appropriate computing

*Thin-client/server computing will allow deployment of hardware as needed.*

resources with their employees' job requirements. Thin-client/server software and hardware solutions allow for the strategic placement of computing resources. Full desktop systems can be deployed only where and when required, instead of everywhere at great cost. Thin-client/server hardware solutions, using Windows-based terminals, for example, can be allocated for specific task-based work. Full desktop workstations can be allocated for power users, who need powerful local processing for performing tasks such as CAD/CAM drawing, high-end graphics design, video production, or multimedia creation. Even for knowledge engineers with powerful local workstations, the thin-client/server solutions can be used to access mission-critical applications, such as e-mail or company-specific databases that are centrally managed by IS. In addition, the same mission-critical applications would be available for people working remotely. The net result would be optimization of funds, computing infrastructure, and human resources for the deployment, management, support, and training of the organization's system and resources.

*Thin-client/server computing will result in significant returns on investment.*

As more organizations benefit from thin-client/server solutions, other organizations will want to use these solutions. And as more organizations see solutions that yield better returns on their hardware and software investments, more software publishers and hardware companies will grow and invest in improvements.

### Solutions That Affect Access for Families and That Empower Organizations and Small Businesses

You know about accelerating the deployment of applications and solutions that enhance and extend existing technology infrastructures in businesses and different types of organizations. Now let's look at how individuals, households, or organizations that usually have neither the funds nor the personnel to take advantage of any type of computing information resource could also greatly benefit from thin-client/server technology.

Computing is expensive for individuals and families who are trying to either keep up with current technology or make sure that their kids have access to the best and most recent information. Not only is the point of entry (that is, the PC) expensive, but figuring out how to use the PC can also be costly in terms of time and resources. I wonder how many people would watch television if viewers were required to add hardware or other components to their televisions every year with the new fall television lineup. It's about time computing resources were made as simple to access as television.

Individuals and households actually present a huge opportunity for a large telecommunications company, such as AT&T, MCI, or WorldCom, that is willing to invest in server "farms" that make applications and information available to consumers through thin-client/server devices. Rather than requiring individual households to update computer hardware or precluding their access to information and applications, a telecommunications provider could provide a thin-client/server computing device, such as a Windows-based terminal, with the costs included in a monthly fee for computing services. This arrangement would make home computing access similar to access to cable television programming or to the method used to distribute cellular phones with a cellular account.

> Telecommunications companies can make computing accessible using thin-client/server solutions.

A European telecommunications company, France Telecom, already provides directory and other database services through terminals installed in every telephone subscriber's home. This model could be extended to offer the use of software applications through the thin-client/server technology.

France Telecom created France Teletel in 1980 to provide telephone directory services to its customers. The company distributed a simple terminal with a keyboard to every household with a telephone, in lieu of a telephone directory. Today customers of France Telecom use a device known as the Minitel not only for directory assistance but also for access to about 25,000 different information databases. Currently, 6.5 million Minitel terminals exist, with an additional 600,000 personal computers that use terminal-emulation software to access the directory and database services. Subscriptions and access via the Internet are also offered to places outside of France. (See Figure 9-3.)

**FIGURE 9-3** *France Telecom uses Minitel devices for directory and other services in every household with a telephone.*

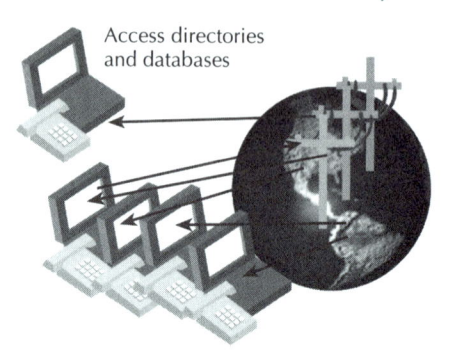

Access directories and databases

To get more information about the Minitel services or access using emulation software through the Web, see the company's Web site at:

http://www.minitel.com

The Minitel terminals are character-based and serve the specific purpose of providing directory services and access to databases. Since France Telecom understands the thin-client/server model for distributing information, it would be a logical step to add an application server farm to its network, for access by the 600,000 customers accessing the services by personal computer. Windows-based terminals could be distributed to households to replace the Minitel text terminals for a wide range of graphical computing offerings from productivity applications, Web-based information, or other more engaging uses of technology. I wouldn't be surprised if France Telecom found the ICA thin-client/server software an effective addition to Minitel terminals in the future.

Imagine the ramifications of a successful pilot project in France that could then be deployed by other telecommunications companies across the globe. Server farms all over the world could host a full complement of productivity, entertainment, research, e-mail, and reference software and services. Students could access their documents from terminals or computers regardless of whether they're working at home or in school, and they wouldn't need to purchase expensive laptop computers. And since thin-client/server software keeps improving, soon users would be able to access multimedia via even the thinnest protocols, such as ICA, which could make the thin-client/server solution useful for all types of curriculum materials and functions within educational institutions, for example. (See Figure 9-4.)

**FIGURE 9-4** *Households and schools can take advantage of thin-client/server computing.*

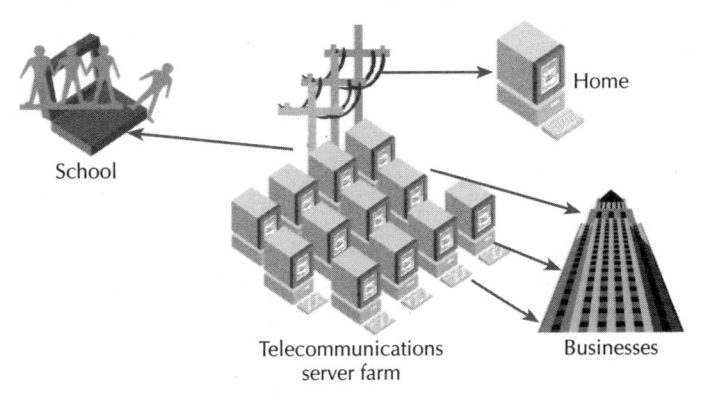

Schools that want to use laptop computer system programs for student access must figure in the cost of entry for the student (that is, how much the student would have to spend to purchase the appropriate hardware), sufficient bandwidth capabilities, and maintenance. Using a thin-client/server model for this type of program would help reduce these kinds of costs and would offer equal access even to students and schools with restricted funds.

While working in my previous position as the academic programs manager for Microsoft's Internet Platform and Tools Division, I encountered the following situation: Often, a barrier to using Microsoft programming languages was the pervasive existence of legacy hardware in institutions of higher education. Academic programs used old versions of programming languages that would run on the old hardware that was available to students. The legacy hardware precluded the schools' use of the most recent versions of programming languages as tools for supporting the technical disciplines, such as computer science, business information systems, engineering, and so on. Many schools simply do not have the funds for either the requisite hardware or adequate IS support. The Idaho State University case study in Chapter 8 illustrates how valuable the thin-client/server solution can be not only for schools but also for organizations constrained by these issues.

*Thin-client/server computing can be used to consolidate IS functions for groups of small businesses.*

In the same way that thin-client/server server farms could provide students and their families with access to computing, regardless of socioeconomic level, telephone companies could economically provide services to small businesses that are unable to afford their own computing infrastructures.

As a small business owner myself, I know what it takes to purchase and set up conventional hardware solutions. It's not as easy as it was when I was working at Microsoft and could call the Help desk, install the latest version of software right off the corporate servers, or send e-mail to some of my colleagues and get answers to technical questions. In setting up and running my small business applications, I learned a great deal about the varying quality of product support from hardware and software vendors. As vendors' software and hardware products get more complex, the vendors try to cut costs by putting information out on the Web. But it's not necessarily easy to find the answers you're looking for on the Internet, and doing so can be quite time-consuming as you try to support your own software needs.

Recently, when I asked my 8-year-old son, Sam, what he thought I did for work, he told me that my job was to support the network and computers in our house. Obviously, since I've been on my own, I've spent too many hours trying to fix system problems, install hardware, or get my internal network to run. I've had to install workarounds, including older or different versions of software, on various computers with different operating systems, just to get my e-mail from a provider (MSN) that didn't support e-mail access by my computer, which is running Microsoft Windows NT as the operating system. As a result of my experiences, I fully intend to off-load some of my internal support work to a thin-client/server solution that will be provided by a local Internet Service Provider (ISP) using WinFrame.

## Where Will the Technology Go from Here?

Citrix predicts that the thin-client/server technology will help to expand the markets for computing solutions. The company also predicts that the thin-client/server model will be deployed in situations with narrow bandwidth, that need thin or light clients, where server-based management is required, and that pose security problems with replication of databases. For a great example of how a thin-client/server solution is working in this context, refer to the case study on Anne E. Biedel & Associates, a medical practice, in Chapter 8.

> Thin-client/server computing will help to make computing ubiquitous.

Messenger or delivery services, law enforcement agencies, and travel agencies are a few of the organizations that could benefit from thin-client/server solutions. These types of organizations need devices that are small and reliable and that have few hardware and software components for support and maintenance. If you've recently returned a rental car or received a package or delivery, think about the devices used by these workers.

## In Conclusion

The driving force behind any decision to implement a thin-client/server solution should be return on investment (ROI). The ROI will start immediately. For example, look at any of the case studies in Chapter 8. The benefits of ROI should alleviate any concerns you might have about the latest and greatest versions of thin-client/server software, especially since both Microsoft and Citrix Systems have made commitments to ensure a smooth upgrade path for their customers.

I believe that the thin-client/server model will accelerate the deployment of solutions in businesses with existing computer infrastructures. I also believe this will energize and accelerate the sales of hardware and software as more businesses are exposed to the model and come to better understand the strengths and weaknesses of thin-client/server solutions vs. desktop workstations with full operating systems.

The thin-client/server technology provides a business opportunity for telecommunications companies and ISPs that can offer thin-client/server business solutions, support, and training to many small businesses. Many small businesses and organizations are caught between a rock and a hard place as they have neither the time nor the resources to implement solutions. The costs and resources associated with thin-client/server solutions offered to small businesses by either telecommunications companies or ISPs could prove to be a great business opportunity for service providers and at the same time a real service to the recipients.

Companies and organizations that take advantage of thin-client/server solutions will begin to realize ROI immediately. I'm thrilled to be working with this technology, and I fully expect to help organizations achieve their aspirations for the effective use of information by developing, deploying, and implementing thin-client/server solutions.

Appendix

# The Thin-Client/ Server Community

The growth of a system-software vendor truly depends on the existence of great solutions for its chosen computing platform. In other venues, "killer applications" have helped bring computing devices to prominence—as was the case with Lotus 1-2-3 and the IBM PC. The thin-client/server technology using Citrix WinFrame is an enabling technology that is paving the way for existing solutions to be used in scenarios and venues that were not previously possible.

To promote the thin-client/server computing model, Citrix Systems created the Citrix Business Alliance program. Members of the Citrix Business Alliance provide the technological building blocks for solutions that include high-performance servers, flexible communications infrastructure, robust client/server development tools, and turnkey corporate applications. The program is for industry vendors that want to work with Citrix to develop innovative new markets for remote computing and Internet and intranet computing. Citrix Systems is committed to providing world-class, cutting-edge solutions for enterprise customers.

The most recent list of Citrix Business Alliance members and their addresses is provided below. The list is divided into the following categories:

- *Application providers* Developers of vertical and horizontal client/server mission-critical applications and development tools
- *Connectivity providers* Providers of network infrastructure connectivity and communications products
- *Platform providers* Manufacturers of high-performance Microsoft Windows NT–compliant SMP server platforms
- *ICA licensees* Manufacturers of ICA-based thin-client/server Windows-based terminals, wireless tablets, PDAs, and NCs

For the most recent information about the Citrix Business Alliance program, its members, and their products, visit the Citrix Web site at:

http://www.citrix.com/channel/cba.htm

## Application Providers

The following table shows developers of vertical and horizontal client/server mission-critical applications and development tools.

| Company | Address |
| --- | --- |
| **Advanced Technologies Support Group, Inc.** | 6 Park Center Court<br>Suite 101<br>Owings Mills, MD 21117 |
| **Amball** | Aussere Bayreuther Str. 350/118<br>Nurnberg 90411<br>Germany |
| **Anmar, Inc.** | 19672 Stevens Creek Boulevard<br>Suite 287<br>Cupertino, CA 95014 |

| Company | Address |
|---|---|
| Arthur Andersen LLP | 2805 Fruitville Road<br>Sarasota, FL 34237 |
| Attachmate Corporation | 3617 131st Avenue SE<br>Bellevue, WA 98006 |
| Automating Peripherals, Inc. | 310 North Wilson Avenue<br>Hartford, WI 53027 |
| Axent Technologies, Inc. | 201 Ravendale Drive<br>Mountain View, CA 94043 |
| Bankers Systems, Inc. | 6815 Sauk View Drive<br>St. Cloud, MN 56301 |
| Best Software | 11413 Isaac Newton Square<br>Reston, VA 20190 |
| Bluebird Systems | 5900 La Place Court<br>Carlsbad, CA 92008 |
| Bull Information Systems | 300 Concord Road<br>MA02/211S<br>Billerica, MA 01821 |
| Burr Wolff, L.P. | 3355 West Alabama<br>Suite 600<br>Houston, TX 77098 |
| Business Object Americas | 2870 Zanker Road<br>San Jose, CA 95134 |
| Ceridian Employer Services | 300 Embassy Row<br>Atlanta, GA 30328 |
| Check Point Software Technologies, Inc. | 400 Seaport Court<br>Suite 105<br>Redwood City, CA 94063 |
| Cognos, Inc. | 3755 Riverside Drive<br>PO Box 9707, Station T<br>Ottawa, ON K1G 4K9<br>Canada |
| Concord Business Systems | 1701 Barrett Lakes Boulevard<br>Suite 160<br>Kennesaw, GA 30144 |
| Consensys Software Corp. | 111 North Market<br>Suite 910<br>San Jose, CA 95113 |
| Control Software, Inc. | 998 Old Eagle School Road<br>Wayne, PA 19087 |

| Company | Address |
|---|---|
| **CoreChange** | 260 Franklin Street<br>Suite 1890<br>Boston, MA 02110 |
| **Cyborg Systems, Inc.** | 2 N. Riverside Plaza<br>12th Floor<br>Chicago, IL 60606 |
| **Daedalus Technology Group, Inc.** | 37 West 28th Street<br>12th Floor<br>New York, NY 10001 |
| **Daly & Wolcott, Inc.** | 141 James P. Murphy Highway<br>West Warwick, RI 02893 |
| **Dorn Technology Group, Inc.** | 38705 Seven Mile Road<br>Suite 450<br>Livonia, MI 48152-1005 |
| **Dr. Solomon's Software Ltd.** | Alton House<br>Gatehouse Way<br>Aylesbury, Buckinghamshire<br>HP19 3XU<br>United Kingdom |
| **Enterprise Systems, Inc.** | 1400 South Wolf Road<br>Wheeling, IL 60090 |
| **Epic Systems Corporation** | 5301 Tokay Boulevard<br>Madison, WI 53711 |
| **Esker, Inc.** | 222 Kearny Street<br>Suite 500<br>San Francisco, CA 94108 |
| **Fast Management Group, Inc.** | 15440 NE 95th Street<br>Suite 240<br>Redmond, WA 98052 |
| **Financial Data Planning** | 2140 South Dixie Highway<br>Miami, FL 33133 |
| **FLX Corporation** | Valleybrooke Corporate Center<br>301 Lindenwood Drive<br>Malvern, PA 19355 |
| **FRx Software Corp.** | One Bay Plaza Building<br>1350 Bayshore Highway<br>Suite 460<br>Burlingame, CA 94010 |
| **Geac Computers, Inc.** | Enterprise Server Division<br>66 Perimeter Center East<br>Atlanta, GA 30346 |

| Company | Address |
| --- | --- |
| Giro Enterprises, Inc. | 75 Port-Royal Street East<br>Suite 500<br>Montreal, QC H3L 3T1<br>Canada |
| Global Village | 1090 Northchase Parkway<br>Suite 350<br>Marietta, GA 30067 |
| Great Plains Software, Inc. | 1701 Southwest 38th Street<br>Fargo, ND 58103 |
| Greentree System, Inc. | 201 San Antonio Circle<br>Suite 120<br>Mountain View, CA 94040 |
| Harland Corporation | 4700 South Syracuse Street<br>Suite 900<br>Denver, CO 80237 |
| Harte-Hanks Data Technologies | 25 Linnel Circle<br>Billerica, MA 01821 |
| HCL America, Inc. | 330 Potrero Avenue<br>Sunnyvale, CA 94086-4194 |
| HealthPoint | 1100 Crescent Green<br>Suite 210<br>Cary, NC 27511 |
| Inventure America, Inc. | 30 Broad Street<br>22nd Floor<br>New York, NY 10004 |
| KBS2, Inc. | 455 South Frontage Road<br>Suite 112<br>Burr Ridge, IL 60521 |
| Keyfile Corporation | 22 Cotton Road<br>Nashua, NH 03063 |
| Kilcare Software | First Floor Dammas House<br>Dammas Lane<br>Wilkshire, Swindon SN1 3EF<br>United Kingdom |
| KLA-Tencor Corp. | 160 Rio Robles<br>San Jose, CA 95134 |
| Kronos, Inc. | 400 5th Avenue<br>Waltham, MA 02154 |
| Lawson Software | 1300 Godward Street<br>Minneapolis, MN 55413 |

| Company | Address |
| --- | --- |
| Logility, Inc. | 470 East Paces Ferry Road<br>Atlanta, GA 30305 |
| Macola | 333 East Center Street<br>Suite 534<br>P.O. Box 1824<br>Marion, OH 43301-1824 |
| MacroSoft | 2523 Product Drive<br>Rochester Hills, MI 48309 |
| Made2Manage Systems, Inc. | 9002 Purdue Road<br>Suite 200<br>Indianapolis, IN 46268 |
| Marcam Solutions, Inc. | 95 Wells Avenue<br>Newton, MA 02159 |
| MDIS | 5310 Beethoven Street<br>Los Angeles, CA 90066 |
| Mediapath Technologies | 125 E/F Gaither Drive<br>Mount Laurel, NJ 08054 |
| Medical Management Solutions, Inc. | 10841 South Parker Road<br>Suite 210<br>Parker, CO 80134 |
| MedicaLogic | 15400 NW Greenbrier Parkway<br>Suite 400<br>Beaverton, OR 97006 |
| MediLife, Inc. | 30 Monument Square<br>Concord, MA 01742 |
| Metrix, Inc. | 20975 Swenson Drive<br>Waukesha, WI 53186-4064 |
| MultiNational Computer | The Eclipse<br>5 Bath Road<br>Slough, Berks SLI3UA<br>United Kingdom |
| Mustang Software, Inc. | 6200 Lank Ming Road<br>Bakersfield, CA 93306 |
| Navision Software a/s | Frydenlunds Alle 6<br>2950 Vedbaek<br>Denmark |
| NCR - Software Division | 3325 Platt Springs Road<br>South Building<br>W. Columbia, SC 29170 |

| Company | Address |
| --- | --- |
| Novalis Technologies | 1505 Barrington Street<br>Suite 1522<br>Halifax, NS B3J 3K5<br>Canada |
| Occupational Health Research | PO Box 900<br>25 Fairview Avenue<br>Skowhegan, ME 04976 |
| Omtool | 8 Industrial Way<br>Salem, NH 03079 |
| Onyx Software | 330 120th Avenue NE<br>Suite 210<br>Bellevue, WA 98005 |
| Optika Imaging Systems, Inc. | 7450 Campus Drive<br>2nd Floor<br>Colorado Springs, CO 80920 |
| Optus Software, Inc. | 100 Davidson Avenue<br>Somerset, NJ 08873-9931 |
| PeopleSoft, Inc. | 4440 Rosewood Drive<br>Pleasanton, CA 94588 |
| PerifiTech | 1265 Ridge Road<br>Hinckley, OH 44233 |
| Platinum Software Corp. | 195 Technology Drive<br>Irvine, CA 92618 |
| Platinum Technology, Inc. | 1815 South Meyers Road<br>Oakbrook Terrace, IL 60181 |
| Profit Systems | 3630 Sinton Road<br>Suite 203<br>Colorado Springs, CO 80907 |
| Progressive Training Solutions Inc. | 8127 Mesa Drive<br>#B 206-104<br>Austin, TX 78759 |
| ProphetLine, Inc. | 2120 South Waldron Road<br>Suite 128B<br>Ft. Smith, AR 72903 |
| Psion Software PLC | 19 Harcourt Street<br>London, W1H 1DT<br>United Kingdom |
| Quality Care Solutions, Inc. | 5030 E. Sunrise Drive<br>Phoenix, AZ 85044 |

| Company | Address |
|---|---|
| Quantum Compliance Systems, Inc. | 4251 Plymouth Road<br>Suite 1200<br>Ann Arbor, MI 48105 |
| Raintree Systems, Inc. | 12842 Valley View Street<br>Suite 204<br>Garden Grove, CA 92645 |
| RightFax | 6303 East Tanqueverde<br>Tucson, AZ 85715 |
| Rothenberg Systems International | 2880 Lake Side Drive<br>Suite 116<br>Santa Clara, CA 95054 |
| SalesLogix Corp. | 8800 North Gainey Center Drive<br>Suite 200<br>Scottsdale, AZ 85258 |
| SBT Internet Systems | 1401 Los Gamos Drive<br>San Rafael, CA 94903 |
| SCT | 4 Country View Road<br>Malvern, PA 19355-1408 |
| Security Dynamics, Inc. | 20 Crosby Drive<br>Bedford, MA 01730 |
| Simplex Time Recorder Co. | 1 Simplex Plaza<br>Gardner, MA 01441 |
| Softlinx | 234 Littleton Road<br>Westford, MA 01886 |
| Solomon Software | 200 E. Hardin Street<br>Findlay, OH 45840 |
| Spectrum Human Resource Systems Corp. | 1625 Broadway<br>Suite 2600<br>Denver, CO 80202 |
| SQL Financials, Inc. | 3950 Johns Creek Court<br>Suwanee, GA 30024 |
| Sybase, Inc. | Powersoft Business Group<br>561 Virginia Road<br>Concord, MA 01742 |
| Symix Systems, Inc. | 2800 Corporate Exchange Drive<br>Columbus, OH 43231 |
| System Innovation | 5951 S. MiddleField Road<br>Suite 201<br>Littleton, CO 80123 |

| Company | Address |
|---|---|
| Systems Union Group Ltd. | Dogmers Field Park<br>Hartley Wintney<br>Hampshire, UK RG27 85E<br>United Kingdom |
| TeleMagic, Inc. | 17950 Preston Road<br>Suite 800<br>Dallas, TX 75252 |
| 3M Health Information Systems | 575 West Murray Boulevard<br>Murray, UT 84157-0900 |
| Triad Resources | 810 South Cincinnati<br>Suite 105<br>Tulsa, OK 74119 |
| TSoft, Inc. | 703 Bells Mills Road<br>West Newton, PA 15089 |
| TSW International | 3301 Windy Ridge Parkway<br>Atlanta, GA 30339 |
| Ultimate Software Group, Inc. | 3111 Stirling Road<br>Ft. Lauderdale, FL 33312 |
| Ungerboeck Systems, Inc. | 1350 Elbridge Payne Road<br>St. Louis, MO 63017 |
| Ventana Corp. | 1430 East Fort Lowell Road<br>Suite 301<br>Tuscon, AZ 85719 |
| Vinca Corp. | 1815 South State Street<br>Orem, UT 84097-8068 |
| Visteon Corporation | 2250 Lucien Way<br>Suite 250<br>Maitland, FL 32751 |
| Wenn/Soft LLC | 2350 South 170th Street<br>PO Box 510948<br>New Berlin, WI 53151 |
| Wincite Systems | 30 West Monroe<br>Suite 300<br>Chicago, IL 60603 |
| Winnebago Software Co. | 457 East South Street<br>Caledonia, MN 55921 |
| Yardi Systems, Inc. | 819 Reddick Avenue<br>Santa Barbara, CA 93103 |
| Zitel Corporation | 47211 Bayside Parkway<br>Fremont, CA 94538 |

# Connectivity Providers

The following table shows providers of network infrastructure connectivity and communications products.

| Company | Address |
| --- | --- |
| Basis International Ltd. | 5901 NE Jefferson Street<br>Albuquerque, NM 87109 |
| Cellsys, Inc. | 14931 Califa Street<br>Suite D<br>Van Nuys, CA 91411-3002 |
| Chase Research, Inc. | 545 Marriott Drive<br>Suite 100<br>Nashville, TN 37214 |
| Comtrol | 900 Long Lake Road<br>Suite 210<br>St. Paul, MN 55112 |
| Digi International | 11001 Bren Road East<br>Minnetonka, MN 55343-9605 |
| Eicon Technology, Inc. | 9800 Cavendish Boulevard<br>Montreal, Quebec H4M 2V9<br>Canada |
| Equinox Systems, Inc. | One Equinox Way<br>Sunrise, FL 33351 |
| Facet Corp. | 4031 W. Plano Parkway<br>Plano, TX 75093 |
| InfoExpress, Inc. | 1270 Payne Drive<br>Los Altos, CA 94024 |
| LANSource Technologies | 221 Dufferin Street<br>Suite 310A<br>Toronto, ON M6K 3J2<br>Canada |
| Multi-Tech Systems, Inc. | 2205 Woodale Drive<br>Mounds View, MN 55112 |
| NDC Communications, Inc. | 265 Santa Ana Court<br>Sunnyvale, CA 94086 |
| Net Access | 18 Keewaydin Drive<br>Salem, NH 03079 |
| Proxim, Inc. | 295 N. Bernando Avenue<br>Mountin View, CA 94043 |

| Company | Address |
| --- | --- |
| **Rascom, Inc.** | 5 Manor Parkway<br>Salem, NH 03079 |
| **RDC** | 551 Foster City Boulevard<br>Suite C<br>Foster City, CA 94404 |
| **Specialix International Ltd.** | 3 Wintersells Road<br>Byfleet, Surrey KT14 7LF<br>United Kingdom |
| **Stallion Technologies, Inc.** | 2880 Research Park Drive<br>Suite 160<br>Soquel, CA 95073 |
| **3Com Corp.** | 5400 Bayfront Plaza<br>Santa Clara, CA 95052-8145 |
| **TSP Companies** | 3425-D Duluth<br>Atlanta, GA 30136 |
| **WRQ, Inc.** | 1500 Dexter Avenue North<br>Seattle, WA 98109-3051 |

## Platform Providers

The following table shows manufactures of high performance Windows NT–compliant SMP server platforms.

| Company | Address |
| --- | --- |
| Amdahl Corporation | 1250 East Arques Avenue<br>MS-380<br>Sunnyvale, CA 94086 |
| Axil Computer, Inc. | 130C Baker Avenue Extension<br>Concord, MA 01742 |
| ChatCom, Inc. | 9600 Topanga Canyon Boulevard<br>Chatsworth, CA 91311-5803 |
| CommVision Corp. | 510 Logue Avenue<br>Mountain View, CA 94043 |
| Compaq Computer | 20555 State Highway 249<br>Houston, TX 77070 |
| Crescent Computers, Inc. | 2979 Pacific Drive<br>Suite B<br>Norcross, GA 30071 |
| Cubix Corporation | 2800 Lockheed Way<br>Carson City, NV 89706 |
| Dell Computer Corporation | One Dell Way<br>Round Rock, TX 78682 |
| Hewlett-Packard | 5301 Stevens Creek Blvd., Bldg. 50<br>Pacific Grove Room–NetServer Training<br>Santa Clara, CA 95052-8059 |
| Intergraph Corporation | One Madison Industrial Park<br>Huntsville, AL 35894-0001 |
| Netframe Systems, Inc. | 1545 Barber Lane<br>Milpitas, CA 95035 |
| Netpower | 545 Oakmead Parkway<br>Sunnyvale, CA 94086-4023 |
| Telegration Associates, Inc. | 9925 Haynes Bridge Road<br>Suite 200–205<br>Alpharetta, GA 30022 |
| Tricord Systems, Inc. | 2800 Northwest Boulevard<br>Plymouth, MN 55441 |
| Unisys Corporation | Township Line &<br>Union Meeting Roads<br>Blue Bell, PA 19424 |

# ICA Licensees

The following table shows manufacturers of thin-client/server ICA Windows-based terminals, wireless tablets, PDAs, and NCs.

| Company | Address |
| --- | --- |
| **Boundless Technologies, Inc.** | 100 Marcus Boulevard<br>Hauppauge, NY 11788 |
| **Cruise Technologies, Inc.** | 115 South Wilke Road<br>Suite 300<br>Arlington Heights, IL 60005 |
| **Neoware Systems, Inc.** | 400 Feheley Drive<br>King of Prussia, PA 19406 |
| **Insignia Solutions, Inc.** | 2200 Lawson Lane<br>Santa Clara, CA 95054 |
| **NCD, Inc.** | 350 North Bernardo Avenue<br>Mountain View, CA 94043-5207 |
| **Plexcom, Inc.** | 2255 Agate Court<br>Simi Valley, CA 93065 |
| **TECO Information Systems, Inc.** | 320 Militas Boulevard<br>Militas, CA 95035 |
| **Tektronix, Inc.** | 14180 SW Karl Braun Drive<br>Video and Networking Division<br>Beaverton, OR 97077 |
| **Telxon Corp** | 3330 West Market Street<br>PO Box 5582<br>Akron, OH 44334-0582 |
| **VXL Instruments Ltd.** | B7, 17th First Main<br>KHB Colony<br>Koramangala<br>Bangalore 560034<br>India |
| **Wyse Technology, Inc.** | 3471 North First Street<br>San Jose, CA 95134 |

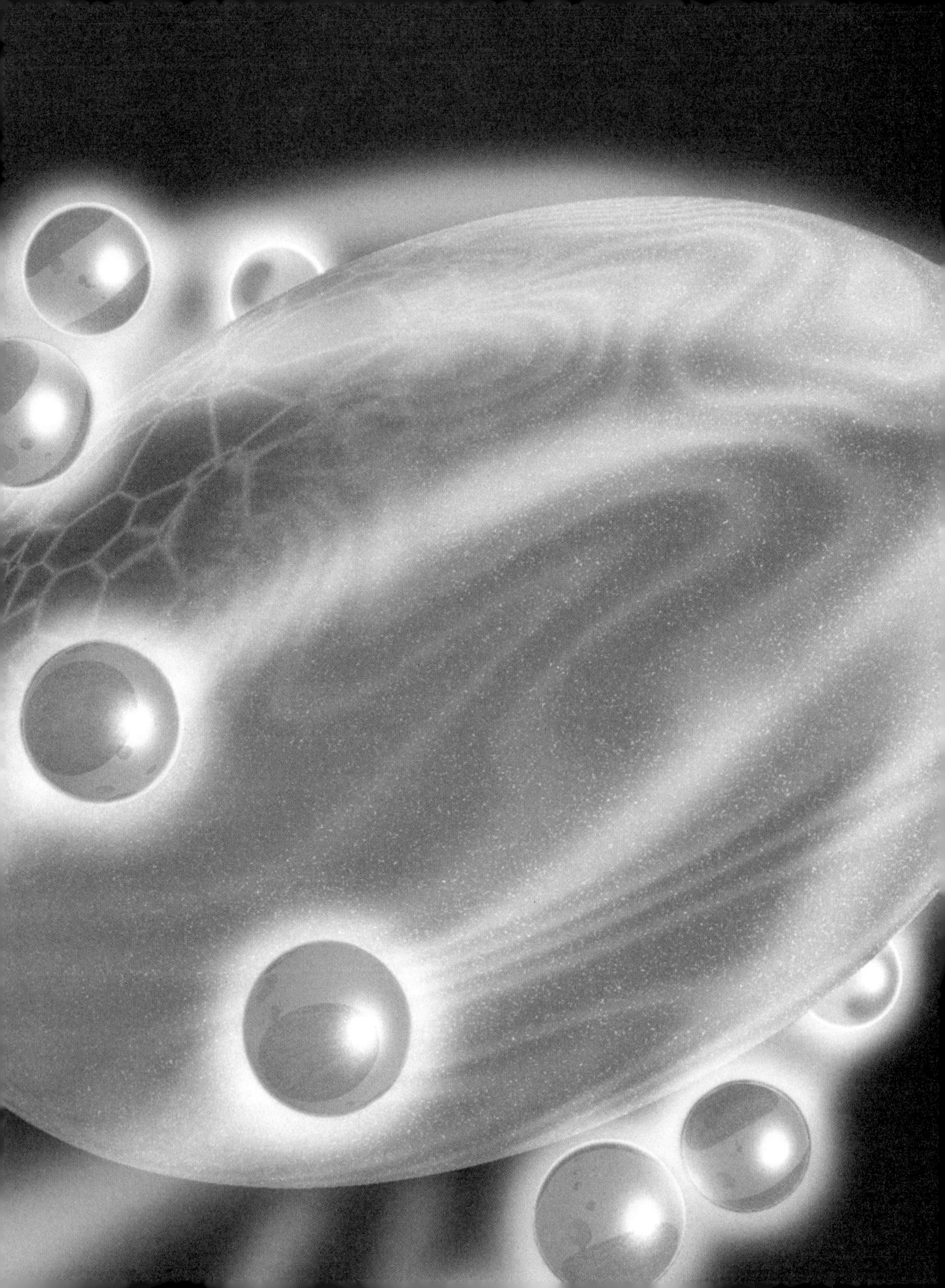

# Index

## Numbers

3Com Corporation, 241
3M Health Information Systems, 239
56-KB lines, 31

## A

<A HREF> tag, 150
abstracting, 32
Access. *See* Microsoft Access
accounting applications, 40, 76, 161, 162–73
ACE/Server (Security Dynamics), 183
ACLCHECK, 112, 155
ACLs (access control lists), 112, 155
ACLSET, 112
ACPI (Advanced Configuration and Power Interface), 79
Action Point, 184, 185
ActiveX controls
   application launching and, 150, 152
   basic description of, 46–47
Administrative Tools group, 96
Advanced Technologies Support Group, 232
ALE (application launching and embedding). *See also* application launching capability
   basic description of, 145, 147, 149–50
   case studies illustrating, 173, 177, 192, 203
Amball, 232
Amdahl Corporation, 242
analysis stage, 121–122
Anamar, 232
animation, 159

Anne E. Biedel & Associates, 161, 177–83, 229
Anon*x* form, 148
Anonymous user group, 147
anonymous users, 147–48
Apache Web server, 149
APIs (Application Programming Interfaces), 27–28, 50
   accessing INI files through, 136
   planning your thin-client/server environment and, 136, 137
   using, instead of custom code, 137
   virtual channel, 63
APP (application execution shell), 112, 155
Apple Computer, 81
Appletalk, 88
applets
   ActiveX controls and, 47
   application deployment strategies and, 41–42, 46–47
   basic description of, 41–42
   GSNW applets, 103–4
   NCs and, 84
   network integration and, 103–4
   Windows-based terminals and, 75
Application Configuration utility, 100, 116, 146–47, 155
application deployment strategies, 121–25
   basic description of, 21–43
   client/server paradigms and, 30–33
   distributed computing architectures and, 30–40
   enterprise-wide application deployment, 41, 56–63

245

application launching capability, 53, 69–71, 144–45, 149–54
   basic description of, 145, 147, 149–50
   case studies illustrating, 173, 177, 192, 203
application logic, 43, 45, 59
Application Registry database, 101
application servers
   application deployment strategies and, 23–29
   evolution of, 24
   redefinition of, 24
APPSEC (application security registration system), 112, 155
APPSRV.INI, 115
architecture(s). *See also* ICA (Independent Computing Architecture)
   comparing, 21–43
   components of, 56–63
   distributed computing architectures, 27, 30–40
   EISA (Extended Industry Standard Architecture), 132
   ISA (Industry Standard Architecture), 132
   MCA (Microchannel Architecture), 132
   *n*-tier (three-tier/multitier) architecture, 28, 32–33
Arthur Anderson LLP, 233
AT&T (American Telephone & Telegraph), 19, 190, 225
ATM (Asynchronous Transfer Mode), 59, 65, 122
Attachmate Corporation, 156, 233
Attachmate Emissary Desktop browser, 156
audio
   cards, 77, 79
   file formats, 83
auditing, 109, 112, 155
AUDITLOG, 112, 155
AU format, 83
authentication, 164
automatic launching, 53, 69–71, 144–45, 149–54
Automating Peripherals, 233
Axent Technologies, 233
Axil Computer, 242

# B

BackOffice. *See* Microsoft BackOffice
Backup Domain Controllers, 107
backup/restore procedures, 124
bandwidth, 6, 68, 138
   accounting systems and, 164
   database sharing and, 204–6
   efficiency and, 206
   the future of thin-client/server computing and, 227
   GUI-based applications and, 23
   low, compensating for, 204–6
   network integration and, 107
   planning your thin-client/server environment and, 123, 126–127, 138
Bankers Systems, 233
base licenses, 95. *See also* licensing
Basis International, 240
batteries, 29
Bell Mobility, 19, 161, 195–97
Berst, Jesse, 37
Best Software, 233
Biedel, Anne E., 161, 177–83, 229
Biedel, Jim, 179, 180
bindery mode, 137
BIOS interrupts, 137
bitmaps, 138, 159
Bluebird Systems, 233
BOOTP, 82
bottlenecks, 131. *See also* bandwidth
Boundless Technologies, 18, 76, 243
Boundless Technologies Web site, 18, 76
browser(s)
   ActiveX controls and, 47
   application deployment strategies and, 33–37, 39, 42, 47
   application launching and, 150, 152
   application setup and, 71
   basic description of, 35–36

browser(s), *continued*
   displaying home pages automatically with, 143–44
   extensions, 37
   ICA client and, 78, 88
   intranets and, 39
   Java applets and, 42
   running, on thin-client/server systems, 158–59
   Web-based paradigms and, 33–37, 39
   WinFrame Web Computing and, 150, 152, 156, 158–59
budgets, 125–30. *See also* cost-effectiveness
Bull Information Systems, 233
Burr Wolff, L.P., 233
business logic, 32
Business Objects Americas, 233

# C

C programming, 47
C++ programming, 41, 47
C2 Security Manager, 155
C2 security specification, 17, 27, 109, 155
Cable & Wireless Company, 165
caching, 62
CAD/CAM drawing, 224
call activation, 195–97
callbacks, roving, 109
capacity planning, 121, 123–124, 126–127. *See also* planning
Carroll, David, 111, 120
case studies. *See also* user scenarios
   in accounting/financial reporting, 161, 162–73
   in communications, 161, 195–200
   in education, 162, 212–17
   in health care services, 161, 177–86
   in legal services, 162, 200–203
   in the nonprofit sector, 162, 203–12
   overview of, 171–217
   in the public sector, 162, 203–12
   in relocation services, 161, 189, 192–94

catalogs, CD-ROM based, 176–77
cc:Mail (Lotus), 184
CD-ROM(s)
   catalogs based on, 176–77
   legal libraries, 201–3
   library systems and, 210–12
   migrating data from print to, 210–12
Cellsys, 240
centralization of user accounts, 50–54
Ceridian Employer Services, 233
CERN (European Particle Physics Laboratory), 35
CGI (Common Gateway Interface), 82, 146
Chameleon NFS, 108
Change User command, 99
Change User /Execute utility, 98–99
Change User /Install utility, 98–99
Chase Research, 240
ChatCom, 242
Check Point Software Technologies, 233
Chevron, 19
Citrix Business Alliance, 231–243
   application providers, 232–241
   connectivity providers, 232
   ICA licensees, 232, 243
   platform providers, 232, 242
*Citrix Solutions Guide*, 138
Citrix Web site, 88, 100, 113, 121, 124, 138, 158, 232
*Citrix WinFrame Solutions Guide*, 121
Claimsnet.com, 145, 161, 186–89
Clarion Health, 161, 177–83
client access licenses, 93. *See also* licensing
Client Creator, 114, 157
Client Networks, 108
client/server paradigms, 29–33
   basic description of, 68–71
   the client/server problem and, 31
   databases and, 30–33, 69
   *n*-tier model of, 28, 32–33, 34
   running applications using, 68–72
   traditional two-tier model of, 30–31, 34
   WinFrame Web Computing and, 155–58

Client tab, 105
Clipboard virtual channel, 62–63
CMOS batteries, 29
Cognos, 233
COM (Component Object Model), 47, 59, 65
COM ports, 59, 65
communications, case studies in, 161, 195–200
CommVision, 242
compact code, 41
Compaq Computers, 77, 242
Compaq Web site, 77
compression, 59, 66
Comtrol, 240
Concord Business Systems, 233
configuring applications, 97–101
connectivity providers, 232
Consensys Software Corporation, 233
contingency plans, 123
contract proposal tracking, 208–9
Control Panel, 105
Control Software, 233
CoreChange, 234
cost-effectiveness, 125–30, 174–77. *See also* budgets
CPUs (central processing units), 12–13, 123, 124
   getting the most out of, 86
   Pentium, 31, 77, 79, 164, 166, 169
   planning your thin-client/server environment and, 127, 131, 132, 134
creativity, 9, 12–13, 21
Cruise Technologies, 85, 243
CTX file extension, 99
Cubix Corporation, 242
curiosity, 21
customer service applications, 195–97
cut and paste, 59
CyberClaim, 186–89
Cybord Systems, 234

# D

data compression, 59, 66
Daedalus Technology, 234
Daly & Wolcott, 234
databases
   application deployment strategies and, 22, 30–33, 38
   client/server paradigms and, 30–33, 69
   product support for, 22
   sharing, over low-bandwidth connections, 204–6
Dell Computer Corporation, 77, 242
Dell Web site, 77
Department of Defense, 17
deployment strategies, 121–25
   basic description of, 21–43
   client/server paradigms and, 30–33
   distributed computing architectures and, 30–40
   enterprise-wide deployment, 41, 56–63
DES (Data Encryption Standard), 65
desktop icons, 69–72, 77
DHCP (Dynamic Host Configuration Protocol), 82, 107
dial-up connections, 65, 78
   accounting systems and, 162–65, 169
   application deployment strategies and, 27, 30
   bandwidth and, 126
   hardware requirements for, 86
   ICA clients and, 159
   starting sessions with, 113
Digi International, 240
Digital Path Defender system, 164
disaster recovery procedures, 124
disk drives, accessing, 53
display logic, 5, 7
distributed computing architectures, 27, 30–40
DLLs (dynamic-link libraries), 8, 99
DNS (Domain Name Server), 107, 150
Domain Admin account, 104

Dorn Technology Group, 234
DOS (Disk Operating System), 23, 43, 77
    application deployment strategies and, 23, 26, 28
    availability of WinFrame Clients for, 114
    configuration files, 54
    NetPCs and, 80
    network integration and, 104
    planning your thin-client/server environment and, 131, 134, 135, 137
    RAS and, 68
    UNIX and, comparison of, 25
downloading
    download-and-run method and, 2, 36, 41–43
    dynamic code, 41
    HTML pages, 33, 34
    installation files, 157, 158
downsizing, 168
DPMI (DOS Protected Mode Interface), 135
Drive Mapping virtual channel, 62
Dr. Solomon's Software, 234
dumb terminals, 22

# E

EaziTC (VXL), 86–87
educational institutions, 145, 162, 212–17, 221, 228
efficiency, 6, 7, 136, 206
Eicon Technology, 240
EISA (Extended Industry Standard Architecture), 132
e-mail, 78, 100, 122, 228–29
<EMBED> tag, 152
embedding. See also ALE (application launching and embedding)
    applications within Web pages, 144–45
    use of the term, 144
Emissary Desktop browser, Attachmate, 156
EMRs (electronic medical records), 177–80
encryption, 59, 60, 65, 66, 67, 109

engineering tasks, 9, 12–13
Enhanced Mosaic browser, 156
Enterprise Systems, 234
enterprise-wide application deployment, 41, 56–63
Epic Systems Corporation, 234
EPOC32 operating system, 86
Equinox Systems, 240
error detection, 59, 60
Esker, 234
Europay security standard, 83
evaluation, 121, 122–123
Excel. See Microsoft Excel
Exchange. See Microsoft Exchange
executable files, 69–71
execution shell, 109
explicit users, 148
extranets
    ALE (application launching and embedding) and, 145
    basic description of, 34, 39–40
    Web-based standards and, 39–40

# F

Facet Corporation, 240
families, access for, 224–29
Fast Management Group, 234
FAT partitions, 112
fault tolerance, 51
file(s)
    creating ICA, 150
    extensions, 99, 150
    lock down feature for, 109
    size, Web-based paradigms and, 33
    system redirection, 59
File Manager, 104, 108, 111
FILENAME.ICA, 116
financial applications, 40, 76, 161, 162–73
Financial Data Planning, 234
firewalls, 40, 154, 155
fixes, notification of, 124

flexibility
    application deployment strategies and, 21
    ICA and, 64–65
    user types and, 13
Florida Water Services, 161, 204–6
FLX Corporation, 234
FoxPro. *See* Microsoft FoxPro
frame relay, 59
framing, 59, 60, 67
France Telecom, 225–26
France Teletel, 225–26
Frontier SuperHighway browser, 156
FRx Software Corporation, 234
FTP (File Transfer Protocol), 82, 107, 111
functionality
    browsers and, 37
    form follows function tenet, 6, 73–89
    user types and, 13
    WinFrame Web Computing and, 149

## G

Gartner Group, 18–19
Gates, Bill, 127
Gateway Web site, 77
GDI (graphical device interface), 63
Geac Computers, 234
GE Capital Services, 19
Gemini, 199
GIF format, 83, 159
Giro Enterprises, 235
Global Village, 235
Goldmine, 194
Goodwill Industries of Southern Arizona, 161, 204, 206–9
Gopher, 107
graphics
    accelerator cards, 80
    bitmaps, 138, 159
    CAD/CAM drawing, 224
    GIF format, 83, 159
    JPEG format, 83, 159
    speed of display, 34, 80

Great Plains Dynamics C/S++, 165–67
Great Plains Software, 235
Greentree System, 235
group accounts, configuring, 50–54
GSNW (Gateway Service for NetWare), 103–4
Guest user group, 147
GUI (graphical user interface), 23, 26–27, 29, 119

## H

Habermacher, Ursula, 22, 31, 44, 55
hackers, 109
handheld computers, 85–86
hard coding, of paths, 137
hardware
    ICA-enabled, 73, 74–88
    leveraging older, for legal research applications, 201–3
    planning your thin-client/server environment and, 122–23, 125, 127–40
    requirements, for building thin-client/server systems, 130–40
hardware-software sales cycle, 127–28
Harland Corporation, 235
Harte-Hanks Data Technology, 235
HCL America, 235
HDS Network Systems, 76
health care services, 161, 177–86, 221–29, 235
HealthPoint, 235
help, 124, 139, 228
Hewlett-Packard, 242
HISs (hospital information systems), 183–86
HMOs (health maintenance organizations), 178
Honeywell Europe S.A., 161, 167–70, 173
HTML (Hypertext Markup Language). *See also* HTML tags
    basic description of, 35–36
    Java and, 36
    pages, downloading of, 33, 34
    standards, 36, 37, 82

HTML (Hypertext Markup Language), *continued*
  Web-based paradigms and, 33–34, 39
  WinFrame Web Computing and, 145–46, 149, 150
HTML tags. *See also* HTML (Hypertext Markup Language)
  <A HREF> tag, 150
  <EMBED> tag, 152
  <OBJECT> tag, 152
  <SCRIPT> tag, 154
HTTP (Hypertext Transfer Protocol), 82
human resource management, 40, 161, 189–94
Hummingbird, 108
Hydra. *See* Microsoft Hydra
Hyperiod Enterprise, 167–70

# I

IBM (International Business Machines)
  AS/400 system, 174, 176
  AT computers, 29
  MCA (Microchannel Architecture), 132
  Model 3151 terminals, 22
  NC Reference Profile, 81–82
  OS/2 system, 22, 25–27, 43, 106–7, 134, 135
  protocols, 175
  Web site, 77, 85
ICA (Independent Computing Architecture), 1, 3, 6–7, 57–59, 88–89
  application deployment strategies and, 28, 33, 37, 43–45
  application setup and, 69–72
  basic description of, 43–44, 59
  connecting to WinFrame sessions with, 65–68
  commands, format for, 60, 61
  computing platforms enabled by, 73–88
  data packets, 63
  embedding applications in Web pages with, 144–45

ICA (Independent Computing Architecture), *continued*
  extensibility, 64–65
  File Editor, 100, 147
  files, creating, 150
  the future of thin-client/server computing and, 222, 226–27
  handshaking, 63
  hardware enabled by, 73, 74–88
  licensing and, 232, 243
  MIME types and, 149
  monitoring sessions and, 54
  multiuser environments and, 50
  printer/disk drive access and, 53
  protocol, 43, 45, 57–59, 62–67, 126–28
  publishing applications and, 100–101
  recap of, 59
  Web client, 78, 155–58
  WinFrame Web Computing and, 144–47, 149, 150, 155–59
ICA32.EXE, 150
icons, desktop, 69–72, 77
Idaho State University, 161, 213–17, 228
IDC, 19
idle time, 148
IMAP4 (Internet Message Access Protocol Version 4), 83
indexing, 32
InfoExpress, 240
INI files, 98–99, 136
initialization, 61, 98–99, 136
Insignia Solutions, 87–88, 243
Insignia Web site, 88
installation, 97–101
  creating user groups during, 147
  disks, 157
  user-global installation method for, 98–99
  user-specific installation method for, 99–100
  WinFrame Web Computing and, 147, 156–58
Intelliquest, 19
Intergraph Corporation, 242

Internet
    basic description of, 34, 35–36
    gateways, 164–65
    Web-based paradigms and, 34, 35–36
Internet Explorer. *See* Microsoft Internet Explorer. *See also* browsers
    application launching and, 150, 152
    application setup and, 71
    extensions, 37
    ICA client and, 88
    intranets and, 39
    WinFrame Web Computing and, 150, 152, 156, 158–59
intranet(s)
    advantages of, 37–39
    ALE (application launching and embedding) and, 145
    applications, three-tier model and, 33
    basic description of, 34, 37–39
    Web-based paradigms and, 37–39
    WinFrame Web Computing and, 145, 154
IntranetWare Client for Windows NT, 105
IntraNetWare GINA, 105
IntraNetWare GUI Login Screen, 105
Inventure America, 235
I/O requests, 137
IP (Internet Protocol), 81, 150, 158, 165
IPX/SPX protocols, 59, 54, 65–67, 102, 103
ISA (Industry Standard Architecture), 132
ISDN (Integrated Services Digital Network), 6, 16, 59, 120, 122, 126, 200
ISO 7816 (SmartCards) security standard, 83
ISPs (Internet Service Providers), 1, 33, 229, 230
ISU. *See* Idaho State University
ITG, Microsoft IS group, 8

# J

Java, 3, 88. *See also* Java applets
    ActiveX and, 47
    availability of WinFrame Clients for, 114
    basic description of, 41–42

Java, *continued*
    development of, 36
    download-and-run method, 2, 36, 41–43
    NCs and, 81
    Virtual Machine, 42, 83, 88
Java applets. *See also* Java
    application deployment strategies and, 41–42, 46–47
    GSNW applets, 103–4
    NCs and, 84
    network integration and, 103–4
    Windows-based terminals and, 75
JavaScript (JScript), 152
JavaStation, Sun Microsystems, 7, 45–46, 84
Jefferson General Hospital, 178
JPEG format, 83, 159
JSB DeskView, 108

# K

KBS2, Inc., 235
keyboards, 61, 75–76, 79
Keyfile Corporation, 235
Kilcare Software, 235
KLA-Tencor Corporation, 235
knowledge workers, 9, 11–12, 13
Kronos, 235

# L

LAN Manager, Microsoft, 22, 106, 108
LANs (local area networks), 6, 58, 60, 71, 78
    accessing WinFrame servers through, 65–67
    accounting systems and, 166
    application deployment strategies and, 22, 28, 29, 31
    embedded applications and, 145
    performance and, 16, 18
    planning your thin-client/server environment and, 120, 122, 123, 134
    starting sessions with, 113

LANSource Technologies, 240
LaSalle Partners, 161, 162–65
launching capability, 149–54
    automatic, 53, 69–71, 144–45, 149–50
    basic description of, 145, 147, 149–50
    case studies illustrating, 173, 177, 192, 203
    use of the term, 144–45
Lawder, Suzanne, 209
Lawson Software, 235
legacy software, 127, 174–77
legal services, 76, 162, 200–203
library systems, 35, 161, 201–4, 209–12
licensing
    basic description of, 91–97
    Citrix WinFrame software, 95–96
    license pooling and, 97
    Microsoft software, 92–95
    multiuser environments and, 96–97
    programs, volume, 128
LIM EMS (Lotus/Intel/Microsoft Expanded Memory Specification), 135
Linux, 25
load-balancing feature, 15–16, 96, 139–40
lock down feature, for files, 109
logic
    application, 43, 45, 59
    business, 32
    display, 5, 7
login
    automatic, 71
    bypassing, 102
    domains, synchronizing passwords with, 54
    embedded, 50
    network integration and, 102
    restricting, 53
    security and, 108–9, 110, 112
    user profiles and, 54–56
    WinFrame Web Computing and, 155
logoff, 148, 155
looping, 137
Lotus, 184, 231
    LIM EMS memory specification, 135
    Lotus Notes, 134, 193

# M

Macintosh, 3, 7, 57, 88, 114
Macola, 236
MacroSoft, 236
Made2Manage Systems, 236
mainframe(s), 131, 169
    application deployment strategies and, 21–22, 23
    terminal-emulation software, deployment of, 174–77
Marcam Solutions, 236
MasterCard security standard, 83
MCI, 225
MCSE (Microsoft Certified Systems Engineer), 130
MDIS, 236
Mecon, 161, 183–86
Mediapath Technologies, 236
Medical Management Solutions, 236
MedicaLogic, 236
MediLife, 236
memory. *See also* RAM (random-access memory)
    caching, 62
    planning your thin-client/server environment and, 123, 131, 133–34
    specifications, 135
META Group, 33, 38, 39
Metaphor, 179
Metrix, 236
Micro Control, 168
Microsoft Access, 8, 14, 16, 214, 220
Microsoft BackOffice, 177, 178
Microsoft Excel, 8, 18, 53, 58, 71
Microsoft Exchange, 178
Microsoft FoxPro, 192–94
Microsoft Hydra, 1, 49, 222
Microsoft Internet Explorer, 8, 35–37
Microsoft Networks, 108
Microsoft Office, 122, 212
Microsoft PowerPoint, 8
Microsoft SQL Server, 30, 38, 102, 107, 134, 214, 216–17

Microsoft Visual Basic, 8, 38, 47, 212–15
Microsoft Visual C++, 212–16
Microsoft Web site
   NetPC page, 80
   NT Server page, 136, 138–39
   Piracy Web page, 92
   Security page, 109
   TechNet page, 136
Microsoft Windows 3.*x*, 77, 222
   application deployment strategies and, 27, 43
   user profiles and, 54, 55
   WinFrame Web Computing and, 155, 158
Microsoft Windows 95, 27, 43, 77
   client/server model and, 69
   NetPCs and, 80
   network integration and, 108
   performance research and, 18
   publishing applications and, 100
   software licensing and, 93
   WinFrame Web Computing and, 146–47, 150, 155, 158
Microsoft Windows for Workgroups, 93, 108
Microsoft Windows NT. *See also* Microsoft Windows NT Server; Microsoft Windows NT Workstation
   application deployment strategies and, 24–27, 43, 46–47
   compatibility issues and, 138–39
   multiuser versions of, 46–47
   network integration and, 101–2
   publishing applications and, 100
   UNIX and, comparison of, 25
   WinFrame Web Computing and, 146–47, 150, 155, 158
Microsoft Windows NT Resource Kit for NT Workstation and NT Server version 3.51, 136
Microsoft Windows NT Server, 1–2, 4–7, 158–59. *See also* Microsoft Hydra
   application deployment strategies and, 26–27
   basic description of, 26–27, 49–72

Microsoft Windows NT Server, *continued*
   the future of thin-client/server computing and, 221
   key components of, 49–72
   multiuser environments and, 50–56
   network integration and, 102
   planning your thin-client/server environment and, 135–36
   security and, 109–13
Microsoft Windows NT Workstation, 31, 93, 136, 222
Microsoft Word, 8, 53, 58, 71
Migration Tool for NetWare, 51
MIME (Multipurpose Internet Mail Extensions) types
   registering, 149
   WinFrame Web Computing and, 149, 156–57
minicomputers, 21, 24–25, 169
Minitel, 225–26
Minitel Web site, 226
Minnesota Power Corporation, 204
MMX technology, 77
mobile task-based users, 9, 10, 13
Modem Control ICA protocol, 67
modem speeds, 6, 33. *See also* bandwidth
monitors, 75–77
mouse, 61, 79
mouse commands, 61
MS-DOS, 23, 43, 77
   application deployment strategies and, 23, 26, 28
   availability of WinFrame Clients for, 114
   configuration files, 54
   NetPCs and, 80
   network integration and, 104
   planning your thin-client/server environment and, 131, 134, 135, 137
   RAS and, 68
   UNIX and, comparison of, 25
MSMail, 111
MSN (Microsoft Network), 228–29
MultiNational Computer, 236

multiprocessing, 27, 40, 132, 139
multitasking, preemptive, 56–58
Multi-Tech Systems, 240
multitier (*n*-tier) architecture, 28, 32–33
multithreading, 27
multiuser technologies, 46–47
　software licensing and, 96–97
　system foundations for, 50–56
MultiWin, 1, 56–63. *See also* Microsoft Hydra
　basic description of, 4–7
　scheduler, 137
Mustang Software, 236

# N

National Educational Computing Conference, 127
Navision Software a/s, 236
NBF (NetBEUI frame), 107
NCD, 18, 76, 243
NCD Web site, 18, 76
NC Reference Profile, 81–82, 84
NCR, Software Division, 236
NCs (network computers), 3, 81–85
NCSA Mosaic browser, 156
NDC Communications, 240
NDS (NetWare Directory Services), 104, 137
Neoware Systems, 76, 243
Neoware Web site, 76
NetBEUI, 59, 54, 65, 67
Netframe Systems, 242
NetManager WebSurfer browser, 156
NetPCs, 3, 7, 79–81, 128
　application deployment strategies and, 33
　basic description of, 79–80
　NCs and, 81
Netpower, 242
Netscape Communications Server, 149
Netscape Communicator, 152
Netscape Corporation, 41, 45–46
　NC Reference Profile, 81–82
　WIP (Web Interoperability Pledge) logo program and, 37

Netscape Navigator browser, 71, 88. *See also* browsers
　application deployment strategies and, 35–37, 39
　application launching and, 150, 152
　extensions, 37
　intranets and, 39
　WinFrame Web Computing and, 150, 152, 156
NetWare (Novell)
　application deployment strategies and, 22, 24–26
　basic description of, 25–26
　Directory Services (NDS), 104, 137
　network integration and, 101–6, 108
network(s)
　application deployment strategies and, 23–29
　bindings, 109
　cards, 77
　computers (NCs), 3, 81–85
　integration, 101–13
　interfaces, Windows-based terminals and, 75–76
newsgroups, 26
nonprofit sector, 162, 203–12, 221
Novalis Technologies, 237
Novell Web site, 104
NPICAx.DLL, 146
*n*-tier (three-tier/multitier) architecture, 28, 32–33
NTFS, 111, 112

# O

Oak, 41
<OBJECT> tag, 152
Occupational Health Research, 237
Office. *See* Microsoft Office
office task-based users, 9, 10–11, 13
OLE (Object Linking and Embedding), 47, 134
Omnes, 161, 165–67

Omtool, 237
On-Line Computing Dictionary, 24–25
OnNow, 79
Open ICA Forum, 50, 59
Open Transport, 88
Optika Imaging Systems, 237
Optimis, 184, 185
Optus Facsys, 178
Optus Software, 178, 237
Oracle, 30, 41, 45–46, 69, 81–82, 85, 134
Oracle Web site, 85
Orange County Public Defender's Office, 161, 201–3
OS/2, IBM, 43, 134, 135
   application deployment strategies and, 22, 25–27, 43
   LAN server, 106–7
   network integration and, 106–7
   Windows NT Server and, 26, 27

# P

PAGEFILE.SYS, 133–34. *See also* paging files
paging files, 123, 131, 133–34
paradigms, 29–40
   client/server, 30–33
   Web-based, 33–40
parallel ports, 62, 75–76, 80
Parallel Port virtual channel, 62
passwords, 109, 111. *See also* security
   application setup and, 69, 70
   changing, 148
   network integration and, 104
   synchronizing, 54
   WinFrame Web Computing and, 148, 150, 155
patches, 138
paths, hard coding of, 137
PCI (Peripheral Component Interconnection) local bus, 132, 134
PCXware, 108
PDAs (personal digital assistants), 85–86
PeerView, 184, 185

Pentium processors, 31, 77, 79, 164, 166, 169. *See also* processors
PeopleSoft, 190–91, 237
performance, 14, 16–18
   the future of thin-client/server computing and, 220
   planning your thin-client/server environment and, 122–23, 125, 139
Performance Monitor, 123
performance/price ratios, 139
PerifiTech, 237
permissions, 148. *See also* security
per-seat licenses, 93–94. *See also* licensing
per-server licenses, 93–95. *See also* licensing
personnel management software, 208–9
pICAsso, 222, 223
PINs (personal identification numbers), 183
planning
   analysis stage, 121–22
   basic description of, 119–41
   capacity planning, 121, 123–24, 126–27
   evaluation, 121, 122–23
   hardware and, 122–23, 125, 127–40
   human resources and, 128–29
   performance and, 122–23, 125, 139
   software requirements and, 130–40
   system deployment and, 121, 124
   system maintenance and, 121 124
platform independence, 41
platform providers, 232, 242
Platinum Software Corporation, 237
Platinum Technology, 237
Plexcom, 243
Polese, Kim, 41
POP3 (Post Office Protocol Version 3), 83
portability, 27
POSIX (Portable Operating System Interface for UNIX), 27, 43, 134, 135
PowerBuilder, 195–97
PowerPoint. *See* Microsoft PowerPoint
power users, 9, 12–13
PPP (Point-to-Point Protocol), 59, 54, 67–68, 176

preemptive multitasking, 56–58
price/performance ratios, 139
printers, 53, 59, 62, 108
Printer Spooling virtual channel, 62
Print Manager, 108
privileges, multilevel, 109
processors, 12–13, 123, 124
   getting the most out of, 86
   Pentium processors, 31, 77, 79, 164, 166, 169
   planning your thin-client/server environment and, 127, 131, 132, 134
Profit Systems, 237
Program Manager, 51, 53, 158
Progressive Training Solutions, 237
ProphetLine, 237
Pro Staff, 161, 189–92
protocols
   DHCP (Dynamic Host Configuration Protocol), 82, 107
   FTP (File Transfer Protocol), 82, 107, 111
   HTTP (Hypertext Transfer Protocol), 82
   IBM protocols, 175
   ICA (Independent Computing Architecture) protocol, 43, 45, 57–59, 62–67, 126–27, 128
   IMAP4 (Internet Message Access Protocol Version 4), 83
   IP (Internet Protocol), 81, 150, 158, 165
   IPX/SPX protocols, 59, 54, 65–67, 102, 103
   Modem Control ICA protocol, 67
   POP3 (Post Office Protocol Version 3), 83
   PPP (Point-to-Point Protocol), 59, 54, 67–68, 176
   Reliable ICA protocol, 67
   SLIP (Serial Line Interface Protocol), 64, 67
   SMTP (Simple Mail Transfer Protocol), 83
   SNA protocol, 175
   SNMP (Simple Network Management Protocol), 82, 107
   TCP/IP (Transmission Control Protocol/Internet Protocol), 54, 59, 65–67, 81, 88, 102, 107, 211

protocols, *continued*
   TCP (Transmission Control Protocol), 66, 81
   UDP (User Datagram Protocol), 82
   X Window System protocol, 43, 59
Proxim, 240
Psion Software PLC, 85, 86, 237
public sector, 162, 203–12
publishing applications, 97–101
Pyramid Breweries, 161, 171–73

# Q

Quality Care Solutions, 237
Quantum Compliance Systems, 238
QuarterDeck Mosaic browser, 156

# R

Raintree Systems, 238
RAM (random-access memory), 8, 77, 86–87. *See also* memory
   accounting systems and, 164, 166, 169, 172
   application deployment strategies and, 29, 31
   client/server models and, 31
   NetPCs and, 79
   planning your thin-client/server environment and,122, 124, 128, 132, 141
   Windows-based terminals and, 75
RAS (Remote Access Service), 67–68, 69–71, 122, 126
Rascom, 241
RDC, 241
recovery procedures, 124
Reflection 5250 terminal-emulation software, 174–75
Registry, 54, 98, 99, 100
Reliable ICA protocol, 67
ReloAction, 161, 189, 192–94

relocation services, 161, 189, 192–94
remote access, 67–68, 161, 173
    productivity applications and, 71–72
    remote-node software, 163
Remote Application Manager, 113–15
remote-control software, 163
resolution, screen, 81
RightFax, 238
ROI (return on investment), 224, 229–30
ROM (read-only memory), 75
Rothenberg Systems International, 238
RSA (Rivest-Shamir-Adleman) encryption, 65, 109
Run command, 158

## S

sales
    cycles, hardware-software, 127–128
    departments, 40, 78, 161, 173–77
SalesLogix Corporation, 238
SBT Internet Systems, 238
scalability, 14–15, 18, 27
Schlumberger, 165–66
screen resolution, 81
<SCRIPT> tag, 154
SCSI (Small Computer Systems Interface) drives, 134
Sears, 19
Secure ICA Encryption Pack, 109
SecurID identification, 183
security
    accounting systems and, 164
    authentication, 164
    basic description of, 109–13
    C2 security specification, 17, 27, 109, 155
    encryption, 59, 60, 66, 67, 109
    Europay security standard, 83
    event logs, 155
    extranets and, 40
    firewalls, 40, 154, 155
    health services and, 180, 183–89
    Microsoft Web page for, 109

security, *continued*
    NCs and, 81, 83
    RSA (Rivest-Shamir-Adleman) encryption, 65, 109
    WinFrame Web Computing and, 147, 148, 154–55
Security Dynamics, 183, 238
serial ports, 62–63, 75–76, 80
Serial Port virtual channel, 62–63
service packs, 138
sessions
    accessing, 113–16
    monitoring, with shadowing, 54, 170
    recovering, 53
    starting, 113–14
shadowing users, 54, 170
Simplex Time Recorder Company, 238
single-point control, 17, 19, 173–74
SIRS (Social Issues Resources Series), 210
SLIP (Serial Line Interface Protocol), 64, 67
small businesses, 224–29
SMBs (server message blocks), 107
Smith, Mark, 125
SMP (symmetrical multiprocessing), 40, 132, 139
SMTP (Simple Mail Transfer Protocol), 83
SNA protocol, 175
SNMP (Simple Network Management Protocol), 82, 107
Softlinx, 238
Solomon Software, 238
SPA (Software Publishers Association) Web site, 92
Specialix International, 241
Spectrum Human Resource Systems Corporation, 238
SpryNet browser, 156
Spyglass, 156
SQL Financials, 238
SQL Server. *See* Microsoft SQL Server
SSL (Secure Sockets Layer), 81
Stallion Technologies, 241
Standard Forms, 161, 174–77

Start menu, 158
storage systems, 131
Sun Microsystems, 36, 41, 81–82
    standards and, 39
    visions of network computing by, 45–46
    Web site, 85
Sybase, 238
Symix Systems, 238
system
    deployment, 121, 124
    failures, contingency plans for, 123
    maintenance, 121, 124
System Innovation, 238
Systems Union Group, 239
SYS volumes, 104

## T

T1 connections, 119–20, 126
T3 connections, 119–20, 126
TCCL (Tulsa City-County Library System), 161, 204, 209–12
TCO (total cost of ownership), 2, 14, 18–19
TCP/IP (Transmission Control Protocol/Internet Protocol), 54, 59, 65, 67, 88, 211
    network integration and, 102
    Print Services, 107
TCP (Transmission Control Protocol), 66, 81
TECO Information Systems, 243
Tektronix, 85, 243
Tektronix Web site, 85
Telegration Associates, 242
TeleMagic, 239
telemarketing, 208–9
Telnet, 82, 107
Telxon Corporation, 85, 243
Telxon Web site, 85
test environments, 123
test.exe, 69–71
ThinWire, 62, 63
three-tier (*n*-tier) architecture, 28, 32–33
Tolly Group, 18, 206

Toshiba Web site, 77
total cost of ownership (TCO), 2, 14, 18–19
trade shows, 29
Triad Resources, 239
Tricord Systems, 242
troubleshooting, 116
trust relationships, 109
TSoft, 239
TSP Companies, 241
TSW International, 239

## U

UDP (User Datagram Protocol), 82
Ultimate Software Group, 239
UNC paths, 104
Ungerboeck Systems, 239
Unisys Corporation, 242
UNIX, 3, 7, 49, 57, 88, 131
    application deployment strategies and, 23–25, 28–29
    availability of WinFrame Clients for, 114
    basic description of, 24–25
    network integration and, 102, 107–8
UnixWare (Novell), 24
upgrades, 124, 125
USB (Universal Serial Bus), 79
U.S. Department of Defense, 17
Usenet newsgroups, 26
user. *See also* user scenarios
    accounts, configuring, 50–54
    profiles, 50, 54–56
    shadowing, 54, 170
User Access for WinFrame Tool, 104
User Configuration Manager, 51–53
user-global installation method, 98–99
User-Global Install utility, 98
User License Pack licenses, 95–97. *See also* licensing
User Manager for Domains, 51, 104, 148
User Manager for Domains dialog box, 104
usernames, 147–48, 150, 155
User Profile Editor, 56

user scenarios
  basic description of, 8, 9–13
  involving knowledge workers, 9, 11–12, 13
  involving mobile task-based users, 9, 10, 13
  involving office task-based users, 9, 10–11, 13
  involving power users with creative, analytic, or engineering tasks, 9, 12–13

# V

var definitions, 152
VDMs (virtual MS-DOS–based machines), 138
vector-based graphics, 138
Ventana Corporation, 239
version control, 42
video, 159
Vinca Corporation, 239
virtual channels, 59–60, 62–63, 65
Visa security standard, 83
Visteon Corporation, 239
Visual Basic. *See* Microsoft Visual Basic
Visual C++. *See* Microsoft Visual C++
Vodac, 161, 195, 197–200
Vodafone Group, 198
Vodastore Communications Centres, 198
volume licensing programs, 128
VT100, 108
VxDs (virtual device drivers), 138
VXL Corporation, 86–87, 243
VXL Web site, 76, 87

# W

WANs (wide area networks), 6, 28, 29, 58
  accessing WinFrame servers through, 65–67
  accounting systems and, 162–65, 166, 167
  application deployment strategies and, 28–31, 44
  performance research and, 18

WANs (wide area networks), *continued*
  planning your thin-client/server environment and, 120, 123
  starting sessions with, 113
  user profiles and, 55
WAV format, 83
Web browser(s)
  ActiveX controls and, 47
  application deployment strategies and, 33–37, 39, 42, 47
  application launching and, 150, 152
  application setup and, 71
  basic description of, 35–36
  displaying home pages automatically with, 143–44
  extensions, 37
  ICA client and, 78, 88
  intranets and, 39
  Java applets and, 42
  running, on thin-client/server systems, 158–59
  Web-based paradigms and, 33–37, 39
  WinFrame Web Computing and, 150, 152, 156, 158–59
Web sites
  Boundless Technologies Web site, 18, 76
  Citrix Web site, 88, 100, 113, 121, 124, 138, 158, 232
  Compaq Web site, 77
  Dell Web site, 77
  Gateway Web site, 77
  Insignia Web site, 88
  Microsoft Web site, 80, 92, 109, 136, 138–39
  Minitel Web site, 226
  NCD Web site, 18, 76
  Neoware Web site, 76
  Novell Web site, 104
  Oracle Web site, 85
  SPA (Software Publishers Association) Web site, 92
  Tektronix Web site, 85
  Telxon Web site, 85

Web sites, *continued*
   Toshiba Web site, 77
   VXL Web site, 76, 87
   Wyse Technology Web site, 75, 76
weekly reviews, 124
Wenn/Soft LLC, 239
WFCMGR32.EXE, 115
WFCMGR.EXE, 115
WFCRUN32.EXE, 115
WFCRUN.EXE, 115
WFICA.OCX, 146
WFICAx.EXE, 146
Williams, Bob, 50
Wincite Systems, 239
Windows NT Magazine, 125
Windows NT Server Concepts and Planning Guide, 136
WinFrame Licensing Utility, 96
WinFrame Load Balancing Option Pack, 96
   setting up Web pages for, 148–49
WinFrame Remote Client Manager, 77
WinFrame Web Computing
   basic description of, 143–59
   configuring Web pages for, 148–49
Winnebago Software Company, 239
WinStation, 53, 67–68
WinStation Configuration utility, 68
Winterm terminals, 85, 179, 208, 189–91
WinView, 22
WIP (Web Interoperability Pledge) logo program, 37

WORD.ICA, 150
Workstation Manager, 105
WorldCOM, 225
WOW.EXE, 136
Write ICA File option, 146
WRQ, Inc., 174, 241
Wyse Technology, 75–76, 179, 189–91, 208, 243
Wyse Technology Web site, 75, 76

# X

XMS (extended memory specification), 135
X Window System, Microsoft, 29, 88, 131
   network integration and, 108
   protocol, 43, 59

# Y

Yardi Systems, 239

# Z

Zenith data systems, 212
Zero Administration Initiative, Microsoft, 80, 97
Ziff-Davis, 37
Zitel Corporation, 239
Zona Research Group, 18–19, 125

**Joel P. Kanter** is president of Kanter Computing, Inc. Joel consults with corporations and schools as well as other public and private organizations, strategizing the use of thin-client/server technologies. The evolution of Joel's interest in thin-client/server computing began while he was the Academic Programs Manager at Microsoft Corporation. In that position, Joel established a $50 million instructional lab grant program that offered software licenses to schools that would share their curriculum materials with other schools through what is now known as the Microsoft Academic Cooperative. Joel's prior positions at Microsoft included instructional design with Microsoft University and technical writing on the Microsoft Excel team. While on the Excel team, he wrote the first book in the Step by Step series for Microsoft Press.

Joel was educated and trained as a special education teacher and, before becoming involved in the computer industry, spent 14 years working to ensure the inclusion within schools and the community of students and adults with different types of disabilities. Joel's interest in computing emerged when he started to use some of the early Apple computers for instructional purposes. It was in 1983, when he purchased his first personal computer (a Morrow with 64 KB of RAM and two 360-KB disk drives that used the CPM operating system), that he realized there would eventually be a place for educators within the computing industry.

In 1986, Joel began his transition from special educator to instructional designer/trainer when he took a position at Boston College. In that position, he developed training materials for IBM PC and Apple Macintosh software during the day and worked on his doctoral dissertation at night. After completing his dissertation in 1987, Joel's search for training or instructional design positions in industry eventually led him to Microsoft.

In addition to his Ph.D. in Education from Boston College, Joel holds a B.A. in Psychology from SUNY Binghamton and an M.A. in Special Education from Teacher's College, Columbia University.

Joel lives with his wife Minna Schiller, a former attorney. Minna is currently the CEO of the Schiller-Kanter household as well as the business manager and legal counsel for Kanter Computing, Inc. She shares Joel's passion for merging the advances of technology with education. Minna also teaches business law courses at Bellevue Community College, in Bellevue, Washington. They have two boys, Sam, age 8, and Matt, age 5, who are very grateful to have their dad working at home.

The manuscript for this book was prepared and submitted to Microsoft Press in electronic form. Text files were prepared using Microsoft Word 97. Pages were composed by Microsoft Press using Adobe PageMaker 6.5 for Windows, with text in Optima and display type in Optima Bold. Composed pages were delivered to the printer as electronic prepress files.

*Cover Graphic Designer*
**Becker Design**

*Interior Graphic Designer*
**Kim Eggleston**

*Interior Graphic Artist*
**Travis Beaven**

*Principal Compositor*
**Peggy Herman**

*Principal Proofreader/Copy Editor*
**Cheryl Penner**

*Indexer*
**Liz Cunningham**

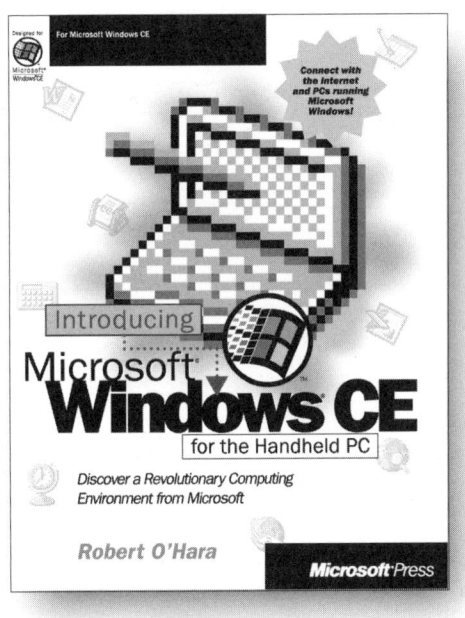

# Grasp the full power of portable computer technology.

INTRODUCING MICROSOFT® WINDOWS® CE FOR THE HANDHELD PC is your guide to the newest member of the Windows family of computing environments, as Microsoft Windows CE applies to handheld personal computers (HPCs). The book shows you how to put the full power of this portable technology to work side by side with existing Windows desktop technology. INTRODUCING MICROSOFT WINDOWS CE FOR THE HANDHELD PC examines the key facets of Windows CE, including:

- How Windows CE can improve productivity and efficiency on the job
- The Address Book, Calendar, Task Manager, Clock, Calculator, and Explorer
- Pocket applications—Microsoft Excel and Microsoft Word
- Control Panel—managing and controlling Windows CE
- Docking with your office PC—moving data between your desktop and pocket office
- Communicating with others—electronic mail, wireless messaging with a pager, and exchanging data with another handheld device
- Surfing the Net with Microsoft Pocket Internet Explorer

**Introducing Microsoft Windows CE for the Handheld PC**
Discover a Revolutionary Computing Environment from Microsoft
Robert O'Hara
*Microsoft* Press

| U.S.A. | $16.99 |
| U.K. | £15.49 |
| Canada | $22.99 |
| ISBN 1-57231-515-6 | |

Microsoft Press® products are available worldwide wherever quality computer books are sold. For more information, contact your book or computer retailer, software reseller, or local Microsoft Sales Office, or visit our Web site at mspress.microsoft.com. To locate your nearest source for Microsoft Press products, or to order directly, call 1-800-MSPRESS in the U.S. (in Canada, call 1-800-268-2222).

Prices and availability dates are subject to change.

*Microsoft* Press

# Profitable strategies for a business revolution.

In five years or less, analysts say, sales transactions on the Internet will total $100 billion annually. In short, online commerce is big and it's growing fast—and here's the book that shows you how to understand and profit from it. This invaluable overview includes:

- **Basics**—how electronic commerce works in the real world
- **Strategies**—the mind-set of companies that will get the most from electronic commerce
- **Consumer applications**—credit cards, digital money, and more
- **Business applications**—purchase orders, invoices, and other large transactions
- **Security**—its paramount importance and the five things it requires
- **The Future**—from electronic agents to microcash and microtransactions
- **Case studies**—insightful snapshots of electronic commerce innovatively applied

The *Strategic Technology* series is for executives, business planners, software designers, and technical managers who need a quick, comprehensive introduction to important technologies and their implications for business.

U.S.A. $19.99
U.K. £18.49
Canada $26.99
ISBN 1-57231-560-1

Microsoft Press® products are available worldwide wherever quality computer books are sold. For more information, contact your book or computer retailer, software reseller, or local Microsoft Sales Office, or visit our Web site at mspress.microsoft.com. To locate your nearest source for Microsoft Press products, or to order directly, call 1-800-MSPRESS in the U.S. (in Canada, call 1-800-268-2222).

Prices and availability dates are subject to change.

**Microsoft**·Press

# A **business technology** so important, it deserves a **nontechnical** explanation.

**STRATEGIC TECHNOLOGY SERIES**

# UNDERSTANDING Groupware IN THE Enterprise

The collaborative environment of LANs, WANs, the Internet, and corporate intranets

JOANNE WOODCOCK

**Microsoft** Press

| | |
|---|---|
| U.S.A. | $19.99 |
| U.K. | £18.49 |
| Canada | $26.99 |
| ISBN 1-57231-561-X | |

In today's enterprise, the way work gets done has changed. People collaborate via groupware, the Internet, and intranets. It's a crucial development that nontechnical professionals must understand—and with this book, you can. Here you'll learn how networking environments are put together, you'll explore the importance of different approaches, and you'll see how collaborative computing can—and can't—advance the goals of your organization. So get an explanation that makes this crucial subject as clear as it ought to be. Get UNDERSTANDING GROUPWARE IN THE ENTERPRISE.

**The *Strategic Technology* series is for executives, business planners, software designers, and technical managers who need a quick, comprehensive introduction to important technologies and their implications for business.**

Microsoft Press® products are available worldwide wherever quality computer books are sold. For more information, contact your book or computer retailer, software reseller, or local Microsoft Sales Office, or visit our Web site at mspress.microsoft.com. To locate your nearest source for Microsoft Press products, or to order directly, call 1-800-MSPRESS in the U.S. (in Canada, call 1-800-268-2222).

Prices and availability dates are subject to change.

**Microsoft**®*Press*

# Intranets *are here.* Where *are you?*

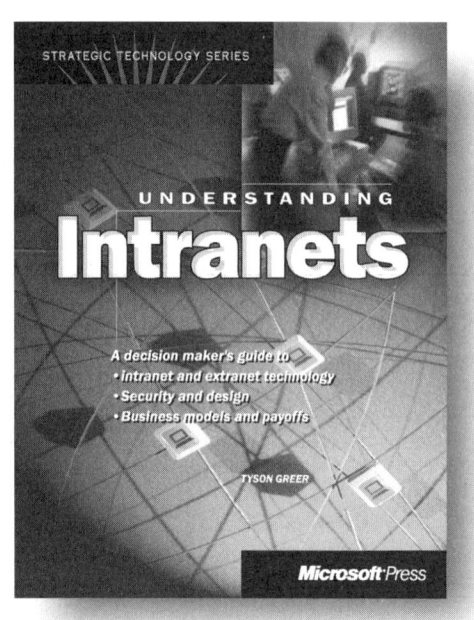

**I**ntranets are becoming the backbone of the corporate information system, transforming communications, data exchange, skills training, applications development, and more. That's why people like you need UNDERSTANDING INTRANETS. It's for technically savvy managers, information professionals, entrepreneurs, and anyone else who wants to grasp the power and potential of this important technology. Here are clear explanations of intranet opportunities, risks, solutions, and lifecycles—all set forth using insightful case studies, fast-paced overviews in quick-reading formats, and plenty of instructive diagrams and illustrations. In short, UNDERSTANDING INTRANETS makes complex issues clear—and gives you the knowledge you need to profit from the intranet revolution.

| | |
|---|---|
| U.S.A. | $22.99 |
| U.K. | £20.99 |
| Canada | $31.99 |
| ISBN | 1-57231-702-7 |

Microsoft Press® products are available worldwide wherever quality computer books are sold. For more information, contact your book or computer retailer, software reseller, or local Microsoft Sales Office, or visit our Web site at mspress.microsoft.com. To locate your nearest source for Microsoft Press products, or to order directly, call 1-800-MSPRESS in the U.S. (in Canada, call 1-800-268-2222).

Prices and availability dates are subject to change.

**Microsoft** Press

# Register Today!

Return this *Understanding Thin-Client/Server Computing* registration card for a copy of the "Big on Thin" CD from Citrix Systems and a Microsoft Press® catalog

Offer for CD expires November 1, 1999.
U.S. and Canada addresses only. Fill in information below and mail postage-free.
Please mail only the bottom half of this page.

---

1-57231-744-2  *Understanding Thin-Client/Server Computing*  *Owner Registration Card*

_____
NAME

_____
INSTITUTION OR COMPANY NAME

_____
ADDRESS

_____
CITY                                    STATE           ZIP

(      )
PHONE NUMBER (optional)           E-MAIL ADDRESS (optional)

# Microsoft® Press
*Quality Computer Books*

For a free catalog of
Microsoft Press® products, call
**1-800-MSPRESS**

---

**BUSINESS REPLY MAIL**
FIRST-CLASS MAIL   PERMIT NO. 53   BOTHELL, WA

POSTAGE WILL BE PAID BY ADDRESSEE

NO POSTAGE
NECESSARY
IF MAILED
IN THE
UNITED STATES

**MICROSOFT PRESS REGISTRATION**
UNDERSTANDING THIN-CLIENT/SERVER
   COMPUTING
PO BOX 3019
BOTHELL  WA   98041-9946